Hillbilly Maidens, Okies, and Cowgirls

MUSIC IN AMERICAN LIFE

A list of books in the series appears at the end of this book.

Hillbilly Maidens, Okies, and Cowgirls
Women's Country Music, 1930–1960

STEPHANIE VANDER WEL

UNIVERSITY OF ILLINOIS PRESS
Urbana, Chicago, and Springfield

Publication of this book was supported by grants from
the Judith McCulloh Endowment for American Music
and from the AMS 75 PAYS Endowment of the American
Musicological Society, funded in part by the National
Endowment for the Humanities and the Andrew W. Mellon
Foundation.

Library of Congress Cataloging-in-Publication Data
Names: Vander Wel, Stephanie, 1969– author.
Title: Hillbilly maidens, okies, and cowgirls : women's
    country music, 1930–1960 / Stephanie Vander Wel.
Description: Urbana : University of Illinois Press, 2020. |
    Series: Music in American life | Includes bibliographical
    references and index.
Identifiers: LCCN 2019052253 (print) | LCCN 2019052254
    (ebook) | ISBN 9780252043086 (hardcover) | ISBN
    9780252084959 (paperback) | 9780252051944 (ebook)
Subjects: LCSH: Country music—To 1951—History and
    criticism. | Country music—1951–1960—History and
    criticism. | Women country musicians—United States.
    | Radio and music—United States—History—20th
    century. | Wells, Kitty. | Montana, Patsy. | Maddox, Rose. |
    Lulu Belle, 1913–1999. | WLS (Radio station : Chicago, Ill.)
Classification: LCC ML3524 .V38 2020 (print) | LCC ML3524
    (ebook) | DDC 781.642082/0973—dc23
LC record available at https://lccn.loc.gov/2019052253
LC ebook record available at https://lccn.loc.gov/2019052254

For Denis and Robert

Contents

Acknowledgments

One of the joys of finishing this book is thanking everyone who contributed to the various stages of its completion. When I was in UCLA's PhD program in musicology, I was fortunate to work with an amazing set of mentors whose creative approaches to music have served as my models. Susan McClary's scholarship has offered invaluable examples of how to conceptualize music's relationship to gender and sexuality, and her graduate seminars exploring the signification of music encouraged my first papers on country music and gender. Susan's continued interest in and keen backing of my work have directed my inquiries into the singing voice in country music. With Mitchell Morris, I have had many dynamic and helpful conversations about southern culture and representations of sexuality, gender, and class in country music, and my work has benefited from his scholarship on Dolly Parton. Moreover, Elisabeth Le Guin's insights about writing and argument contributed to the development of my research. But I am most indebted to Robert Walser for his conscientious guidance as a mentor. He always pushed me to articulate, with conviction, why the study of country music is so important at a time when the field of musicology was just opening up to it. His continued encouragement did not end once I graduated and got a job. He has read many chapter drafts of this book and has offered invaluable edits and suggestions, giving me the confidence to see the project through. I have many fond memories of my time as a graduate student at UCLA, where I was surrounded by a community of faculty, peers, and friends whose imaginative scholarly pursuits have fueled my own. From our time in the seminar room to conversations at academic conferences, I thank the following people, in no particular order: Dale Chapman, Tamara Levitz, Charles Hiroshi Garrett, Raymond Knapp, Loren Kajikawa, Ewelina Boczkowska, Robert Fink, Cecilia Sun, Louis Niebur, Lester Feder, Des Harmon, Olivia Carter Mather,

Caroline O'Meara, Stephen Pennington, Erica Scheinberg, Erik Leidal, Ross Fenimore, Griffin Woodworth, Maria Cizmic, Andrew Berish, Gordon Haramaki, Jacqueline Warwick, Steven Bauer, Gwyneth Bravo, and Jonathan Greenberg. Glenn Pillsbury especially has been a dear friend and colleague whose generosity and close readings of individual chapters have been instrumental in the completion of this book.

Many other mentors and colleagues have had a hand in shaping my approaches to music history and the development and completion of this book. From my interests in music and gender I pursued an MA in music history and music criticism at the University of Virginia, where I had the opportunity to benefit from the guidance and direction of Suzanne Cusick, Fred Maus, and Kyra Gaunt. It has been a privilege to have Suzanne's continuing support of my work as I finished this book. Dale Cockrell and David Brackett have been unstinting in their professional support over the years, and their respective work has influenced the inquiries of this book. I have enjoyed many conversations with Lydia Hamessley about country music, banjo playing, and the singing voice, and I am grateful for Travis Stimeling's friendship, help, and sage advice regarding this project at its earliest stages. It has been incredibly helpful to present my research at the following academic conferences: the Society for American Music, the American Musicological Society, the International Country Music Conference, the Experience Music Project, the Rock and Roll Hall of Fame, and the International Association for the Study of Popular Music. Invitations from Youngstown State University, Case Western Reserve University, and the University at Buffalo's Gender Institute and the Humanities Institute provided opportunities to share my inchoate ideas that formed the basis of the book. In these various forums, I have appreciated the insightful feedback and support of Larry Hamberlin, Jocelyn Neal, Jason Hanley, Mary Simonson, Gregory Reish, and Daniel Goldmark. I thank my colleagues at the University at Buffalo for their encouragement and critical engagement with my work while I was writing this book. Michael Long offered astute criticisms and suggestions of early chapter drafts. Jamie Currie continually engaged with my ideas of the singing voice, yodeling, and humor in country music, and he has been a champion of my research at UB. Margarita Vargas and Gwynn Thomas have cheered my work on gender in country music. My many conversations with Brian Moseley in the halls of UB and at his dinner parties provided welcome retreats from the solitary hours of writing.

It was while conducting the archival research for the project that I learned the most about country music. I want to acknowledge the assistance and wealth of knowledge of John Rumble, the senior historian at the Country Music Hall of Fame and Museum, where I did the bulk of the primary research for this book. His advice and suggestions have been indispensable. I thank Sharon Marie, the daughter of Carolina Cotton, for providing so much important information and documentation that fueled much of my work on Cotton's musical career in California. I also carried out primary research at the Southern Folklife Collection at the Library of the University of North Carolina, Chapel Hill and at the Rock and Roll Hall of Fame Archives with the assistance of the Senior Director Andy Leach. My primary research was funded by a research grant and travel grant awarded by the Gender Institute at the University at Buffalo, SUNY.

Special thanks go to Laurie Matheson, my editor at the University of Illinois Press. Laurie always believed in this book, and her encouragement and advice gave me the confidence to keep going. I cannot say enough wonderful things about Barbara Wojhoski's editorial guidance and the help of Jennifer Comeau, Julie Laut, and Jennifer Fisher in getting the book through the production process. I also value the critical engagement of the two anonymous readers of this book, whose incisive criticisms helped me sharpen my arguments and clarify key concepts.

Finally I would not have been able to complete this project without the generosity, love, and support of my family and close friends. The words of wisdom and strength of Susan Griffin have sustained and nourished all aspects of my life, including the writing of this book. Kirsten Eurenius, Orsolina Sepe, Jaynelle Nash (my childhood partner in crime), and Colin Nash have each offered immeasurable moments of inspiration, adventure, and fun. My heartfelt thanks go to my mother, Karen, for always believing in me and to my father and stepmother, Louie and Danene, for their help over the years. My grandmother Lorraine did not live to see the completion of this book, but in more ways than one, the journey of her life and her enjoyment of country music continue to inspire my own passions. Most of all, I am grateful for the unwavering encouragement of my husband, Denis (who has listened to hours of my yodeling without judgment), and for the unfailing cheer that our son, Robert, brings to our lives.

Introduction

Eager to watch the glittering performances of 1950s country music legends, I purchased the twelve-DVD collection *Memories: Grand Ole Opry Stars
of the Fifties*. Compiled in 1996, *Memories* features individual episodes of the
television program *The Country Show: With Stars of the Grand Ole Opry*, produced by Albert C. Gannaway Jr. and Flamingo Films. For two years, beginning
in 1955, television viewers could watch a twenty-two-minute weekly program
that was an extension of the *Grand Ole Opry*, the popular radio barn-dance
program launched by Nashville's WSM in 1925.[1] Staged in what appeared to be
a barn (but was really a Quonset hut), *The Country Show* brought the luminaries
of the *Opry* to a new medium, television. Though the program was broadcast in
black and white, audiences could still experience the stagy vividness of country
music entertainment. Clothed in flashy rhinestone-studded suits, Webb Pierce,
Ray Price, Faron Young, and Carl Smith took turns hosting the program and
greeting the audience with their honky-tonk hits and upbeat rockabilly tunes.
The master of ceremonies would be surrounded by his accompanying instrumentalists (guitarists, fiddlers, pianist, and pedal steelist), the featured musicians who would perform throughout the show, as well as country music "fans,"
perched on bales of hay clapping and swaying to the rhythms of the music.

The rustic setting, informed by the tropes of variety entertainment, gave the
impression of a spontaneous barn-dance party where an impressive range of
performers—including many female artists—displayed their talents. Introduced
as the "number one girl singer," Kitty Wells performed honky-tonk songs, in a
musical style integral to 1950s country music, by playing the part of the wanton
woman in her televised performance of "I Don't Claim to Be an Angel" (recorded
in 1953).[2] Jean Shepard and Goldie Hill also sang honky-tonk numbers that
placed the strife and turmoil of adult love in the center of their narratives of

female subjectivity. June Webb and Rita Robbins crooned love ballads in their sonorous voices (predating the career of country torch singer Patsy Cline). In contrast to these songs of the heart, Minnie Pearl or June Carter would play the role of the archetypical hillbilly buffoon in slapstick routines that often outshone or purposely undermined the male authority of the emcee (vaudevillian tactics dating back at least to 1930s barn-dance radio). Watching this television program, I was struck by the diverse ways that women participated in and helped shape the predominant practices of country music.[3] Though women did not host the show, they were not simply typecast in supporting roles meant to be "window dressing" for the male stars of the program, a still-common perception of this era of country music.[4] Rather, their compelling performances engendered distinct visions of womanhood within a mosaic of musical and theatrical expressions that intertwined conventions of the past with contemporary idioms.

This vibrant presence of women in country music can be found throughout its history as it was dispersed through radio, recordings, film, and later television well before Nashville had emerged as the center of country music production. This book is an interdisciplinary study that considers important cultural junctures of commercial expansion in which the voices and performances of women came to the forefront of the country music industry. Focusing on the significant formats that helped catapult country music into the American consciousness in the 1930s, 1940s, and 1950s, it explores the musical and theatrical roles and reception of female performers in barn-dance radio, dance-hall culture, and honky-tonk music. Specifically I focus on Lulu Belle and Patsy Montana on Chicago's WLS radio station and the *National Barn Dance* in the 1930s; Carolina Cotton and Rose Maddox in the Los Angeles country music scene of the 1940s and 1950s; and Kitty Wells, Jean Shepard, and Goldie Hill in the 1950s country music industry in Nashville.

Women's early country music, bound to the cultural currents of these three decades, presents several avenues for inquiry that are central to a range of discourses involving gender, place, and class in popular musicology. Place and displacement in relation to musical style and performance, for example, are main themes throughout the book. Displacement informed specific musical discourses (including western swing, rockabilly, and honky-tonk) and dispersed country music throughout the nation. Chicago was the creative center of country music in the 1930s; California dominated the dispersal of country music in the 1940s; and Nashville emerged in the late 1940s and early 1950s as a major production hub.[5] This study connects women's performances in a range of media (radio, film, television, and recordings) to these geographic locales as well as to the imagined places and spaces (including the symbolic western frontier and the idealizations of a southern past) that played a formative role in the reception of country music.

Like Andrew Berish's recent work on the relationship between jazz and the "conceptions and experiences of place and mobility," I argue that women's country music in these years engendered "new ways to make sense of the changing spaces and places of American life."[6] Country music has been instrumental in reconceptualizing the public and private spaces (such as the home, the dance hall, and the honky-tonk) that were integral to the real and imagined lives of women striving for upward social mobility and/or resisting the rigidity of middle-class codes of behavior in historical settings of migration and displacement. Assuaging the fears and anxieties arising from the social and economic upheavals of industrialism, the commercial imagery of women's country music often provided modernist notions of "tradition, nostalgia, and the feminine" linked to the domestic.[7] Yet against these gendered concepts of familial and geographic stability, the actual music and performances of women artists pointed in the direction of change and mobility. This book thus underlines the general tensions emerging from dominant concepts of femininity, likened to the ideals of traditionalism, and gendered performances in country music that simultaneously indicate and embody societal shifts, for example, the singing cowgirl rejecting the trappings of domesticity to roam the imagined wild West, the hillbilly comedienne critiquing the gender economy of the southern home, or the honky-tonk angel longing for the security of the domestic while frequenting the licentious working-class juke joint. All these representations encapsulated the concerns of their audiences regarding historical junctures of disruption and uncertainty. Women's country music wielded an array of gendered imagery to signify these cultural contentions. Rather than simply alleviating the worries of its appreciators, it also underscored their ambivalent relationships to the ideological pressures of industrialism and middle-class security, especially when it became increasingly difficult to maintain a level of economic and geographic stability.

Along with the notion of place and the cultural transformations of the 1930s-1950s, the book's conceptual frame also connects musical expression (vocal idioms and timbres, melodic and harmonic language, song arrangements, and instrumentation) to the dynamic and paradoxical tensions of white, rural, working-class women's relationships to dominant norms of gender. Each chapter maintains a dialogue between musical enactments of gender and conventional notions of gender norms rooted in the historical processes of class relations and geographical dislocation. The working class has historically been defined against what it is not, such as the appearance and behavior of the middle class.[8] Since the nineteenth-century formation and social dominance of the middle class, it has self-consciously asserted its identity in everyday practices and living patterns, including cultural tastes, eating habits, recreational activities, physical comportment, and manners of dress and speech in specific places and spaces, in short, what Pierre Bourdieu has identified as *habitus*, the cultural practices and dispositions that distinguish and classify specific social groups.[9] One of the key concepts that have traditionally defined the middle class, on the other hand, has been a sense of character, largely based on a Victorian belief system of self-control and morality, which relied heavily on notions of femininity.[10] The so-called cult of true womanhood (a nineteenth-century social construction) made a feminine ideal a goal of the middle and upper classes, in which women, according to gender scholar Angela McRobbie, came to be the "standard bearers for middle-class family values, for certain norms of citizenship and also for safeguarding the valuable cultural capital accruing to them and their families through access to education, refinement and other privileges."[11] Within this context, femininity became a sign of the middle-class woman.[12]

In contrast to the gendered premises of bourgeois culture, rural and working-class women—domestic servants laboring in the homes of the upper classes, factory workers earning a wage to help support themselves and their families, farm women laboring inside or outside the home, and homemakers maintaining households without domestic help—were associated with physical forms of labor that coded them as hardy, robust, and strong.[13] The physicality and by extension sexuality associated with working-class women aligned them more with depictions of male laborers or with nineteenth-century sexologists' perceptions of female inverts than with the passivity and ideals of femininity itself. As musicologist Nadine Hubbs has noted, working-class constructions of womanhood have given rise to elements of gender variance that have much in common with the look and manner of queer women.[14] These gendered and sexual intersections of class and queerness have informed cultural expressions of rustic and unruly women. The asexual tomboy imagery of nineteenth-century female figures of the West, such as Calamity Jane, or the unruly vaudevillian women who recast male-defined roles of the scolding wife or temptress, all contributed to the gendered and theatrical tropes of women in early country music.

Historical perceptions of working-class women have positioned them as crossing the conventional demarcations of gender and sexuality, tied to distinct categories built around middle-class constructs that were part of U.S. society well before the 1930s, the period in which my study begins. As Beverley Skeggs writes, "For working-class women femininity was never a given (as was sexuality); they were not automatically positioned by it in the same way as middle- and upper-class White women. Working-class women—both Black and White—were coded as the sexual and deviant other against which femininity was defined."[15] In this context, working-class women have had to negotiate their gendered identities in ways that middle-class women have not. My own background is representative of this: having grown up in a rural, working-class family, I still recall how impressed my mother's cousins were with my maternal grandmother's abilities to do strenuous farm labor, "work like a man," while maintaining her feminin- ity largely by achieving a fashionable hairstyle with pin curls. Thus I approach working-class womanhood not simply as striving for middle-class acceptance but also as a complex process with its own specific concerns.

Throughout this study, I emphasize the fact that respectability and glamour have been powerful tropes that working-class women have used to dissociate themselves from the overt sexuality linked to the lower classes, as the work of Skeggs and others demonstrates.[16] Yet there is nothing simple or straightforward culturally or socially about the process of adopting or performing the look and physicality of middle-class decorum. Within this complicated play in which the unrefined, prurient, or masculinized body is up against corporal propriety and discipline, working-class women have occupied a "series of contradictory subject positions."[17] They are continually confronting dominant norms of gender, grounded in the idealized notions of bourgeois womanhood, while distanc- ing themselves from the sexually based metaphors that define the low Other. Commenting on Skeggs's ethnography of white working-class women, Lois McNay summarizes the situation: "In short, the women both identified and dis- identified with their class position and lived these ambivalences as the 'hidden injuries' of shame, awkwardness and the sense of being judged by others." There is more to the working class, however, than confronting and mediating dominant society. Elements of working-class culture, such as "the anti-pretentious humour, the dignity, the high ethical standards of honor, loyalty, and caring," are highly valued outside the lower classes and appropriated by the middle class.[18]

I build on these insights of feminist scholars to relate music to the complexity and contradictory nature of gender and class via the embodied performances and sonic details of women's early country music. Throughout my book, I jux- tapose women's performances with commercial and societal expectations to focus on the ways women artists wielded various performative devices to work within and against social norms. Women's sonic and performative narratives in barn-dance radio, western swing, rockabilly, and honky-tonk could evoke the dreams of upward mobility, the fears of social and economic upheaval, and the sexual and subaltern images that pointed to the hidden injuries of working- class womanhood. Performers not only voiced (culturally and acoustically) the vulnerabilities of working-class women but also critiqued the social restrictions and rigidity of gender conventions. The 1930s "Queen of Radio," Lulu Belle, for example, often projected a brazen model of womanhood that purposely defied the decorum of the bourgeois. Her unruly hillbilly persona, a performative mask of sorts, could be a source of either pride or embarrassment for her listening audiences, particularly southern migrants, rural or former rural denizens, and working women encountering the biases and increased scrutiny of midwestern and northern urban societies. At the same time, however, Lulu Belle could draw on domestic ideals of rural sentimentality to distance her gendered imagery from low and debased images to create fantasies of pastoralism informed by the feminine ideal.

With a focus on musical performance, the book aims to broaden the conceptual approach to country music from the thirties and the fifties. Chroniclers have largely traced the commercial forces that shaped female artists into domestic examples of rustic propriety. Kristine McCusker finds that the gendered representations in radio programming of early country music reinforced "gendered binary models, meaning there were men and there were women, cast in country terms as cowboys and cowgirls, southern matriarchs and hillbillies (typically, though not exclusively, gendered as masculine)."[19] Analyzing the particular ways in which the radio industry marketed women in barn-dance radio, McCusker's historical study argues that women usually adopted the guise of the "Southern sentimental mother" to promote "a more wholesome and moral national culture" for a country facing the chaos of the Great Depression and the uncertainty of the Second World War.[20]

Pamela Fox reaches similar conclusions about how the commercial formulas of the country music industry, including the gendered biases of country authenticity, channeled female artists into traditional gender roles. "At least through the immediate postwar period," women were seen as the "guardians of both conventional domesticity and rural 'folk' culture."[21] Yet male musicians, particularly those of 1930s barn-dance radio and 1940s honky-tonk, inhabited a cultural space of authenticity that could disclose the complexities of the working class. For Fox "poor or working-class white men serve as the normative model for authenticity in representational figures such as the country hillbilly and the more urban honky-tonk loner."[22]

By revisiting the musical careers of female and male artists and shedding new light on the performances of lesser-known artists, I pick up the interpretive threads of these previous studies of gender and move them in a musicological direction. Music has the power to complicate and exceed the significance of other cultural forms as it takes an active role in creating fluid and multiple interpretations of historical and social processes that concern the formation of social categories. That is, the meaning of the music cannot solely be found in the lyrical narratives of songs or in the marketing strategies of the country music industry.[23] I examine the promotional tactics that the country music industry employed in trying to relegate women to the home and the idyllic past. However, I do so in a way that highlights the contradictions between the country music industry's conservatism, grounded in its notions of respectability, and the musical voices, theatrical displays, and commercial success of female artists that could not be contained within the marketable packages of rustic, domestic propriety.

The book has been inspired by recent intersectional approaches that have emphasized the complexities and contestations of class in women's country music of later periods. A predominant topic is the music and imagery of Dolly Parton, an artist who has crafted a performative persona that theatricalizes the sexualized tropes of class, region, and womanhood while enabling her to reach the heights of commercial success and fame. Musicologist Mitchell Morris explores the ways Parton managed her crossover success musically in the 1970s while still maintaining an audience of country fans with her "self-cartooning" image of the "ultimate glamourpuss as seen by a naïve farm girl."[24] Leigh Edwards also suggests that Dolly Parton's "enactment of excessive femininity" formed important strategies of camp, parody, and irony that have broadened gendered notions of country authenticity.[25] Moreover, Lydia Hamessley's forthcoming book explores Parton's songwriting strategies and techniques that have drawn on traditional Appalachian mountain music to create narratives that disclose the complexities of womanhood, sexuality, class, and poverty.[26]

Also Hubbs demonstrates how the country artist Gretchen Wilson more recently has reconfigured the usual paradoxes of class and womanhood to project her musical image of the "Redneck Woman" (2004). Wilson unequivocally celebrates a "white working-class female subjectivity" without falling into the typical "twofold trap in which working-class women (a) symbolize a revered-and-resented middle-class respectability within their own class, even as they (b) embody disrespectability for the middle class."[27] In other words, working-class men's particular views of their wives cast them as pushy agents for middle-class comforts while dominant society link their class standing to an exaggerated sexuality.[28] "Redneck Woman" thus serves as a "gender and class manifesto that outsmarts the pitfalls and double binds attending its narrator's doubly devalued identity position and that calls attention to gender's contingency on class."[29]

The women in my study also resisted or challenged the gender codes of respectability by being in constant dialogue with normative culture. Their enactments, in turn, were not simply a celebration of class rebellion but rather also involved the complicated process of identification and disavowal for their audiences.[30] Country fans of various socioeconomic and regional backgrounds could identify with or appreciate the rebellious tones that confronted the rigidity of middle-class and heteronormative respectability. They could also distance their own rural or class identities from the parodies and masks of rusticity or take pleasure in the "exotic fantasies" of otherness.[31] Though the performative modes of the women in my study have had a lasting influence on artists like Parton and Wilson (as discussed in the conclusion), they continually confronted and played with the expectations of gender roles to highlight as well as contest class formation within a period of industrial modernity.

Given my interest in applying larger cultural factors to the particularities of country music, I examine the acoustic qualities of women's singing voices in a variety of musical settings that combined folk idioms with the theatrical traditions of the plebeian stage (notably the conventions rooted in minstrelsy and vaudeville) and the practices of popular music. Stylistic breadth has long been part of country music. Musicologist David Brackett, for example, demonstrates how the phonograph industry could not agree on a conceptual category for marketing the assemblage of disparate musical styles in 1920s rural white music making.[32] Yet within vernacular and popular idioms, particular practices and codes indeed emerge. The rhetorical cogency of music, as argued by musicologist Susan McClary, largely lies in the "shared procedures" of particular practices. Musical "conventions always operate as part of the signifying apparatus, even when they occupy the ground over which explicit references and encoding occur: in other words, it is not the deviations alone that signify but the norms as well."[33] Analyzing the ways in which the music of Bessie Smith articulates "desire and pleasure from the woman's point of view" within a twelve-bar blues form, McClary demonstrates that the blues performer balanced form and structure with individual expression to mold her visions of female sexual agency.[34]

Similarly, the book connects musical practice and shared sonic experiences to individual utterances. Considering the fact that most country artists entered the commercial spotlight as singers, the book emphasizes the role of vocality in relation to country music theatrics. I am interested in the sonic signification of the singing voice, how artistic choices in relation to vocal style, technique, and production have contributed to or subverted lyrical content or even the commercial packaging of performance identity within particular musical contexts. Musicological approaches to the voice in country music specifically and popular music in general have been especially helpful in illustrating the ways in which singing style can bear musical signification. In their collaborative study, Richard Leppert and George Lipsitz locate the power of Hank Williams's expressions not only in the text of songs but also in the sonic qualities of the performer's voice. The nasal timbre of Williams's higher vocal range produced a significant level of "acoustic tension" that effectively contrasted with "the culturally coded paternal assuredness of the deeper male sounds," representing "a significant refusal to accept dominant cultural narratives."[35] Against the historical backdrop of post–World War II domesticity, Williams musically "spoke directly to the internal psychic wounds generated by the gap between lived experience and an ideology that promised universal bliss through the emergence of romance and family as unchallenged centres of personal life."[36] As demonstrated in Williams's music, the singing voice can be a sonic form of cultural agency. Leppert has also written about the ways that Patsy Cline's vocality provided an aural model of gender that reclaimed "the very agency that many of the songs she sang, still duty-bound to 'traditional' values, eschew."[37] Moreover, Jocelyn Neal describes Cline's skillful use of phrasing as she moved away from the "hillbilly twang" of earlier performers and "mastered how to own a song, how to command it, and how to make it belong to her alone, even though she had not written it."[38]

Other analyses of the singing voice in country music have overturned previous understandings of specific artists and country styles. Robynn Stilwell, for example, explores how Brenda Lee's vocal production in her rockabilly numbers showcased a level of skill and agency that runs counter to the historiography of women in rockabilly that has rendered Lee "invisible and mute."[39] Travis Stimeling's astute interpretation of the vocal staging deployed in many of Waylon Jennings's outlaw songs complicates the usual perceptions of Jennings's "hard country" persona. Instead of supporting the appearance of "danger, unpredictability, and potential violence," Jennings's vocal production converted this stance into a "façade that masks profound insecurity."[40] More recently, Stimeling has interrogated the concept of authenticity through a study of Taylor Swift's vocal performances and her appeal to her target audience of teenage girls. As he underlines the ways "masculine notions of country music authenticity" have worked to marginalize female country performers, especially those like Swift who incorporate a more mainstream popular music aesthetic, Stimeling turns the gendering of authenticity on its head.[41] He argues that the vocal techniques of rawness and inexact intonation for which critics have faulted Swift are the same ones that have marked male vocalists like Hank Williams and Gram Parsons as authentic and sincere for decades.

Inspired by these insights into how the encoded meaning of vocal expression can overturn common (mis)perceptions of musical identity and aesthetic categories, I take into account the physiological demands placed on the singing voice that engendered various styles that could work for or against vocal and genre expectations.[42] In doing so, I engage with and contribute to musicological studies that have explored the relationship between the performing body and the cultural production of gender. Musicologist Suzanne Cusick has laid the discursive foundation of how the body of the instrumentalist or the singer enacts gender and sexuality by applying to musical performance Judith Butler's theories indicating that gender is constituted by performative acts.[43] Regarding the intricate connection between the voice and the body, Cusick writes that "we believe the voice *is* the body, its very breath and interior shapes projected outward into the world as a way others might know us, even know us intimately." Yet even though the singing voice emanates from the lungs, throat, and mouth, voices are still "culturally constructed. Voices are always performances of a relationship negotiated between the individual vocalizer and the vocalizer's culture." That is, the very act of singing can constitute "performances of sex, gender, and even sexuality."[44]

Extending these insights about the voice to country music, I analyze the role of the performing body in relation to the production of sound. I ask, What are the interior shapes of the body during moments of vocal production? What is physically involved in projecting particular vocal timbres, registers, and ranges? and What is the role of vocal style in shaping the aural metaphors of class, region, and gender? To answer these questions, I suggest that the vocal practices of southern vernacular singing provided a predominant vocal sonority, the nasal-inflected "twang" that so many scholars and journalists refer to in their accounts of country music.

Women vocalists, in particular, have typically sung in their chest voices even for notes that lay in their midrange or higher head register above the vocal break.[45] To help carry the chest voices to a higher range, many country singers propel air through the nasal chamber. In such instances, the singer raises the larynx, which helps in reaching notes of an upper range, and lowers the soft palate at the back of the throat, singing with what feels like a slightly closed throat. With this vocal approach (referred to as postnasality or hypernasality), the singer often produces a nasally pinched timbre. For a brighter and louder tone, as Jocelyn Neal notes, the performer can sing with twang, a vocal timbre associated with southern accents and speech patterns (such as diphthongs and vowel elongation).[46] Though (oral) twang is used in an array of vocal styles in popular music, musical theater, and opera to produce bright and high-frequency vocal tones that carry to the back of the performance hall, country musicians have long included nasal twang in their vocal deliveries.[47] Twang, in general, involves the constricting and narrowing of the pharynx (located behind the nose, mouth, and larynx), elevation of the larynx, and the tightening of the epiglottis and surrounding muscles (referred to as the aryepiglottic sphincter and located above the laryngeal tube). The turning of the epiglottis, made of flexible cartilage, to the back of the throat forms a "curled leaf shape" that acts as an additional resonator of high frequencies in the vocal tract.[48] In the process of constricting the throat muscles, the country singer often keeps the tongue in a high and flat position limiting the oral space and producing the sound at the front of the mouth and behind the nose.

The singer does not need to close the back of the throat and propel air through the nasal cavity to provide nasality. Nasal twang, otherwise referred to as "forced nasality" by vocal pedagogue James C. McKinney, sends the vibrations through the nose.[49] Many vocalists, however, combine nasal singing or hypernasality with nasal twang by keeping the nasal port partly opened so that air can move through the nose and the mouth simultaneously. Both of these singing approaches, particularly in the upper chest register, result in physical and vocal tensions (the tightening of the tongue, mouth, and throat muscles) and provide an aesthetic of strain (such as the "acoustic tension" of Hank Williams's singing voice in his higher range) associated with southern, white, rural, working-class musical culture.

Sammie Ann Wicks demonstrates that these particular vocal modes of production, hypernasality and nasal twang, have been a long-held tradition of southern vernacular singing evidenced by the ways that prominent nine-teenth-century southern singing masters reacted negatively to their students' "untutored" loud, nasal singing.[50] The institution of the singing school that had spread from eighteenth-century New England to the Midwest and the South largely sought to address low levels of musical literacy and to standardize singing practices.[51] B. F. White and E. J. King, the compilers of the *Sacred Harp* (which became the most prominent southern shape-note hymnal), were proponents of reforming and sanitizing the vocal traditions of "lining out" psalms wherein church deacons read or chanted lines aloud and congregations responded by embellishing the tune, producing an improvised performance that bore little resemblance to the printed music. In particular, they opposed the melodic embellishments rendered by loud, nasal voices straining in higher registers. The introduction to White and King's 1859 edition of the *Sacred Harp*, for example, declares, "Yet how hard it is to make some believe soft singing is the most melodious; when, at the same time, loud singing is more like the hootings of the midnight bird than refined music."[52] They go on to explain that words should be "properly pronounced, and not torn to pieces between the teeth, nor forced through the nose. Let the mouth be freely opened, but not too wide . . . and let the sound come from the lungs."[53] Similar to White and King, Joe S. James (editor of the 1911 version of the *Sacred Harp*) also reacted against "the twisted rills and trills of the unnatural snaking of the voice" and instructed singers to "avoid any unnatural contraction or distension of the mouth or throat" and to forgo directing "the sound into the nasal cavities."[54] In many ways, these edi-tors and teachers were insisting that students of shape-note singing adopt the European aesthetics of bel canto or classical singing, which had come to the conceptual forefront in the latter half of the nineteenth century and remained integral throughout the twentieth century.

Examples of this traditional vocal art that these singing instructors so firmly opposed can be heard in Alan Lomax's 1959 recording of the Alabama Sacred Harp Convention. In the spiritual "David's Lamentation" and the folk hymn "Melancholy Day," for instance, the women singers work to stay in their chest ranges, increasing in volume to realize the higher-pitched melodies without transitioning to their head voices.[55] This tendency is especially noticeable dur-ing a stepwise ascent to D_5 in "David's Lamentation," which at least one of the sopranos manages to sing in the chest register with a loud and piercing vocal timbre clearly inflected by nasal twang without any sort of vibrato. From the early recordings of Roba Stanley and the Carter Family to the honky-tonk recordings of Kitty Wells, female singers have incorporated these elements of southern vernacular singing into their performances by combining an expressive chest register inflected by the use of twang and nasality with additional vocal techniques influenced by popular music and microphone technology, such as the use of vibrato and vocal slides and breaks for expressive effect.

Focusing on the singing voice in country music, I explore how individual vocalist's artistic choices of register, range, and timbre have helped shape musical narratives involving notions of class inflected by gender and region. Trying to modify the volume of her singing voice for the microphone, Lulu Belle, for example, initially departed from southern vernacular traditions to sing in a quiet head voice above the vocal break. Yet she still sang with an explicit use of nasal twang producing an aural impression of a naive young country girl unacquainted with the rituals of heterosexual courtship and marriage. When playing the part of the wench (a theatrical incarnation of the unruly woman), however, she would purposely caricaturize the tone, timbre, and register of southern vernacular singing with vocal excess and exaggeration. Yet in other settings, Lulu Belle would abandon nasality and sing with rounded tones love ballads in duet with Scotty Wiseman. In the cavernous space of the dance hall, Rose Maddox projected her chest voice with an open-throat technique similar to that of a "belter" to perform songs that cast contrasting representations of Okie womanhood against the gendered convention of post–World War II. Yet she would also inflect her vocal timbre nasally in parodies of well-known country songs. A few years later, Kitty Wells performed honky-tonk songs by pushing her chest register to a higher range where she highlighted her nasal-twang tone. In this way, her piercing and strained voice convincingly depicted the honky-tonk angel's desperate desire for material comfort and security. Using the microphone for expressive means, Jean Shepard and Goldie Hill similarly modified their nasal-sounding voices to offer subtle shades of dynamics and phrasing in their honky-tonk ballads, which also addressed the desires and fears of a 1950s audience who found the era's promises of socioeconomic mobility out of their reach.

Yet, importantly, not all the women in my study sang with the nasal twang that characterizes country singing. The singing cowgirls discussed here—Patsy Montana, the Girls of the Golden West, Louise Massey, and Carolina Cotton—purposely adopted the vocal styles of more-mainstream popular artists, like Kate Smith, who performed Tin Pan Alley tunes in a pseudo-classical style. As Stilwell has pointed out, female popular singers of the big-band era were expected to follow the assumptions of "vocal decorum," that is, singing in tune in a smooth manner.[56] In front of the microphone, the singing cowgirls, who were often lead singers of western swing ensembles, cultivated rounded tones in both their chest and their head registers without overly emphasizing nasal-twang timbres, thereby projecting aural versions of femininity that resonated with mainstream or middle-class popular aesthetics. But this decorous vocal mode nevertheless stood in direct contrast to the virtuosic yodels that suggested the cowgirl's bold presence on the mythical landscape of the West. Following this aural and theatrical trend, Carolina Cotton, as a 1940s singing cowgirl, combined the virtuosity of the yodel with its comedic legacy in her western swing performances, which continued the thespian fluidity of barn-dance radio.

In addition to the vocal modes of production in country music, vernacular and popular singing styles have been just as varied. For example, African American women vocalists in both sacred and secular styles, such as gospel and blues, have often combined chest-dominant vocal techniques with various timbral affects for expressive means.[57] A choreographic mixture of chest and head voice can be heard in the singing of Mahalia Jackson and Aretha Franklin, who acquired their vocal training in the church and by listening to the recordings of the 1920s blues queens. In particular, Bessie Smith employed an array of vocal devices that showcased the different shades of her chest-dominant register, such as growling in her lower range, singing with a quiet vibrato, and belting melodies in her upper range. The dynamic singing of the blues queens like Smith extended to the technical and artistic choices of rhythm-and-blues artists, notably Big Mama Thornton and Ruth Brown, who could inflect their full-bodied chest voice with slides, breaks, and melodies in the upper head register in narratives that confronted the ideals of romantic love and voiced sexual desire and heartache.

Timbral inflections of the lower range of women's singing voices, particularly chest dominant vocal techniques combined with an open-throat approach, have often constituted vocal signs of strength and agency that have defied common notions of gender, especially those that involve bodily refinement and containment. As Nina Eidsheim reminds us, however, "the perceived meaning of vocal timbre and vocalization" is contingent on listening practices of the listener. "Voice is already produced through social relationships, within which it is heard and reproduced."[58] Because we, as listeners, often get our perceptions of voice types from the gendered playing field of opera (particularly nineteenth-century opera), we have learned that the high-voice part of the soprano is the sonic embodiment of virginal innocence, while the lower mezzo-soprano, like Bizet's sultry Carmen or Verdi's Amneris, project visions of sexuality, resistance, and worldliness.[59] The usual typecasting of vocal roles has led critics to describe Ethel Merman's belting chest voice in terms of masculine power, far removed from notions of femininity and linked to working-class aesthetics (even though Merman's background was middle class).[60] This reception has extended to blues queens and rhythm-and-blues artists, as well as to contemporary popular and country singers.[61]

But not all chest-dominant techniques suggest a (dangerous) level of vocal power. Laurie Stras's study of the vocal production of early girl groups (such as the Shirelles, the Ronettes, and the Shangri-Las) reveals that their male producers encouraged a particular vocal aesthetic of vulnerability in songs about teenage love. Though lead singers typically pushed their voices to the higher range, they did not project a strong belting chest tone. Instead, girl groups would often produce a strained, thin, often nasal, and out-of-tune vocality.[62] Singing with a closed throat and high larynx to render heightened melodic passages, they infused their narratives of adolescent romance with the sounds that suggested naivete and fragility.

As Motown emerged as a major center for the production of girl groups, Berry Gordy and Smoky Robinson pushed for their female ensembles to sing even higher with light timbres often located in the head voice, as Jacqueline Warwick's work demonstrates. The Marvelettes (who gave Motown its first hit recording) initially featured Gladys Horton's husky purrs and robust, chest-dominated tone. But this vocal production of "robust sass" (as Warwick calls it) with clear ties to rhythm-and-blues singing practices "was set aside in favor of [Wanda] Young's soprano whisper-sweetness."[63] The aesthetic differences between the use of a predominant chest voice and a high, light vocal timbre also played out in the singing careers of Florence Ballard and Diana Ross of the Supremes.

As these studies of vocal practice demonstrate, the singing voice carries important elements of musical signification that can exceed, complicate, or reinforce the marketing of female vocalists within the popular music industry. By placing vocal production in relation to the theatrical staging of country music, I focus on how the "sonic dynamisms" of performance stood in tension with the conventions associated with prevalent commercial or social environments. In this book I seek to complicate the usual understandings of how commercial culture and patriarchal values worked in tandem to delimit women's avenues of musical expression. The marketing strategies employed to press the musical and performative spectacles of women into ideal portraits of gender often came undone. It was as if the singing voices of the hillbilly buffoon, the singing cowgirl, or the honky-tonk angel could not be completely contained within the commercial images of respectability and domesticity. Instead radio and the country music industry tried to come to terms with Lulu Belle's parodic displays of femininity (often vocally enacted), Montana singing about the musical promises and freedoms of the West, and Wells's success in providing a sonic voice for the honky-tonk angel as the first "Queen of Country Music."

• • •

The book is divided into three parts. Part 1 focuses on radio's role in propelling country music into the national spotlight, while part 2 concentrates on the performance contexts of California country music. The third part examines Nashville's emergence as a major production center of country music that competed in a popular music market. Chapter 1 sets the stage for understanding the theatrical context of early country music as a hybrid form that reaches a heterogeneous audience. On Chicago's WLS and the *National Barn Dance*, "oldtime" or "hillbilly" music were part of the eclectic blend of styles and genres that transgressed cultural divides of high, middle, and low during the Depression era. Chapters 2 and 3 focus on the musical treatments of gender by WLS's radio stars Lulu Belle and Patsy Montana and their use of a fluid mix of styles and the vaudevillian practices of early country music to respond to their listeners' fraught relationship with the socioeconomic upheavals of the 1930s. Lulu Belle's lowbrow theatrics expressed the class, gendered, and regional tensions stemming from the vilification of southern migrants in the Midwest and the North and the changing roles of men and women. To bring into focus Lulu Belle's artistic agency in her stage routines, I connect her theatrics and vocal styling to a historical lineage of comediennes, including the Elinore Sisters, Sophie Tucker, and Fanny Brice, who assumed the roles originally defined by female impersonators of the popular stage. Though Montana could also perform gender-bending songs that challenged social norms, she developed a cowgirl persona that engendered a sense of glamour. Nevertheless, she addressed the gender strife and change of the 1930s by refashioning the West into a place where standard models of gender could include autonomous cowgirls who yodeled to the heights of their vocal range while singing sweetly about the symbolic freedoms associated with frontier individualism.

Part 2 begins with chapters 4 and 5 and considers the musical and performative roles of women in the dance hall culture of California. Chapter 4 focuses on the relationship between Carolina Cotton's vocal performances with the leading western swing bands of the 1940s and her appearance in Hollywood films that reached both a regional and a national audience of transplanted Okies, wartime women, servicemen, and mainstream appreciators. Like her predecessors and peers in barn-dance radio, Cotton contributed to California's theatrical staging of country music by using the yodel as a means to slip in and out of a range of rustic characters. Chapter 5 examines how Rose Maddox magnified the buffoonery of the rube, bringing the burlesque humor of the hillbilly to the roadhouses and nightspots of California, while she developed an open-throat singing style that still drew on southern vernacular traditions. Her bold theatrics and vocal production carved out a performance space for honky-tonk singer Jean Shepard and the "Queen of Rockabilly," Wanda Jackson, in Los Angeles's country music industry.

Chapter 6, the first chapter in part 3, analyzes Kitty Wells's musical expressions of yearning and loss within 1950s honky-tonk, a style that encapsulated the burdens of a newly founded white working class. Wells, who honed her singing voice in the gospel traditions of the Church of the Nazarene, provided a vocal means to articulate the sexual codes of working-class womanhood. Joining Wells in the Nashville music industry were Jean Shepard and Goldie Hill, who also included vocal elements of southern vernacular singing in their narratives about sexual desire, resistance to the double standards of gender, and the anguish and vulnerability of women abandoned in love by men. Chapter 7 positions the singing voices of Wells, Hill, Shepard, and their male contemporaries against the marketing strategies of 1950s country music. As the country music business strove for commercial acceptance in the popular-music market, it promoted performers, including male honky-tonk artists, as examples of middle-class propriety. The conclusion considers the ways in which the female artists of the 1960s and 1970s—Loretta Lynn and Dolly Parton—and more contemporary artists—the Dixie Chicks and Miranda Lambert—have drawn on the performative and singing practices of the women in my study to form their own individual voices.

Taken as a whole, this interdisciplinary study highlights the significance of women in early country music. Connecting the singing voice to the theatrics of the popular stage, the politics of marketing country to mass-mediated audiences, and the historical processes of class and gender, I bring country music to the center of many musical and social concerns of scholars of various backgrounds. At the same time, I sharpen the focus on the dynamics of class and gender by locating the meaning of women's country music within working-class women's uneasy and fraught relationship with the ideals of femininity. Each chapter works to convey the artistic agency and vibrancy of the individuals considered in my study. Their voices articulated the paradoxes of gender norms in relation to social and geographical mobility. In sound recordings, film, and radio transcriptions, the immediacy of their voices has reached our ears, casting light on the historical nuances and complexities of both real experiences and the cultural representations of gendered and classed lives.

PART ONE

WLS and the *National Barn Dance*

1 Early Country Music

*The Crossing of Musical Hierarchies
on Chicago's WLS*

Country music gained its foothold in the commercial establishment
of popular music largely through radio programming in the 1930s and 1940s.[1]
Before the recording industry stumbled onto the appeal of southern vernacular music, Atlanta's WSB had become the first radio station to introduce white
southern folk and popular musicians over the airwaves. Fiddlin' John Carson,
for example, could be heard on WSB in 1922, a year prior to his recording debut
with Okeh Records, which launched not only the "old-time" series for the record
label but also the phonograph industry's business pursuits of recording and
circulating the various strands of white, rural, and southern vernacular music.[2]
While the recording industry contributed significantly to building a market for
what was referred to as "mountain music," "old time-tunes," or "hill country
music," radio stations followed WSB's model of capitalizing on the commercial
interests of musicians connected to the South.[3] Fort Worth's WBAP introduced
the first barn-dance program in 1923, replete with an evening of square-dance
music. The succeeding year Chicago's WLS established the *National Barn Dance*,
which emerged as the reigning Saturday-evening barn-dance show throughout
the 1930s as it acquired network status and transmitted southern vernacular
music into the homes of listeners across the Midwest and the nation.

Of particular interest in this study is radio's role in shaping and popularizing
the theatrical and musical conventions of early country music on one of the
most prominent radio stations. This achievement catapulted some of the biggest
names in country music into the national spotlight. Among them were Lulu
Belle, the "Queen of Radio"; Red Foley, who was not only a successful recording
and radio artist but also emceed a portion of the *Grand Ole Opry* from 1946
to 1953; the singing cowgirl Patsy Montana with her hit song "I Want to Be a
Cowboy's Sweetheart"; and the singing cowboy Gene Autry, who crooned his

way from radio to the silver screen. Yet WLS did not broadcast only the syncretic styles of early country music, composed of sentimental ballads, comic numbers, southern string-band playing, western swing, and Tin Pan Alley cowboy songs. The radio station also mixed the diverse strands of vernacular expression with music that pointed to the high and popular aesthetics of the middle-class mainstream. Listeners could tune their radios to the serenades of the WLS Orchestra or to the polished singing of numerous soloists and singing ensembles who swung the melodies of popular tunes in sweet-sounding harmony. The programming of "classical" music or "cultivated" popular music contrasted starkly with the rustic buffoonery that included southern backwoods characters, blackface comedians, and ethnic personalities. In transmitting a multitude of styles and genres, WLS and radio in general largely continued vaudeville's pursuit of bringing together listeners of different musical tastes and social backgrounds while still striving to attract a middle-class consumer base.[4]

This chapter examines country music's dynamic role in WLS's enterprise of catering to a divergent audience of women, men, midwestern farm families, former rural dwellers, European immigrants, and white southern migrants within the historical setting of the Great Depression. Previous scholars of barn-dance radio have argued that WLS's historical significance is predominantly its programming of rural music that provided bucolic reveries of escape from the economic distress and uncertainty of the 1930s.[5] Though WLS did strive to create fantasies that enabled its audience to retreat from the harsh material realities that plagued the decade, early country music did not offer only nostalgic portraits of a premodern past. Providing a counterpoint to the dominant narrative of WLS and the *National Barn Dance*, I argue that the various strands of old-time music or hillbilly music achieved a regional and national consciousness by circulating within a mix of high, middle, and low entertainment associated with the various cultural configurations of taste. In this setting, radio's eclectic programming enabled a complex and contradictory play of social negotiations tied to regionalism, dislocation, and the shifting parameters of gender conventions during the Great Depression.

WLS's Programming for a Heterogeneous Audience

WLS, an independent radio station, was established by Sears, Roebuck, and Company in 1924 and then sold to Burridge D. Butler, the publisher of the *Prairie Farmer* newspaper, in 1928. The station initially catered to the midwestern farm family, an audience overlooked by radio's predominantly urban-centered programming. Billing WLS as the "Prairie Farmer Station," Butler believed that radio technology could tap into the midwestern readership he had carefully cultivated through his newspaper, which he had owned since 1908. With the marriage of radio and print, Butler could hope for the creation of an "imagined community" of listeners who resided in the Midwest.[6] The essays collected in *The Hayloft Gang: The Story of the National Barn Dance* provide historical accounts of how WLS managed to draw a rural populace into the folds of its audience.[7] Its clear-channel signal and fifty-thousand-watt transmitter (acquired in 1931) sent WLS's programs into the homes of people living in the central part of the country. The daily and weekly broadcasts—agricultural reports and weather updates for the farmer, programs such as the *Homemaker's Hour* about fashion, cooking, and child rearing for the farmwife, and bedtime stories for the children—made WLS's programs a vital element in the daily lives of all members of the farm family. Thus in 1930 the *WLS Family Album*, a trade magazine published by the *Prairie Farmer* from 1930 to 1957, could state, "With clean entertainment, new market, and weather reports, WLS has a great audience in rural communities. Thousands of letters daily assure us that our human interest programs reach the hearts of WLS listeners."[8]

The "farm" station further strengthened its relationship with its target audience by transmitting music that seemed compatible with the lifestyle of rural denizens. The *WLS Family Album*, for example, announced that the early-morning daily program *Smile-A-While* was ideal for "farm families and other early risers who enjoy[ed] lively popular and old-time music to start the day off right."[9] As this advertising blurb for *Smile-A-While* suggested, WLS mingled popular tunes with folk or old-time music and other musical genres on the same programs. Yet WLS often cloaked its multitude of genres in regional and pastoral imagery. The instrumental quartet the Hoosier Hot Shots often played swing numbers and comic songs, the Maple City Four sang Tin Pan Alley songs and church hymns, and the many sister and female acts, such as the Three Little Maids, harmonized old standards as well as current popular songs. Verne, Lee, and Mary, another successful trio, were billed as the "Three Wisconsin Honey Bees" or "sweet harmonizers" who, at times, sung to the accompaniment of the WLS Orchestra (see figure 1).[10]

WLS's programming, however, drew more than just the farm families of the Midwest into its listening community. Historian Chad Berry has written of how the Chicago radio station also marketed its music to a growing body of white southern migrants.[11] Since World War I, black and white southerners had been leaving the depressed conditions of the South for the economic promises of such manufacturing cities as Chicago, Detroit, and Cincinnati.[12] By 1930, close to three million white southerners (mostly from the Upland South region of the southeastern United States) had settled in the Midwest.[13] The contemporary sociologist Vivien M. Palmer even noticed a "distinct colony" of Tennesseans in the North Center of Chicago in 1930 that had joined the various ethnic communities of the city.[14] Acknowledging the increased presence of southern migrants

Figure 1. Verne, Lee, and Mary. *WLS Family Album*, 1936.

in the Midwest, WLS encouraged an array of singing and instrumental styles associated with the vernacular traditions and folk theatrics of the rural South. From 1926 to 1930, Bradley Kincaid played the part of the "singing mountaineer" performing folk ballads supposedly plucked from southern Appalachia. Beginning in the 1930s, the Cumberland Ridge Runners offered instrumental renditions of southern vernacular music, and rustic buffoon figures, such as Lulu Belle or Arkie the Woodchopper, highlighted the humor connected with hillbilly music.

I want to extend Berry's historic account of WLS's audience of southern migrants to argue that the radio station's fans were not simply a homogenous coterie of prosperous "farm folks" but rather consisted of a diverse body of listeners who crossed class, gender, regional, and ethnic lines.[15] The varied nature of WLS's programming was intended for a heterogeneous white audience. The agricultural Midwest included those of German-Swiss descent, many of whom later moved to the industrial centers of the region.[16] During the first third of the twentieth century, when rural dwellers were leaving the countryside for the city, places like Chicago also attracted European immigrants from Poland and Czechoslovakia in addition to migrants from the American South.[17] These groups constituted the rank and file of working-class waitresses, sales clerks, laborers, and foremen and lower-middle-class factory managers.

In navigating the musical tastes of a multifarious audience, WLS and radio in general followed the theatrical conventions of vaudeville, a format of entertainment entwined with the contested debates of high and low culture that had emerged in the closing decades of the nineteenth century.[18] Much has been written about vaudeville's attempts to negotiate this crossing of high and low by creating an aura of respectability on stage and in the audience. Featuring music and skits consistent with a middle-class ethos, entrepreneurs hoped to draw bourgeois women into their audiences to connect their halls to "the sacralized feminized culture that emerged in the second half of the nineteenth century."[19] Yet even though "vaudeville houses marketed themselves as a sanitized, family-friendly" venue, as noted by Lori Harrison-Kahan, they continually negotiated the conflicting illustrations of refinement, on the one hand, and the bawdy, on the other.[20] Vaudeville thus did not simply adopt the standards of propriety couched in the nineteenth-century ideology of the feminine (i.e., the "angel in the house").[21] Instead, it emerged, according to M. Alison Kibler, as a "site of debate over cultural hierarchy and 'refinement'" as it appealed to a "mass audience: a heterogeneous crowd of white men and women of different classes and ethnic groups."[22]

Continuing the goals of vaudeville, radio encouraged a multitude of musical idioms that brought together popular and folk music and serious and comic expressions. David Goodman's recent research demonstrates that radio revived "older traditions from before the sacralization and rigid separation of highbrow from lowbrow culture, while at the same time ostentatiously proclaiming and surrounding itself with the sacred aura of classical musical tradition and its great performers." Radio then was not simply a democratizing vehicle meant to edify the masses by broadcasting "serious" music. Rather, "radio's commercial but civically responsible public sphere was being filled with an often self-conscious juxtaposition of higher and low, classical and popular."[23] In other words, radio was a medium that upheld the divides between musical hierarchies as it jumbled together classical music with a wide range of vernacular musics.

Following the general trends of radio programming, WLS radio managers worked to create a listening space for a middle-class consumer base of leisure (lower-middle-class farm women or manufacturing managers, for example) while meeting the cultural tastes of a disparate audience of male and female southern migrants, immigrants, and urbanites. Just as vaudeville mediated the intersections of high and low entertainment, radio highlighted programs that projected a bourgeois sensibility onto the staging of slapstick comedy based in the theatrics of minstrelsy (including blackface and rube and ethnic humor).

Middlebrow culture, associated with an expanding middle class, had taken root in American society in the 1920s, finding a place between high cultural forms couched in modernist aesthetics (avant-garde music) and plebeian humor and entertainment (burlesque).[24] Much of WLS's programming seemed to be part of this "genial middle ground" even as it highlighted rural and working-class amusements.[25]

For those of German-Swiss ethnicity, for example, WLS's daily and weekly programs featured instrumental German music and Swiss vocal performances aimed at transmitting a European lineage of middlebrow respectability. WLS took pride in being the "first station to bring a Little German Band to the air" and included a photo of this ensemble rehearsing in the 1934 issue of the *WLS Family Album*. The picture's caption noted that the members of the band had "a collection of numbers brought directly from Germany, which [were] not to be found in any American music library."[26] Apart from programming rarified instrumental music, WLS also promoted Christine, the "Little Swiss Miss," who could sing yodel songs that soared "almost as high as the Swiss Alps where her ancestors used to live."[27] In her Swiss costume, Christine projected a pastoral image that helped position an ethnic version of femininity in the romanticized past, underscoring the feminine ideals of sentimentality for farm families and urbanites with a northern European background (see figure 2). In addition to promoting a repository of musical traditions, WLS demonstrated how German-Swiss acts could fit in the contemporary terrain of vocal harmony groups. The Three Hired Men were an ensemble of "Swedish boys with plenty of 'mean' harmony," a description that can be compared to many other WLS harmony acts, such as the Maple City Four or the Melody Men.[28]

The esteemed lineage and acculturation of German-Swiss music promoted by WLS, however, contrasted with the stage antics of "Ole Yonson," a comic ethnic figure known for his musical parodies of popular songs sung in Swedish (see figure 3). As WLS advertised, the Swedish rube "is especially comical to watch, as he keeps time with those long arms. Ole usually is somewhere out in the crowd when his turn comes on the program, and he gallops up and climbs onto the stage at the very last minute."[29] Ole Yonson, joining other rube comedians and comediennes before the WLS microphone, was part of a theatrical lineage of humor that emphasized crude caricatures of ethnic traits. Satirical displays of immigrant culture could mock the aura of refinement that WLS cultivated in its broadcasts of the "Swiss Miss" or traditional German music, thereby traversing cultural divides between respectability and grotesque humor.

Apart from German or Swiss music, WLS also entertained an emerging Polish and Czech population then settling in Chicago. The singing cowgirl Patsy Montana wrote her hit song "I Want to Be a Cowboy's Sweetheart" (1935) with this diverse audience in mind. Montana recalled in a 1984 interview, "We always

Figure 2. Christine, the "Swiss Miss." *WLS Family Album*, 1937.

had a good following right in the city of Chicago, because of a lot of Polish people there and Irish and, you know, just all kinds of nationalities."[30] Featuring the rhythmic language of swing that predominated in 1930s dance bands, Montana shaped her cowgirl tune into a jazz-inflected polka replete with yodels. As her virtuosic yodels evoked the Swiss-Alpine tradition, popularized by her WLS peers (notably Christine, the "Swiss Miss"), her polka song resonated with the musical sensibilities of German, Polish, and Czech immigrants.

Moreover, WLS made a conscious effort to connect with a growing urban audience located in the industrial centers of the Midwest. As billed in WLS's fan magazine *Stand By!* (a *Prairie Farmer* publication launched in 1935), the daily *Dinnerbell* program offered "a wide variety of musical features, guest speakers, market news, and information on many subjects of interest in both town and country."[31] Furthermore, WLS tried to blur the divide between rural dwellers and urban listeners in an article titled "Chicago—A Farm Town," emphasizing

Figure 3. "Ole Yonson."
WLS Family Album, 1934.

that the Windy City was the "the national's agricultural capital" and "the biggest farming town in the country."[32] It placed the buying and selling of livestock within the industrial and manufacturing complex of Chicago, demonstrating that the interests of the midwestern farmer were not far removed from those of the urbanite. And for those listeners with a more urban sensibility, WLS included genres like the blues in *Merry-Go-Round*, its Saturday afternoon "variety" program of "harmony teams, male quartets, banjo selections, piano novelties, 'blues' numbers, and other features [that] help[ed] to make this fast-moving show."[33]

With broadcasts of competing vernaculars, including early country music, WLS positioned them against the aggrandizement of western art music and made it clear that it was a radio station that upheld the civilizing and aesthetic principles of classical music. The station's publicity billed "the WLS Orchestra, under the direction of Herman Felber, Jr." as "a group of the finest musicians in Chicago," proclaiming, "Every member is a distinguished soloist." The orchestra could evocatively play "stirring marches, dreamy melodies" and permeate the airwaves with "the mellow tones of the wood-winds" and "the sweetness of strings."[34] WLS's programming included vocal ensembles that also signaled the esteemed position of "classical" music. The contralto Carol Hammond, "a Chicago Girl," projected "a grand voice," and the Three Contraltos, each artist "a soloist and accomplished musician," performed to orchestral or piano accompaniment.[35] In fact, WLS underscored that one of the singers of the Three Contraltos, Adele Brandt, was a distant relative of Franz Schubert and enjoyed singing the composer's acclaimed "Ave Maria."[36]

The panoply of styles and genres proliferating on the daily programs was the precise goal of WLS, as explained by the station manager Edgar Bill: "We featured high-brow music on one night, dance bands on another; then programs featuring large choruses. Other nights, we'd have variety or we might have a radio play. When it came to Saturday night, it was quite natural to book in old-time music, including old-time fiddling, banjo and guitar music and cowboy songs."[37] WLS's Saturday-evening program the *National Barn Dance* emerged as one of the most successful shows that helped launch early country music into the national limelight. First broadcast in 1924, this weekly hoedown reached a broad regional audience that could also attend live performances of the show in the radio station's Eighth Street Theatre, built in Chicago in 1932. By the following year, listeners throughout the country could tune their radios for a one-hour segment of the *National Barn Dance* transmitted by the NBC Blue network.

Sponsored by Keystone Steel and Wire Company, the barn-dance program, billed as the *Keystone Barn Dance*, usually began the evening with a regional broadcast that featured Lulu Belle (the "Belle of the Barn Dance") with her husband and duet partner, Scotty, in performances of comic and sentimental numbers. The duo was also part of the national broadcast (sponsored by Alka-Seltzer and billed as the *National Barn Dance: NBC Hour*), which included a varied selection of entertainment: the vocal trio Verne, Lee, and Mary with orchestral accompaniment, the jazz-inflected playing of the instrumental ensemble Hoosier Hot Shots, the harmonized hymns and popular numbers of the Maple City Four, the southern string-band playing of the Cumberland Ridge Runners, the polished cowboy songs of the Westerners, and the blackface performances of "Spareribs." Either before or after the national broadcast, WLS broadcast various segments of the barn dance, supported by an array of sponsors, such as the *Gillette Hayloft Party*, *Barn Dance Jamboree* (sponsored by the Murphy's Products Company), *Barn Dance Frolic*, or *Barn Dance* (sponsored by the Jordon Clothing Company). Later in the evening (beginning sometime between 9:00 and 11:00 and continuing until midnight), the *Prairie Farmer–WLS National Barn Dance* continued to reach regional listeners with the western swing numbers and cowgirl songs of Patsy Montana and the Prairie Ramblers; the popular and sentimental numbers of contralto Grace Wilson; Christine, the "Swiss Miss"; the Irish tenor Bill O' Connor; and Arkie's comic performances of old-time songs.[38] The Saturday-night programs (which drew from WLS's extensive array of artists) featured not only popular and early country music but also concert hall music in a variety-show format. It was in this context of mingled musical sounds and categories that radio transmitted early country music to a divergent audience.[39]

To negotiate the cultural and musical divides of serious and popular, urban and rural, sentimental and parodic, WLS tried to frame its eclectic mix of styles and genres (even ethnic and rube humor and popular urban music) nostalgically, as if the modern methods of radio transmission could effectively pull music from a bygone era, predating the rise of modernity and mass consumerism. In this vein, WLS's artists were not advertised as sophisticated performers with highly polished stage acts but rather as "home folks, striving to do their best to lighten your cares by bringing you wholesome fun and entertainment." Their goal was categorical: "They hope that you will enjoy their show from the ringing of the first cowbell until 'Home Sweet Home.'"[40] WLS's publicity continually marketed its radio personalities with overdetermined language to project an image of old-fashioned propriety: "In every branch of WLS activities the fireside and the family are emphasized. That's because we are home and fireside folks and we love our homes and our families."[41]

WLS, attempting to mediate the continual crossing of cultural divides in its broadcasts, linked notions of sentimentality to a middle-class ethos by regularly emphasizing that its managers, announcers, and performers came from respectable circumstances. Photographs and reports in the *WLS Family Album* were used to encourage fans to forge personal connections with their favorite radio personalities by learning about their private domestic lives, for instance, how they met their spouses and the delightful activities of their children.[42] Historian Kristine McCusker has argued that barn-dance radio, like its predecessor vaudeville, emphasized the virtue of its artists to attract a broader-based audience. Especially during the two world wars, radio wanted its artists (in particular women performers) to "promote a more wholesome and moral national culture."[43] Along those lines, radio executives of WLS and the *National Barn Dance* hoped to establish a sense of stability for their listeners as well as attract the support of sponsors, the economic basis of the radio business. Thus it was essential for performers to come across as upstanding individuals, especially since the radio industry aspired to cultivate a culture of consumerism based in social convention, even during the tumultuous conditions of the Great Depression, when middle-class stability was becoming an impossible ideal.

The Great Depression and WLS's Audience

The sentimental and middle-class imagery promulgated in WLS's trade magazines carried additional symbolic weight during the Depression era, when the threats of dispossession pervaded the lives of many of its listeners. In her study examining 1930s women's novels in relation to middle-class ideology, Jennifer Haytock argues that downward mobility made "it ever more important to stake out lines of class identity—to cling to signs of middle-class status and to identify even indirectly, those who 'did not belong,' a category that might include immigrants and African Americans but also included the working class, the poor, those who had slid backward, even those who violated middle-class proprieties."[44] WLS's emphasis on sentimentality and domesticity largely continued the era's debates over cultural hierarchy and respectability. The crossing of cultural divides could cordon off genteel culture from the "low others" (immigrant or southern rubes) who failed to live up to bourgeois expectations and at the same time remind appreciators that they were part of a larger community of listeners who could immerse themselves in the fantasies of the past—the ideals of home, family, and community.

Despite WLS's nostalgic portraits, real divisions along gender, class, and region were increasingly exacerbated by the economic and social crisis of the Great Depression. Farmers believed that the federal government was more concerned about the welfare of those in the city than those in the agricultural industry; men lost their jobs and resented the increased presence of women in the work force; and midwestern society regarded southern migrants as an economic drain in an economy with few resources. Even before the market crash of 1929, WLS's particular audience of farm families found themselves hard-pressed to maintain their livelihoods in the midst of falling crop prices. As Daniel Nelson notes, "For the nearly half-million midwestern farm families that earned no more than a semiskilled factory worker, the depression was more than a debt crisis."[45] With the cost of production far outweighing the selling price of crops, many farm families lived in fear of losing their farms. Those fears became a reality as bankruptcy doubled in the agricultural Midwest between 1931 and 1933 and reached even higher levels in Minnesota and Iowa.[46]

The 1930s rural Midwest was far from being a harmonious region of farmers enjoying a middle-class standard of living. Though WLS station manager Edgar Bill may have initially targeted the "the prosperous and pious farmers of the Midwest," the Midwest was not a homogenous region of economic stability during the 1930s, when the *National Barn Dance* was at its most popular.[47] Half of the midwestern farming community included tenant farmers, who were even more vulnerable to the economic upheavals of the agricultural industry than landowners. In response, farmers banded together to form organizations such as the radical Farmers' Holiday Association and the more moderate National Farmers' Union (in which women had an equal voice) to protest the low prices of products and to demand government subsidy plans that would address the growing economic disparities of the region.[48] Along with this activism, the voices of farm women increased in volume to advocate for "economic justice for themselves and their families," as demonstrated by Katherine Jellison's study of the Midwest.[49] To national leaders and the editors of farm-life publications circulating throughout the region, farm women wrote impassioned letters about the conditions of rural poverty and the lack of domestic and agricultural technology.[50]

Just as rural women emerged as "a political and economic force that could not be ignored," the industrial Midwest also witnessed a growing presence of women in the public sphere.[51] The closing of production industries (including Chicago's construction, manufacturing, and mining industries, to name a few) decimated their working-class labor and lower-middle-class managerial force, pushing the male unemployment rate in Chicago up to a staggering 50 percent in the early 1930s, double the national rate.[52] Stripped of their livelihoods, these men found it impossible to assert their patriarchal status as breadwinners.[53] With the basis of patriarchy seemingly crumbling under the economic pressures of the era, more married and single women entered the public sphere to secure jobs in the increasingly feminized service industries.[54] Working-class women or women who had slipped from their former middle-class position now found employment as waitresses, sales clerks, or secretaries.[55] Despite the gendered, stratified employment market, contemporary social commentators grew incredibly alarmed over the increased number of women in the public labor force, accusing working women not only of stealing jobs from men but also of robbing them of their masculinized position of cultural authority in both the public and the private realms of society.[56]

Concomitant with the economic and social changes that pervaded the countryside and the city, the Midwest grew increasingly resentful of white southern migrants, such as that "distinct colony" of Tennesseans located in the neighborhoods of Chicago. Midwestern and northern cities had condemned the influx of African Americans since the beginning of the Great Migration, scapegoating newly arrived black southerners for the increase in urban crime and racial tensions. Yet those same industrial centers did not notice the arrival of white migrants until the 1930s, when the high unemployment rate caused the region to become wary of any southern newcomers, who threatened to consume the few available resources.[57]

Midwestern society articulated its growing resentment of white migrants and emphasized their outsider position by underlining the hillbilly stereotype at a time when WLS started to broadcast southern rural music making (including the theatrics of rube comedy). The "hillbilly" (a term that had entered print media in the United States at the start of the twentieth century) was thought to be an Anglo-Saxon of Scotch-Irish lineage, living in the impoverished isolation of southern Appalachia. The *Nation's* 1935 article "Hill-Billies Come to Detroit" serves as one of the first public acknowledgments of the tensions surrounding the arrival of southern whites in a midwestern city. In his report about the automobile industry's active recruitment of "hillbillies from Kentucky, Tennessee, Louisiana, and Alabama," Louis Adamic characterized southerners as "hillbillies," "impoverished whites," and "white trash," with a "low standard of living and lack of acquaintance with modern plumbing."[58] With unemployment still relatively high in the mid-1930s, Detroit residents—former automobile workers along with the middle class—blamed the arrival of these "hillbillies" for thwarting the city's economic recovery from the effects of the Depression.

In response to the continued influx of southerners, several midwestern states expanded their settlement laws. Illinois and Indiana in the 1930s changed their one-year residency requirement for state aid to three years, and Michigan required any new arrivals to meet a certain income bracket in order to stay in the state. For many migrants, who often returned to the South during the summer months when the automobile industry shut down or when it was harvesting season on the family farm, the stringent settlement laws made it impossible to receive economic assistance.[59] As Berry states, displaced people in need of aid were "caught in the middle of an inhumane game of returning the unwanted to their states of origin, where they were unable to earn a living."[60]

Further heightening awareness of white southern transients were the numerous national reports that made public the widespread economic and social conditions of the South. By the 1930s, a majority of southern Appalachian residents were attempting to extract a living from small plots of land, and 60 percent of farmers in the Cotton Belt had resorted to the exploitative system of tenancy and sharecropping.[61] Settlement laws thus were intended to keep the economic troubles of the South out of the Midwest and the North (and, in other contexts, the West). During the 1930s, the white southern migrant thus became the embodiment of individual failure, magnifying midwestern and northern society's fears of dispossession and dislocation.

Country Music on WLS

It was within this historical context of migration and economic instability that early country music came to the forefront of radio. During its peak success in the 1930s, when WLS's Saturday-evening program emerged as the most prominent barn dance (before WSM's *Grand Ole Opry* acquired network status in 1939), the radio station launched the careers of several singing mountaineers, rustic maidens, and hillbilly entertainers who continually traversed the cultural divides of middle/low and sentimentality/parody. Given this performative context, the *National Barn Dance* was not simply a bastion of "old-time music" linked to an idyllic past meant to assuage the concerns of those southern migrants and rural dwellers of the Midwest. The syncretic nature of early country music that crossed and blurred categories of culture could also articulate the anxieties of dispossession, dislocation, and the shifting roles of men and women that had disrupted gendered social conventions.

In spite of the station's projected aura of decorum and good taste, WLS highlighted a contradictory approach to its broadcasts of country music that played out in the dualistic dynamic between the pastoral mountaineer and the comic hillbilly. As mentioned earlier, WLS introduced Bradley Kincaid as a singing mountaineer, one of the performative archetypes associated with the marketing of southern vernacular music. With folklorists like Cecil Sharp and John Lomax collecting and documenting the sonic artifacts of folk culture (believed to be removed from the effects of modernity and mass consumerism), many early country artists strove to align themselves with the ideals of an untainted, noncommercial form of music making.[62] Even though Kincaid acquired commercial success through radio (a medium intricately tied to consumer culture and modernity), WLS still billed him as "The Mountain Boy," "a barefoot mountain lad, natural ballad singer," who brought to radio "old songs [that] had been buried in the hill country, in quiet places off the main road."[63] As WLS painted the image of Kincaid in pastoral and "authentic" tones, his musical expressions included folk remnants, notably "Barbara Allen," a ballad inherited from the British Isles, in addition to comedic songs and laments coming from the minstrel stage's racialized depictions of southern black culture (such as "How the Banjo Was Invented," "Little Old Log Cabin in the Lane," or "Old Dan Tucker"), as well as newly composed music.[64] Kincaid's performances underlined the fact that early country music was not simply an extension of rural culture but also a form of entertainment that incorporated strands of commercialism and popular theater in its staged displays of the folk.[65]

However, in his published songbooks (which were in high demand among WLS listeners) and radio broadcasts, Kincaid downplayed the theatrical elements of his repertory and further emphasized that his musical performances "grew out of the life and experiences of hardy Scotch, Irish, German, English and Dutch natives, who came to American."[66] McCusker demonstrates that in his radio scripts Kincaid bolstered a connection between southern Appalachia and the pioneering history of America. He, in turn, appeared as a respectable, stalwart figure tied to frontier culture, where men could assert their patriarchal standing to counter the social and economic uncertainties of the Great

Depression.[67] In other words, Kincaid did not cast his southern identity as an unwanted Other to midwestern listeners. Instead, he aligned the white southerner with social norms that stood in contrast to the current circumstances of displacement.

Kincaid's musical representations, however, did not necessarily connote a conventional model of masculinity. That is, he played the part of a *singing* mountaineer, a figure whose emotive expressions often disclosed a doleful longing for a premodern era.[68] In his high tenor voice, Kincaid popularized the ballad "Barbara Allen," a song about unrequited love and young death. Accompanied by the quiet strumming of his guitar, Kincaid sang directly into the microphone and offered a vocal sound of immediacy and intimacy with his use of tremolos, rounded tones, and legato phrasing that emphasized his expressive upper range to portray the emotionally heightened narrative of a young man dying for the love of the fair maiden Barbara Allen. In the morose tale, Barbara Allen also dies from remorse and thus is reunited with her beloved through death. In effectively conveying these sentimental matters of the heart, Kincaid's vocal production was far from sounding like that of an authoritarian rustic man forging his way with pioneering valor.

Kincaid's radio career emerged at a time when social commentators were deeply disturbed by how microphone technology could convey the vocal techniques of crooning tenors like Rudy Vallee.[69] For conservative cultural critics, Vallee's higher range and intimate style that emphasized longing and romance could signal an emasculated vocality. During these cultural debates about radio, microphone technology transmitted Kincaid's clear tenor voice into the homes of his listeners. Like his contemporaries in popular music, Kincaid demonstrated a level of control of his upper register, enabling him to convey a higher tone for dramatic affect.[70] With a singing voice informed by contemporary practices of popular music and transmitted by modern technology, Kincaid carried his listeners to a premodern pastoral era marked by vocal expressions of nostalgia and remorse.

Though Kincaid left WLS in 1930, the performative mode of the singing mountaineer (a purveyor of both musical tradition and sentimentality) formed the theatrical basis of a number of later performers. Billed as Skyland Scotty, Scotty Wiseman played the mountaineer character who brought the music of his North Carolina home to a midwestern and national audience. When he teamed up with Lulu Belle, he often acted as a genteel foil to her hayseed comedic image. Further, when Gene Autry launched his career on WLS in 1932, he largely adapted the nostalgic idioms of the southern mountaineer to the singing cowboy, whose crooning voice imparted a sentimental masculinity to songs like "That Silver-Haired Daddy of Mine" (1931) or "Cowboy's Heaven" (1933). With his weepy narratives mapped onto the topography of the West, Autry infused the cowboy persona of independence with tender idioms, bringing together a heroic representation of masculinity with perceivably effeminate modes of expression. In this context, the music of mountaineers and cowboys did not simply rescue masculinity from the emasculating forces of the Great Depression, but rather they gestured to the fragile position of rural and urban men unable to assert their patriarchal status.[71]

Apart from conveying the sentimental expressions of the mountaineer and cowboy, WLS encouraged other forms of southern vernacular expression. Joining WLS in 1930s, the Kentuckian John Lair formed the first southern string-band ensemble of WLS, the Cumberland Ridge Runners, which included prominent musicians Clyde "Red" Foley, Hugh Cross, Linda Parker (aka "the Sunbonnet Girl"), Slim Miller, Doc Hopkins, Hartford Taylor, and Karl Davis. As one of WLS's most successful acts, the Cumberland Ridge Runners had their own daily program and appeared on the early-morning program *Smile-A-While* as well as the weekly NBC broadcast of the *National Barn Dance*, in which they frequently "cut loose with an old-fashioned hoedown" or a "breakdown" that set "the feet a-tapping and the hands clapping in time to the music."[72]

Like Kincaid, Lair was billed as "a leading authority on American folk music."[73] He established WLS's Music Library and collected "valuable music books, some that [went] back to 1600. . . . Old books, rare sheet music, reference books, source books containing most of the hill-billy tunes [made] the library one of the most complete in radioland," as stated in *Stand By!*[74] In many ways, Lair acted like a folklorist collecting musical relics of various traditions. He even had a weekly column titled "Notes from the Music Library" in *Stand By!*, where he would answer fans' questions about the origins of specific songs and include the lyrics of tunes not available in sheet music.

Despite his role as music collector and librarian for WLS, Lair's radio persona often blurred the distinctions between a guardian of Anglo-Saxon culture and a performer who highlighted the staged buffoonery of the comedic rube. For example, *WLS Family Album* pointed to Lair's "tireless research into the history and background of old time music," noting, "He has been able to bring out from the hidden places back in the hills, old melodies that have never been written, but only carried along by ear." In the same article, the trade magazine stated that when Lair is in front of the microphone with "his happy crew of Cumberland Ridge Runners, he relaxes and drops back into the native dialect of the mountains" and "says 'you-all' and 'hain't got no more time this mawnin', but mebbe we'll play it fer you tomorrer.'"[75] In other words, Lair could appear as a hillbilly clown in performance, speaking in a regional class-based dialect with his raucous-sounding string band joining him on the stage of the *National Barn Dance*.[76] He even insisted that the members of the Cumberland Ridge Runners dress in checkered shirts, suspenders, and boots or go shoeless, and that Homer

Slim Miller, the comic character of the ensemble, blacken his teeth to mimic the look of an uncouth yokel to play up the hillbilly stereotype (see figure 4).[77]

The performative contexts of the Cumberland Ridge Runners signaled a level of musical and cultural complexity in WLS's programming of white southern music. Intertwining parody with sentimentality, the Cumberland Ridge Runners' rhythmically driven hoedowns could easily be followed by nostalgic numbers to counterbalance their boisterous performances or Tin Pan Alley cowboy songs, depending on the lead vocalist. Linda Parker, billed as the "Little Sunbonnet Girl," was the so-called girl singer of the string band whose idyllic persona embodied the traditions and gendered ideals of Anglo-Saxon culture, preserved in isolated southern Appalachia. Similar to the singing mountaineer, Parker played the part of the mountain maiden. Lair, however, discovered Parker's talents not in the southern hills of Kentucky but rather in a Chicago nightclub, where Jean Muenich (Parker's original name) regularly performed.[78] Leaving behind an urban setting, Parker (under Lair's direction) played the part of a young rustic maiden dressed in gingham frocks who regularly performed the woeful ballad "Bury Me beneath the Willow."

Pristine as those mountains of Appalachia, Parker's virginal persona was tied to a maternal lineage of folk balladry that lent an aura of tradition and gentility to the music making of the Cumberland Ridge Runners. *WLS Family Album,*

Figure 4. Cumberland Ridge Runners: *from left to right,* Slim Miller, John Lair, Karl Davis, Linda Parker, Red Foley, and Hartford Taylor. *WLS Family Album,* 1934.

contributing to Parker's bucolic image, gave the impression that the singer had "learned many of the old ballads of the hills" from her mother and grandmother in Covington, Kentucky. The *Album* told its readers, "Probably when her mother put a little sunbonnet on her head and sent her out to pull weeds in the garden, she little dreamed that some day this little girl would be captioned as 'The Sunbonnet Girl,' singing those same old songs for millions of people."[79] Parker's performance identity, steeped in a past when women remained in the domestic maternal world of morality, helped make southern music making more palatable to middle-class tastes and gendered expectations, especially during a time when women's emerging presence in the public labor force caused great alarm and consternation. But by 1932, Lair had helped shape the persona of another female performer, Lulu Belle. Instead of playing the tenderhearted maiden, Lulu Belle adopted the theatrics of the hillbilly. As discussed in the following chapter, Lulu Belle's incarnations of an "unruly" southern woman rebelled against the parameters of social normativity while stealing the show from the well-behaved "Little Sunbonnet Girl."[80]

WLS's combination of sentimentality and buffoonery carried on the conventions not only of vaudeville but also of blackface minstrelsy. The pastoral was not only a middle-class guise of respectability but also a performative mode dialectically related to lowbrow humor. Blackface performance, according to Dale Cockrell, could promote discordant songs of defiance that mocked and refused to adhere to the aesthetic of the bourgeois. "Jim Crow," for example, consisted of "music for the croaking voice and the wild fiddle," sounds that contributed to a rebellious noise.[81] Yet Stephen Foster's nineteenth-century "plantation songs" (unlike his rhythmically derived "Oh! Susanna") extended blackface minstrelsy to the expressive realm of nostalgia. With a heightened melodic line unfolding in a verse-chorus form, Foster's maudlin "Old Folks at Home" (1851) could be appropriate for the middle-class parlor or the popular stage where a blackface performer enacted the part of an African American protagonist longing for the plantation South.[82] The grotesque mockery that could erupt in rebellion and the maudlin expressions of yearning for home informed early country music's portrayals of an illusory South.[83]

On WLS in the 1930s, the vestiges of minstrelsy were a central component of the *National Barn Dance*, "encompassing and forever entangling the performance of 'black' and 'white' rustic identities," as noted by historian Pamela Fox.[84] The white actor Clifford Soubier, for example, played the role of "Old Pappy," who had "long fascinated WLS radio audiences with his old darky sketches," and white vaudevillian Malcolm Clair enacted the blackface character "Spareribs," a "story-teller and jokester" who related his tales "in the soft dialect of the 'deep south' negro."[85] In addition to airing on the *National Barn Dance*, Spareribs's comic routines could be heard on the daily program *Morning Minstrels*, where he would join "'Possum' and 'Porkchops' Dean [and] Arthur (Tiny) Stowe, [the] interlocutor" in a broadcast redolent of nineteenth-century minstrelsy.[86]

Apart from John Lair and his Cumberland Ridge Runners, prominent white comedians Arkie the Arkansas Woodchopper, "a farm boy from the Ozarks" (who started his career at WLS in 1929), and Pat Buttram, known for his "back-woods humor of the Old South" (who first appeared on WLS in 1934), joined blackface performers to depict a fictionalized South.[87] WLS's publicity continu-ally explained that Buttram's exaggerated nasal speaking voice that constantly broke to his head voice was his natural mode of speech: "He really does talk most of the time the same way as he does on the stage or on the radio. He was just born with a comical streak."[88] Arkie's buffoonery often involved singing a tune while other comics such as Poke Martin or the slapstick antics of the Maple City Four disrupted his performance by making the Woodchopper break out in maniacal "dangerous" laughter, "known to start a whole studio full of folks to laughing, and nearly disrupt the program schedules."[89] *WLS Family Album* described such a scene for its radio listeners: "Imagine the Maple City Four down on all fours like a drove of pigs, and Ralph Emerson [WLS's organist] waving his arms and chasing them right in front of Arkie. You'd laugh too."[90] As with the slapstick acts of others, Arkie's ability to throw a show into humorous confusion and revelry contrasted with his performances of nostalgic songs, some tied to blackface minstrelsy, that also evoked the figure of the sentimental mountaineer or cowboy. As one listener put it in a letter to *Stand By!*, "I always feel like Arkie is singing to me when he sings 'Little Green Valley'" or "when Red Foley sings 'Echoes of My Plantation Home,' well it is perfect."[91] As with the fluidity of Lair's persona, Arkie could be a guardian of southern folk tradition or a hillbilly buffoon, traversing the divide between these two stock characters.[92]

Fan Responses to WLS's Programming

The eclectic mix of early country music, including the dialectic dynamic between sentimentality and parody, met the ears of a diverse regional and national radio audience. In turn, listeners voiced their preferences and dislikes of the different components of early country music as well as other musical forms—classical music and popular music—that crossed the cultural divides of the era. Previous scholars have argued that WLS's panoply of musical styles and genres never appeared to be an issue for its 1930s audience.[93] As long as WLS could market its broadcasts as belonging to a bygone era of gentility and middle-class ethos, the effective intimacy of radio could seamlessly create an amalgam of musical expressions and bring them into the homes of its listeners. But as Goodman and Susan Douglas have individually demonstrated, radio was a "site of great cultural conflict" that highlighted the class tensions of the 1930s and the "pull between cultural homogeneity and diversity."[94] Radio "expos[ed] many to an identical aural experience," which according to Goodman, "drew attention to the very different ways that people could respond to the same thing," thereby underlining the "differences in beliefs, tastes, and ways of listening."[95] Thus, despite the attempts to market barn-dance musicians as exemplars of respectability and homespun traditions, listeners still took issue with the particularities of radio programming.[96]

WLS encouraged listeners to express their views, including those that contested the mingling of genres and styles, by publishing their fan letters in *Stand By!* Though radio executives were probably highly selective in choosing letters to include in the weekly fan magazine, the radio station nonetheless created a space for an ongoing dialogue among radio appreciators. Farm women, manufacturing managers, middle-class urban householders, steel-plant laborers, and waitresses all could articulate their preferences for disparate but specific types of music (operatic singing, popular music, old-time tunes, Swedish folk songs, German band music, and slapstick routines) that involved the cultural resonances of taste and social identity.

Several listeners, for example, viewed early country music, especially its comedic or parodic side, as a low form of entertainment that did not meet their standards of amusement. One writer, Charles of East Chicago, Indiana, disparagingly evoked hayseed imagery to complain that the "barn dance program" was full of "guff haws and it sound[ed] like a bunch of chickens cackling in the back yard instead of laughter."[97] In similar terms, another critic denounced the early morning show *Smile-A-While* as the "silliest program on the air," stating, "I didn't think you could find such a gang of yokels in the United States but you got them all in one station. Can't you give us some music, and if there's a reason to smile or laugh, let us do it?"[98]

The complaints against the lowbrow humor that pervaded WLS's daily and weekly programs specifically pointed to the singing and stage antics of Arkie the Woodchopper (a featured performer of *Smile-A-While*). Arkie's comic performances of breaking out into laughter surely contrasted with broadcasts that featured stylized renditions of art music, popular songs, and even old standards. Gordon Mattson of Illinois wrote, "I don't like the Arkansas Woodchopper's singing. Why has he been on the air so long? . . . Also I can't understand why some people like that silly laugh of his."[99] Another commentator also ridiculed the comic elements of Arkie's act: "I would just like to know who that hillbilly 'singer' is who just has to try to laugh and sing at the same time, and can do neither. . . . Is he supposed to be cute? Buy him a lollypop."[100] A listener from Chicago pitted the sentimental against the comic to argue that Arkie's staged antics disrupted what would otherwise be enjoyable performances of old-time music: "I wonder if Arkie wouldn't be much more popular if he sings his songs without laughing. Once when he was in our city, I wished some of the others would quit acting up and spoiling really pretty songs. I've heard the same complaint about Lulu Belle."[101] No matter how carefully WLS created a nostalgic backdrop, the rustic caricatures of country musicians stood out and were contested by listeners.

Listeners interested in "respectable" entertainment, however, could be attracted by WLS's incorporation of highbrow or middlebrow music, which moderated the parodic humor of hillbilly music. While Mrs. Hackett of Wisconsin believed that "a little nonsense now and then is relished by the best of men," she preferred to listen to "more of the sacred and semi-classical type of music," specifically the cultivated singing of tenor Henry Burr on the *Smile-A-While* program.[102] For Mary E. Stewart of Indiana, the singing of Bill O'Connor, an Irish tenor, and Sophia Germanich, billed as a "soprano with a gentle, quiet voice," countered the monotony of listening to hours of cowboy songs on the *National Barn Dance*.[103] Similarly, Mrs. Gaumer from Iowa asked, "Why not have more songs by Sally Foster or Verne, Lee and Mary accompanied by the symphony orchestra?"[104] Another listener from Illinois made a case for the inclusion of orchestra and band music: "I haven't ever seen an item in *Stand By!* about the orchestra. I think they are grand. I like the March pieces they play. I always listen to them on dinner bell time [the *Dinnerbell* program] and every time they are on the air. Keep up the good work boys. The German Band is good, too."[105] Farm families and urban dwellers, clinging to the ideals of social mobility during the 1930s, could enjoy the broadcasts of WLS's orchestra, the German Band, or nineteenth-century popular or art songs—music that evoked aurally the sacralized concert hall, a revered past, or the domestic sanctity of the middle-class parlor.

Along with embracing WLS's programming of "classical" or "refined" music, fans welcomed broadcasts that featured a combination of styles and genres instead of only rural music making. James Armstrong of Wisconsin stated, "I have lived on a farm all my life and when I come in from a hard day's work I want something to listen to besides a mouth organ and guitar. Let's have a little variety."[106] Other fans championed shows that included both popular music and country music. Mrs. Earle Compton of Illinois wrote, "On the subject of popular [and country] music I have this to say: I like both and my favorite artists are those who do each equally well. I should hate to have to listen to either all the time, and I don't have to, for WLS gives a pleasing mixture."[107] Likewise, a fan from Ohio made it clear that he got a "kick out of both popular and old-time music," declaring, "I think I am like most of the listeners and that is, I should not like to listen to either all the time."[108]

Even though several listeners of WLS embraced the station's genial middle ground, many fans advocated the expulsion of classical and popular music from the *National Barn Dance*. These particular fans of old-time music responded to the many ways that WLS acts participated in the popular trends of the 1930s. Comparable to the singing styles of the Andrews Sisters, WLS's female trios (the Dinning Sisters, for example) could easily translate the popular idioms of jazz syncopation to homophonic rhythms gently swung by voices blending in close harmony. Similarly, the Hoosier Hot Shots or the western swing ensemble the Prairie Ramblers, who could play in a style that signaled a folk aesthetic, also highlighted the syncopated dance rhythms of the era.

In reaction against the programming of dance music and popular songs, Gladys Corbin of Michigan wrote, "Can you imagine our keen disappointment when last Saturday night, fully half the music on the Barn Dance was popular music? Not that the hayloft boys and girls cannot sing and play popular airs as well as anyone else, for they can; but we hear that type of music all week and we have looked forward to hearing old-time music for at least one hour."[109] Many other appreciators of the *National Barn Dance* opined that it was one of the rare shows that highlighted rural music making. A married couple from Wisconsin stated, "The more old-time music the better. These people who like popular music can get it on almost any other station, so why not let good enough alone."[110] Other fans echoed these sentiments, including a woman from Wisconsin who declared, "[The] barn dance is not a hit parade, plus a few folk songs."[111] A fan from Minnesota reminisced about the "golden" years of the *National Barn Dance*: "All of us enjoy the Barn Dance programs but we also agree that we really liked them better a few years ago." The fan recalled when Chubby Parker (a banjoist billed as the "Kentucky Wonder Bean"), Walter Peterson (who played the guitar and harmonica), and the singing mountaineer Kincaid were part of the cast. Like many others, this listener believed that there was "too much modern music on the programs now," reminding WLS station managers, "One can get all the modern jazz at any time from other stations," especially in a city like Chicago, which was known for its radio broadcasts of jazz music.[112] For its fan base, the *National Barn Dance* could be a white enclave tied to the past against the modern sounds of black popular music.

Another trend among enthusiasts of old-time music was the complete rejection of mingling art music with vernacular expressions. The inclusion of orchestral serenades or bel canto singing represented a cultural invasion of bourgeois pretension in a program created to offer down-home entertainment. A fan from Chicago wrote in 1936, "I am very much displeased with what you call a barn dance. I've never heard a concert orchestra with a barn dance yet."[113] Another devotee of hillbilly music, identified only as "Disappointed Listener," reacted against the stylized singing practices of art music vocalists: "I have been listening to the barn dance every Saturday night for five years and I think it gets worse every week. It does not sound like a barn dance but more like an opera house. . . . I never heard of a classical orchestra being in a barn dance and never heard of sopranos and baritones singing classical songs in any kind of a barn dance."[114] Another advocate of old-time music put it this way: "I certainly agree with 'Disappointed Listener' about the classical or symphony orchestras heard on the barn dance. That kind of music spoils the program. You have real entertainment in the Prairie Ramblers and Patsy Montana, Lulu Belle and Scotty, Red Foley, also in the mountain and cowboy songs and real good old-timers."[115] In resisting the pretense of "classical" music, Mr. and Mrs. Dave Gamache of North Dakota wanted less opera and more of Arkie on the *National Barn Dance*: "We wish you would leave out some of the opera singing Saturday nights and don't be so stingy with Arkie's jolly singing."[116] Another follower explained that the comedy acts served as a salve for the pressures of the 1930s: "You have helped us keep up our morale. Moments when tired and discouraged, it has been a great help to laugh with Arkie and Jolly Joe, to listen to Red Foley" and "to share some more serious moments with Dr. Holland, Jack Holden and others, to listen to Sophia Germanich sing the good old hymns of the church with such earnest interpretation."[117] For this listener and probably many others, the palliative effects of humor combined with religious sermons and music offered comfort and relief from the uncertainties of the 1930s.

How does one make sense of these different responses to the same aural experiences transmitted over the airwaves by WLS? The heated and contested debates of aesthetics and radio listening point to the fact that the symbolic boundaries of styles and genres played a central role in how radio fans made sense of their changing worlds. For southern migrants or rural dwellers of the Midwest, the rustic buffoonery of hillbilly music could offer material for inside jokes that helped them forge a sense of inclusion within the region. Listeners could respond to rube humor as a respite from the onslaught of uncertainty or a defense against bourgeois pretension and the pressures of acculturation. On the other hand, the process of laughing at radio's rube caricatures enabled not just southern migrants but also former and current rural dwellers to dissociate themselves from those acts of mimicry, self-conscious performances of Otherness, at a time when many were attempting to stave off the socioeconomic effects of downward mobility. For urban denizens, hillbilly music could offer nostalgic and comedic fantasies of geographical locales (the southern mountains or the western prairies of the United States) that deflected the uncertain immediacy of the 1930s. In the mingling of high and low that gravitated to the middle, radio broadcasting magnified the interplay of inclusion and exclusion or identification and disavowal of early country music to regional and national listeners.[118]

Conclusion

Through the technology of radio, early country music first secured a place in the American consciousness by commingling with other genres and styles that transgressed cultural and musical divides within the historical setting of the Great Depression. The *National Barn Dance* pulled together the diverse strands of country music—folk balladry, rube humor and comic songs, string-band music, nineteenth-century parlor songs, Tin Pan Alley songs, and western tunes—to market barn-dance radio to a heterogeneous regional and national audience. This amalgam of musical expression that fit with aesthetics of sentimentality and amplified the thespian conventions of plebeian humor also created a performative atmosphere of theatrical fluidity, enabling performers to slip in and out of rustic roles.

The following chapters examine how Lulu Belle, the "Belle of the Barn Dance," and Patsy Montana, WLS's most successful singing cowgirl, fit in the musical landscape of 1930s radio. Each performer highlighted the staginess of early country music, drawing on vaudevillian practices to project performance personae of protean transformations. Lulu Belle could play the comic white southern rube as well as the devoted wife and mother, and Patsy Montana enacted the role of the glamorous cowgirl from the West with songs that could bend gender norms as well as gesture to heterosexual tropes of romance. In their own way, these artists called into question societal conventions while addressing the geographic and material upheavals of the era. From the stage of the *National Barn Dance*, WLS successfully projected the diverse components of early country music, including the performances of Lulu Belle and Patsy Montana, not just in the idyllic past but also in the contested present of the 1930s.

2 The Rural Masquerades of Gender

Lulu Belle and Her Radio Audience

Within the performative context of WLS and the *National Barn Dance*, Lulu Belle emerged as one of the most successful women in radio. In 1936, the subscribers of *Radio Guide* magazine voted Lulu Belle "Radio Queen" in a contest where she came in fifth after male luminaries Jack Benny, Eddie Cantor, Nelson Eddy, and Lanny Ross.[1] While she ruled the airwaves, she popularized the theatrics of the rustic rube, becoming the first female performer on Chicago's WLS to base her act on parodic displays of southern culture and womanhood. In essence, Lulu Belle extended the performance traditions of theater—minstrelsy and vaudeville to be specific—to her stage acts as a vibrant performer who was not locked into a single performance identity. Her embrace of theatrical elements provided a space for fluidity, where she slipped in and out of characters, including her highly publicized but private roles as wife and mother. She also enacted the role of the naive country girl in duets with Red Foley, such as "Hi Rinktum Inktum" (1934), and solo vocal numbers, such as "Little Black Moustache" (1934), and played the part of the demanding shrew in "Wish I Was a Single Girl Again" (1939) with a vocal style that parodied southern vernacular singing practices to heighten her portraits of marital and gender discord (themes that had dominated the gender depictions of the minstrel stage). Yet in duets with Scotty, she could slip into a sentimental character in "Homecoming Time in Happy Valley" (copyrighted 1937) or sing with rounded, resonant vocal tones about the ideals of romantic love in "Have I Told You Lately That I Love You?" (initially performed in the film *Sing, Neighbor, Sing*, 1944).[2] Yet against these examples of nostalgic and romantic expressions, Lulu Belle (with Scotty playing the straight man) continued to enact the brazen southern woman in comic sketches and songs, critiquing the tropes of marriage not only in radio but also in film.

Previous scholars have focused on the ways that WLS's publicity marketed Lulu Belle within conventional understandings of gender and folk culture so that she gave the appearance of a "sentimental mother" or a preserver of "family mores and traditional mountain arts" even as she "threatened the more sanitized representations of female folk culture in her on-stage antics."[3] WLS certainly did attempt to reign in Lulu Belle's rebellious and slippery performance personae by stressing the domestic side of her mass-mediated radio character and marketing Lulu Belle and Scotty as the "Hayloft Sweethearts," which projected a marital image of rusticity, stability, and nostalgia for Depression-era audiences. In performance, however, Lulu Belle fashioned rustic white southern womanhood into models "capable of protean transformation," in that she "both invoked and undermined a persona of the self, highlighting the theatrical construction of the star on stage."[4]

By playing the part of the "funny ole gal," the wench figure, the devoted wife, or the naive rustic maiden, Lulu Belle was part of a legacy of comediennes and actresses (such as Sophie Tucker and Fanny Brice) who continually blurred their biographical selves with their performative personae, thereby challenging the parameters of middle-class normativity and acculturation. Lulu Belle's hyperboles of rural southern womanhood came to the forefront of radio at a time when listeners struggled with their own class standing and white southern migrants came under public scrutiny in the Midwest. Hence, her theatrical fluidity could encapsulate her radio audiences' shaken, conflicted relationship to the gendered and material standards of the middle class, which were unraveling during the fraught socioeconomic circumstances of the 1930s.

Lulu Belle's Stage Act of Grotesque Humor

Lulu Belle's stage antics and musical performances grew out of a performative context that continually blended sentimental expression with comedic displays of rebellion, playing to the cultural divides of respectable entertainment and low-brow humor, broadcast by radio.[5] In 1932, John Lair, an impresario of southern talent for WLS, convinced the radio management to hire Lulu Belle, originally Myrtle Cooper, although she had no experience with microphone technology.[6] Lair oversaw the young performer's transformation into an outspoken comedic rube, joining Linda Parker, the "Sunbonnet Girl," as part of the cast of female performers of rural southern music on the *National Barn Dance*.

While Parker acted as the fair maiden of Lair's string band the Cumberland Ridge Runners, Lulu Belle's guise of the outlandish young woman from southern Appalachia served as Parker's dialectic opposite. Her rustic persona, drawing on a well-defined legacy of plebeian humor and nostalgia inherited from minstrelsy, evoked the wench figure. Black-faced "white men in drag" typically played the part of the unattractive masculine "funny ole gal" in mismatched clothing or the hypersexual coquettish "plantation yellow girl," thereby casting black womanhood as an object of derision, desire, and humor.[7] Within an industrialized nineteenth-century context of precarious economic conditions for the lower classes, white working-class men, usually of Irish ethnicity, acted out their fears and anxieties of being "ineffectual breadwinners" largely through racialized masks and heterosexual pantomimes of courtship and marriage. Specifically the grotesque mockery largely involved mixing the visual signs of femininity with those of masculinity. One could not help but notice the large arms and legs and oversized shoes appearing under the skirts of the wench character who purposely disregarded patriarchal authority and defied the ideals of femininity.[8]

Though blackface performance was still featured in WLS's daily and weekly programs when Lulu Belle first started her career on the radio station, she likely modeled her look and manner after June Weaver, one of the most famous comedic rubes of vaudeville, whose stage name was Elviry Weaver (1891–1977). Encouraged by Lair, Lulu Belle attended performances of Elviry and the Weaver Brothers, Abner and Cicero, in Chicago, where she found the vaudevillian to be "real feisty." In an interview, Lulu Belle stated, "I think that's what he [Lair] wanted me do to. Well, I know he did. And so I did it insofar as I could."[9] Lulu Belle took note of Elviry Weaver's hyperbolic mix of masculine and feminine traits by adopting her disruptive rustic manner and old-fashioned country costume of high-top boots with a petticoat showing underneath a gingham dress.

Apart from Elviry's costume, we do not know exactly what Lulu Belle witnessed in those vaudeville performances. Elviry and the Weaver Brothers, however, did leave behind vestiges of their act in a number of Republic films of the late 1930s and early 1940s. Referred to as "ignorant hillbillies" by an urbanite in their 1939 film, *Jeepers Creepers*, the trio appeared as hayseeds, outsiders to modern society.[10] Yet their simplistic agrarian ways formed the basis of their moral integrity, enabling them to confront the corruption of wealthy capitalists and protect the disadvantaged, a common narrative in the populist films of the Depression. In such plots, Elviry's assertive bearing resembled Al Capp's well-known hillbilly character Mammy (in his cartoon strip *Li'l Abner*) with a pipe sticking out of her mouth and the ability to defend herself and those closest to her in a fistfight with men twice her size. Similarly, Elviry physically and verbally confronted authority figures—men of high political and business standing and pretentious women of the upper classes. In demonstrating her prowess and incorruptible principles, Elviry's comedy shaped a rough confrontational manner that could easily be coded as masculine, especially against the prim and proper airs of upper-crust women. Yet the humor of her image and demeanor largely resided in the incongruity between her assertive manly behavior and her exaggerated feminine dress, replete with a bow in her hair.

Within this spectrum of gender variance, Elviry could slip in and out of various characters. She played the man-starved woman, chasing after a beau in the aforementioned *Jeepers Creepers*, and she also appeared as the wife and partner of equal standing to Abner in the 1940 film *Grand Ole Opry*.[11]

Music played a central role in fueling the confrontational mode and class standing of Elviry. In the film *Grand Ole Opry*, named after WSM's barn dance, the Weavers attempt to undermine the governor's political designs to defeat the passing of a farm bill, legislation that would provide economic support to rural communities. The Weavers first meet the governor when he is arrested and imprisoned for speeding through their small community. Yet even in jail, the governor attempts to deliver a radio address encouraging his wealthy and urban constituents to vote against the farm legislation. To stymie the media event, Elviry decides to hold a hoedown in the local courthouse where the governor plans to broadcast his divisive speech. Prominent acts from the actual radio show the *Grand Ole Opry* join the Weavers in this raucous and disruptive moment of music making aimed at drowning out the governor's radio address. George Hay (the Solemn Old Judge character and the master of ceremonies of the *Opry*), Roy Acuff and his Smokey Mountain Boys with Rachel Veach on banjo, and Uncle Dave Macon also on banjo with his son on guitar provide the rowdy, boisterous music for the square dance. Still worried that the governor might be heard over the music, Elviry grabs the microphone away from him to call out square dance configurations to the string-band music. Thus the social noise of the powerless (hillbilly music, in this case) disrupts and obliterates the voice of the powerful.

Elviry's assertive rube character, anachronistic and exaggerated feminine dress, and use of rural southern music and imagery to challenge figures of social authority were salient features that informed Lulu Belle's act. Lair first introduced Lulu Belle to the Midwest as the girlfriend of Red "Burrhead" Foley, a member of the Cumberland Ridge Runners. But instead of being a feminine embodiment of mountain folk culture and music as Parker was, Lulu Belle played the man-hungry rube in pursuit of her beau. Supposedly, when Lulu Belle heard the radio broadcast of Foley's singing from her home in Kentucky, she decided to hitch a ride to Chicago to track her long-lost love.[12]

Lulu Belle's introduction to WLS listeners not only feminized the migratory experience but also turned it into a comic narrative. Far from the economic realities of white southern migrants searching for work in Chicago during the economic upheavals of the Great Depression, Lulu Belle's motivations to leave her southern mountain home involved following her love interest (who had escaped momentarily from her affections) to the urban Midwest. Clad in rustic attire with a faux fifty-carat diamond ring on her finger, Lulu Belle enacted a hyperbolic, sexualized version of rural womanhood while magnifying the rebellious aspects of the uncouth rube. The account of Lulu Belle's arrival on the *National Barn Dance* may have reminded listeners of another character of Al Capp's comic strip *Li'l Abner*, the hypersexual Daisy Mae, who continually chased the object of her affection, Li'l Abner, over the hills of Dogpatch.

Though Lair intended for Lulu Belle to present a female incarnation of the hayseed to radio audiences, the Cumberland Ridge Runners resented the ways she literally stole the show from their "Sunbonnet Girl."[13] Lulu Belle later stated in an interview, "That gang on the Barn Dance got so they hated my insides" for the ways she continually drew attention to herself.[14] The stage setting of the *National Barn Dance* in the Eight Street Theatre (where acts performed for both live audiences and radio listeners) created a communal scene of music making intertwined with comic skits. Performers for the evening's show would gather around, sitting on bales of hay, listening to the other ensembles until it was their turn to entertain. Instead of Lulu Belle sitting quietly while the Cumberland Ridge Runners and Parker performed, her physical comedy came to the forefront of the show at a time when the comic routines were not always scripted on the *National Barn Dance*. The comedienne concocted a humorous skit of dragging onstage "a little wooden box" with the words "Hope Chest" painted on the side during the performances of other artists.[15] She recalled, "What I had in it was food, candy and sandwiches and grapes, and every week I'd sit over on a bale of hay at a corner of the stage and get into my hope chest and make myself a sandwich and squish it down and give one to somebody in the audience."[16] Lulu Belle's absurd misuse of an emblem of domestic promise—where a young woman keeps her trousseau in hope of marriage and children—easily elicited the laughter of her audience.

As she stole the show from the other ensembles, Lulu Belle realized that her kinetic comedy act was a huge source of appeal: "I had already gotten the reputation in this business, in a short time, of doing something all the time. And if I *moved* the audience would laugh, whether it was funny or not." Apart from her routine involving the hope chest, Lulu Belle's stage buffoonery included chewing large amounts of bubble gum. She recalled, "I'd blow a great big bubble and it would go all over my face ... and everybody hated me. Even on the commercials I would."[17] She even published the song "Chewing Chawing Gum" (1941) about how her gum-chewing ways rebuked polite society.[18] Lulu Belle's bodily humor evoked the look and manner of the manly female hillbilly with a wad of chew or tobacco bulging from her mouth, an image that had been in circulation since turn-of-the-century humorists had begun dramatizing the social depravities of southern rural life for a middle-class urban readership.[19]

Attempting to control the young comedienne, the announcer of the barn-dance program, Hal O'Halloran, would chastise her to the point where she would stay backstage until it was her time to perform. The production manager, however, would demand that she "go on back out there and sit on that stage and don't open that hope chest." And when she didn't adhere to these directives and reverted to her slapstick humor, O'Halloran openly criticized her behavior on the air and in front of live audiences. One evening after a performance, Lulu Belle was so upset over the announcer's scalding comments that she turned to her mother, who encouraged her daughter to verbally outwit the announcer of the show. "So I got to be a smart aleck," Lulu Belle explained. "Anything he'd say to me, I'd come right back at him. The audience just loved that."[20]

With her comedic mask, Lulu Belle questioned male authority, becoming at times a threat to the social order of patriarchy and to middle-class values at a time when more women were entering the paid work force to help support their families as male unemployment rose. Lulu Belle's verbal and physical excesses underlined not only the shifting roles of women but also the increased presence of white southern migrants in the Midwest. By refusing to conform to the demands of the authoritative male announcer, Lulu Belle's unruly southern persona could be a source of pride for southern migrants encountering the biases and increased scrutiny of midwestern and northern urban societies. Lulu Belle, however, continually reminded listeners that her physical humor was a parody of womanhood and southern culture (a mask that could be taken off and on), as she played a variety of characters—the man-hungry rube, the shrewish wife, or the youthful rustic maiden.

Lulu Belle's Songs of Gender Discord

Lulu Belle extended the performative modes of the popular stage to her musical numbers, including her early duets with Foley. In the song "Hi Rinktum Inktum Doodle" (recorded in 1934 for Conqueror Records), Lulu Belle declares that she is eager "to catch me a fellar," a proclamation that fits well with Lair's introduction of Lulu Belle as the southern "girlfriend" intent on holding Foley to his promise of marriage.[21] Foley begins the song with a series of questions to see if Lulu Belle, as a young maiden of seventeen (her actual age at the time), would make a suitable wife. Though she might be eager to find a "fellar," Lulu Belle repudiates the idea of committing herself to a lifetime of backbreaking work as a householder. In response, Foley concludes that he couldn't possibly marry such a churlish woman who will not abide by the usual gendered divisions of labor in heterosexual marriage. Indignant that a suitor beneath her romantic standards would ask her to marry him and then reject her, Lulu Belle emphatically concludes, "Well, there ain't nobody asked you to, you old red-headed Burrhead" (the stage name that Lair had given Foley).

The heated dialogue between Lulu Belle and Foley unfolds within a setting of lively dancing and music making that likely extended to the plebeian theater.

In the refrain, Lulu Belle and Foley sing in harmony a series of what initially appears to be nonsense syllables, "hi rinktum inktum doodle dummy dum." The lyrics, however, evoke a scene of dancing and revelry replete with the sounds of banjo playing. The etymology of the verb "to rink" means to prowl, range, or move restlessly about. In the eighteenth century, the term's meaning shifted to refer to skating on a rink and, in some contexts, to dancing. "To tum" involved producing "the sound made by plucking a tense string of a musical instrument, such as the banjo." With "rinktum" connecting the image of dancing to banjo music, the following lyrics—"doodle dummy dum"—were often used in folk or theatrical songs to illustrate the actual rhythmic component of banjo playing. The ballad "Devilish Mary," for example, includes a similar lyrical refrain—"sing a roddle on a ring tum."[22]

The banjo, originally an African instrument, was integral to African American vernacular music and to blackface theater, both of which influenced the developments of old-time music.[23] Within these musical contexts, the banjo was heard as an instrument of noise and clamor that disrupted the aesthetics of the bourgeois well before it transitioned to white old-time music, converting the aural codes of noise to hillbilly music, as demonstrated in the Weavers' film *Grand Ole Opry*.[24] Steeped in the practices of southern vernacular music, "Hi Rinktum Inktum" includes a pentatonic, rhythmically derived melody in a verse-refrain form with lyrics that gesture to the ruckus of banjo playing. Thus the clamor to which the song alludes contributes to the very discord between Foley, trying to find a dutiful wife, and Lulu Belle, scorning the gender division of the patriarchal home.

The actual recorded performance of the song, however, is not that noisy. Instead of the banjo, the accompaniment instrument is the quieter guitar, and Foley's vocal style of rounded tones in his resonant baritone range offers an aesthetic that is more aligned with the vocal practices of mainstream popular music. Lulu Belle's vocal manner, however, shapes the aural impression of a young southern country girl so naive of gender norms that she rejects her suitor's romantic pursuits. In her vocal performance, Lulu Belle deviates from a predominant vocal praxis of southern vernacular singing, as exemplified by many of her contemporaries associated with 1930s old-time or folk music, such as Roba Stanley, the Carter Family, Cousin Emmy, and the Coon Creek Girls (the first female string band). Instead of pushing the chest voice to a higher range, where nasal-twang timbres are intensified, as did Sara Carter in one of the Carter Family's first hits, "Single Girl, Married Girl" (1927), Lulu Belle offers a singing voice that deliberately mixes chest and head registers with a nasally inflected tone.[25]

When Lulu Belle first auditioned for WLS, the station managers refused to hire the young performer because she lacked vocal training in front of a microphone. According to Lulu Belle, she first started singing for the chamber of commerce on a stage without a microphone: "All by myself I'd go and sit there on the stage with that guitar and bleat [out] those songs." It's interesting that Lulu Belle uses the verb "bleat" to describe her vocal production. Bleating usually refers to the cries of a sheep or a goat.[26] Lulu Belle's vocal style may have combined a belting chest voice and nasal-twang techniques to produce loud tones of high frequencies meant for large spaces, for she recalls how the dynamic level of her voice did not fit aesthetically with the microphone technology: "I got up close to that microphone and started in 'projecting' and they were going crazy in the control room."[27] When she returned to audition again for WLS, she purposely did not sing as loudly. To dampen the vocal dynamics of her voice, Lulu Belle developed a technique of transitioning to her head voice even though it is clear that the strength of her voice lies in her lower range. Lulu Belle raised the larynx to reach the upper notes in her higher range and constricted the pharynx to include a nasal-twang vocal quality, thereby producing a nasal vocal sound in the head register, the ideal sonority to enact the character of a young country girl.

The arched melodic line of "Hi Rinktum Inktum" begins squarely in Lulu Belle's chest range, and as the melody ascends stepwise to the middle range of the voice, she switches registers to sing in her head register before returning to the chest. While singing in the range immediately above the speaking voice, Lulu Belle produces a lighter tone, which is common for young female vocalists whose vocal folds are still developing.[28] Her nasally inflected higher timbre contrasts with Red Foley's resonant, open-throat baritone voice that extends to his lower range, offering the sonic impression of a mature man in search of a wife. The marked difference between Foley's and Lulu Belle's singing styles and registers gives the impression that Lulu Belle's vocal character is that of a southern maiden trying to sound like a proper lady but failing to execute a well-developed head voice. Foley, on the other hand, convincingly plays the sonic part of an authoritative, mature man.

Lulu Belle started her radio career at a time when bel canto singers had successful radio careers and helped establish the elements of "good" singing in this new medium.[29] On WLS, women performers with clear, well-developed alto and soprano voices surrounded Lulu Belle. The mellifluous harmonies of the Three Little Maids, the bel canto singing of the soprano Sophia Germanich, and the crystalline voice of Christine, the "Little Swiss Miss," signaled an aesthetic associated with a bel canto tradition of rounded tones, smooth transitions between registers, and well-developed chest and head registers. "Thinking of singing as an aesthetically circumscribed activity," as Jonathan Greenberg argues, "was commonplace during the decade . . . 1925–1935."[30] Critics debated what vocal elements constituted "good" singing, and radio, including WLS, featured operatic performers singing arias, sentimental songs, and patriotic numbers. Against this backdrop, Lulu Belle's explicit use of nasal twang involved constricting the throat muscles, keeping the tongue in a high and flat position, and propelling the sound from the front of the mouth without making use of its oral space. This particular singing approach did not fit with the vocal "refinement" or fullness of tone of WLS's popular or operatic singers. Amplified by her southern accent, she aurally produced the image of a young, rural woman feigning "ladylike" behavior.

Lulu Belle included additional material that evoked the theatrical conventions of the popular stage. In "Little Black Moustache" (a popular tune among Lulu Belle's fans), the comedienne again played the naive country girl.[31] The song appears to be a satirical vignette of heterosexual courtship replete with stock characters—the gentlemanly villain, the unassuming young woman, and the old maid.[32] In the beginning of the tune, Lulu Belle sings of once having a charming and wealthy beau who dons a "charming black moustache" and seduces her with promises of domestic comfort: "He said we'd live in grandest style for all he'd lots of cash."[33] The seemingly sophisticated suitor, however, turns out to be the archetypical debonair villain (who often sports a black moustache), cultivated in nineteenth-century melodramas and twentieth-century silent films. Though he repeatedly flashes his fortune, he abandons Lulu Belle for the wealth of a middle-aged woman disguised as an "old maid."

Against this seriocomic backdrop of love and betrayal, Lulu Belle vocally enacts the smitten agrarian woman by wielding a vocal style that underlines the humor of the song. To the basic chordal accompaniment played on the guitar, Lulu Belle's nasal-sounding voice sings the full range of the pentatonic melody, which falls comfortably in her lower range. Yet to underscore the allure and promises of romance, she jumps momentarily to her head register, producing a lilting timbre on the word "moustache" in the phrase "Oh, the little black moustache, charming black moustache." Again with her lighter-sounding upper range, Lulu Belle convincingly plays the part of a smitten young southern white woman, enchanted with the villain's charming "moustache." Yet she fails to secure his affection as he pursues the vaudevillian old maid. In a song that brings together theatrical figures of the popular stage, Lulu Belle's vocal enactments heightened the comedy and drama of this ballad.

Lulu Belle continued to perform songs embroiled in the ritualized strife of heterosexual romance, even after her 1934 marriage to her duet partner, Scotty Wiseman. In 1933, Wiseman (billed as Skyland Scotty, a singing mountaineer) joined the cast of the *National Barn Dance*, after which the station manager decided that Lulu Belle and Wiseman should develop an act.[34] To introduce Scotty as Lulu Belle's new duet partner, replacing Foley, they performed "Madam, I've Come to Marry You" (1935).[35] Though the title points to conjugal promise, the song is about the failed negotiations of marriage.[36] In the song Scotty attempts to convince Lulu Belle that he can provide a life of social comfort with his impressive array of possessions—an acceptable home and a well-managed farm. Unlike the rustic girl who falls for the promises of the gentlemanly villain in "Little Black Moustache," Lulu Belle scoffs at Scotty's material assets, insinuating that his display of wealth is simply a ruse. Scotty, frustrated with Lulu Belle's rejection, wishes on the recalcitrant woman a lonely and forsaken life: "While sleeping by yourself some night, I hope to my soul you'll freeze." Lulu Belle, who once again gets the last word, explains that she is looking for true love, suggesting that Scotty is not her ideal mate. Distancing herself from the material trappings of wedlock, Lulu Belle demonstrates the artificiality of marrying only for middle-class comforts and stability.

Lulu Belle and Scotty contested the terms of heterosexual unions in a variety of musical songs, including "Wish I Was a Single Girl Again." Their version of the tune circulated among the primary media of popular or hillbilly music—radio, recording, and sheet music—demonstrating the centrality of the song in their stage act for the *National Barn Dance*.[37] The narrative of "Wish I Was a Single Girl Again" presents a subject reminiscing about the pleasures and even past worries as a young single woman in the first half of each verse and lamenting her disillusionment with marriage in the second half.

This account of marital woe appears in many folklike songs, including the Carter Family's "Single Girl, Married Girl," which Linda Parker often performed on WLS.[38] Lulu Belle's rendition, though, wasn't musically related to "Single Girl, Married Girl."[39] "Wish I Was a Single Girl" consists of a verse-chorus form (unlike "Single Girl, Married Girl") with a completely different melodic line. Instead, her version of domestic strife adopted the tune "I Wish I Were Single Again," originally composed by James Cox Beckel (1811–1889) and performed by WLS's guitar and mandolin duo Mac and Bob.[40] Though the composer is best remembered for his Civil War battle songs and sacred music, Beckel also wrote and arranged comic songs for lowbrow venues. "I Wish I Were Single Again" includes syncopated and declamatory melodic lines supported by static harmonies, suggesting that Beckel composed the song for the banjo and fiddle—primary instruments in blackface minstrel ensembles. Moreover, the song's lyrical setting involves a male protagonist reminiscing about his past freedoms as a single man before he married his "wife . . . the plague of his life." It's easy to imagine a white performer in blackface providing an account of marital strife, while the shrewish wench, played by a white man in black drag, affects a ladylike manner.[41]

In performance, Lulu Belle converts the song into a feminized protest of the gendered labor of women in the rural home by giving the wench character a strident voice of dissent. In rendering this account of marital discord, a string band—fiddle, banjo, and guitar—plays in the stylistic idiom of old-time music.[42] The fiddle, for example, introduces the folklike melody with strong down bows embellished with double stops or harmonic drones.[43] Wiseman plays the banjo in a two-finger style in which the thumb plays the melody while plucking the fifth string and the index finger plucks the first string, both strings acting as drones.

With this accompaniment, Lulu Belle's singing style makes this tale of discontent into a comic portrait of gender by parodying southern vocal conventions. Unlike "Hi Rinktum Inktum" and "Little Black Moustache," Lulu Belle's vocal style is more obviously based in parody. As in the recording of "Madam, I've Come to Marry You," Lulu Belle embellishes her vocal lines with an explicit use of nasal twang in her higher range and clear glottal stops for comic effect. In "Wish I Was a Single Girl Again," she continues to develop and use these particular vocal devices to enact the complaining wench. Lulu Belle begins each four-bar phrase of the verse with the same melodic line ascending to her head voice by accentuating the use of vocal hiccups or glottal stops, as if she were playing the part of an "untrained" singer who is unable to manage registral shifts with any sort of skilled transition. At the same time, though, her pronounced use of nasal twang in the chorus makes it clear that she is impersonating a southern vocalist. She launches into the chorus with another vocal hiccup, accenting her chest voice, followed by an ascending nasal slide realized by pushing the chest register to her middle range, where she cries out, "Lord," before singing the title phrase, "I wish I was a single girl again." She concludes the line with an emphatic glottal stop on the word "again," underlining the hard *g* on the downbeat, elongates the vowel, and stresses the nasal *n*.

Her vocal exclamation could be heard as a desperate plea to break free from the burdens of domesticity. Yet the abrupt switch of vocal timbre and register and the exaggerated use of nasality (by means of nasal-twang techniques and emphatic nasal pronunciations) suggest that Lulu Belle's performance is a caricature of a lament, not an actual lament. Lulu Belle further underlines the parodic display of her vocal delivery by singing in a self-conscious "hillbilly" dialect to depict her uncouth husband who "chaws tobaccer," wears a "flannel under suit," and gives her a gingham apron before showing her to a sink of dirty dishes.

In contrast to Lulu Belle's comic performance, Cousin Emmy's 1947 recording of "I Wish I Was a Single Girl Again" is a lament, similar in tone to Sara Carter's sorrowful account of the plights of rural working-class women in "Single Girl, Married Girl."[44] Even though Cousin Emmy enacted a "hillbilly girl" from Kentucky in a costume comparable to that of Lulu Belle on

WHAS's barn dance in Louisville, Kentucky, and as a guest artist on WLS, her vocal performances captured, rather than parodied, southern vernacular expressions.[45] Like Carter, Cousin Emmy's use of a strident nasal vocal timbre, specifically strained and pronounced as she pushes the chest register to the middle range, underscores the travails of rural poverty for mothers bearing the responsibilities of child rearing. Unlike Lulu Belle, Cousin Emmy does not switch registers or exaggerate her nasal-twang tones. Rather, she sings above the vocal break in her chest voice in the beginning of each short phrase of the verse. First, she offers a plaintive nasal cry on the word "when" ("when I was single, marrying was my crave") and elongates the word "crave." In the following phrase, she stresses the immediate present and her troubles, "Now, I am married and I'm troubled to my grave," again sustaining the last word, "grave." In effect, Cousin Emmy's use of her upper-chest register with a consistent nasal-twang timbre forms an anguished cry of desperation. Without enough food to feed her children ("so hungry, oh, they can't raise up their heads"), the subject stresses that rural married women of the underclass usually spend their adult lives toiling yet despairing of being able to care for their families with severely limited means. Whereas Lulu Belle's mimicry of southern music and culture provided a comic critique of patriarchy and domesticity, Cousin Emmy's performance made use of southern vocal idioms to articulate the abjection of rural poverty.

Lulu Belle and the History of Manly Comediennes

Lulu Belle's impersonations of rustic womanhood, redolent of the theatrical tropes of minstrelsy, can be interpreted as part of a legacy of comediennes who adopted and reconfigured male-defined blackface and ethnic female characters for the popular stage. At the turn of the century, vaudevillian Kate Elinore, for example, rose to success largely by assuming the roles of the coarse, assertive Irish maid or old maid, thespian parts that had been developed by cross-dressed male comics. Comic acts played up the lasciviousness associated with working-class immigrant women, for example, the Russell Brothers in their 1870s transvestite skits.[46] In turn, Elinore's theatrical incarnations, as M. Alison Kibler argues, combined "male comic styles of performance" with ethnic humor that defined "particular groups of women (immigrant women, working-class women) as sexually, physically, and verbally excessive."[47] Like Lulu Belle's rustic image, Elinore's brash, rebellious Irish stage persona projected a disruptive agency that challenged the restrictions of the bourgeoisie social order while at the same time risking the reinscription of the bawdy behavior associated with working-class women's bodies.

The cultural work of women in vaudeville involved grappling with what it meant for an audience of European immigrants to be part of a marginalized ethnic category. Kate Elinore's various incarnations of the manly and rebellious Irish maid were often juxtaposed with the persona of Kate's sister, May Elinore, who often enacted the Irish girl or young woman attempting to secure middle-class social standing. Playing to the anxieties of Irish immigrants, including the pressures of assimilation, the Elinore Sisters' act magnified the discord between Kate's boisterous, rowdy conduct and May's middle-class ambitions and embodied grace and elegance.

A similar dynamic arose between Lulu Belle, the audacious, outspoken hillbilly, and Linda Parker, the quiet, demure "Sunbonnet Girl." The dueling portraits of rebellion and sentimentality emphasized the tensions of class and gender for southern migrants, who had been lured from their southern homes by promises of social mobility. While Parker embodied an idealized stable past, rescuing southern femininity from base representations, Lulu Belle's disruptive, defiant humor questioned social convention for listeners who resisted assimilation into a dominant midwestern or northern urban society.

The famous comediennes of the first half of the twentieth century, notably Sophie Tucker and Fanny Brice (whose careers overlapped with Lulu Belle's), also devised routines, based on male-defined minstrel formulas, to introduce "elements of unruly womanhood" into their versions of "slighted Jewish identities," as Pamela Brown Lavitt argues.[48] Tucker, who began her career performing in blackface in 1906, incorporated the tropes of the cross-dressed wench to enact the role of the gender-ambiguous mammy. Tucker's racialized impersonation projected a defiant, brash mode devoid of middle-class values in her performances of "coon" songs, popular songs in black dialect (written by Tin Pan Alley composers).[49] Known for her ample girth that exceeded the boundaries of femininity, she often made it clear in performance that she was wearing a black mask, pulling off a glove to reveal her white skin underneath her racialized image. Responding to the audience's laughter, Tucker would then speak in Yiddish, demonstrating that though she looked white, her ethnic identity fell short of contemporary dominant definitions of whiteness.[50] She would further elaborate on her Jewish identity in performances of "My Yiddishe Momme" (beginning in 1925), a sentimental number about the Jewish mother who continually makes sacrifices for her children. Tucker thus could switch from her rebellious persona of a "coon shouter" (later she would be billed as a sexualized "Red Hot Mama") to embody a Jewish past by singing a maudlin song about maternal devotion.[51]

Fanny Brice also built a comedic persona largely on the conventions of ethnic humor. Singing the Yiddish dialect song "Sadie Salome, Go Home" (composed by Irving Berlin and Edgar Leslie) in the 1909 burlesque *The College Girls*, Brice offered a satirical representation of the seductive femme fatale. Not only did she parody the speech patterns of Jewish immigrants speaking English, but she also incorporated physical slapstick with exaggerated contortions and ogling eyes, drawing attention to her kinetic humor.[52] Similar to Tucker, Brice crossed racialized codes with ethnic comedy to play a variety of characters related to the practices of female impersonation. In Ziegfeld's *Follies*, Brice sang Joe Jordan and Will Marion Cook's "Lovie Joe" (1910) in black dialect; debunked the pretentions of highbrow culture by playing the part of a graceless Jewish girl in the number "Becky Is Back in the Ballet" (1916); portrayed the working-class Jewish immigrant girl (from Second Avenue) clad in preowned clothing in the tune "Second Hand Rose" (1921); and enacted the shrewish Jewish mother nagging her children and emasculating her husband in the monologue "Mrs. Cohen at the Beach" (1927).[53] Yet Brice moved out of her parodies of race and ethnicity in her performance of the torch song "My Man," a genre commonly coded as white and middle class. Brice delivered the lyrics without her typical Yiddish accent to underscore the heartache of loving a duplicitous man. In fact, Brice's audience believed the song to be an autobiographical account of her unstable marriage to the gambler and embezzler Nick Arnstein.[54]

In her memoirs, Brice, who later left her ethnic comedy behind to play the infantilized "Baby Snooks" in radio (CBS, 1936–1951), explained that her earlier skits were primarily for a Jewish audience: "In anything Jewish I ever did, I wasn't standing apart making fun. . . . They identified with me, which made it all right to get a laugh. Because they were laughing at me as much as themselves."[55] For Brice her performances provided a means to connect to a Jewish audience who regularly confronted the complexities and contradictions of striving for acculturation while not meeting the prevailing definition of Anglo-Saxon whiteness. Just as the performances of the Elinore Sisters, Tucker, and Brice encapsulated the anxieties, cultural barriers, and desires of many first- and second-generation European immigrants, Lulu Belle's comic routines and songs also magnified the paradoxes of white southern rusticity. During the Depression era, when midwestern culture demonized the increased presence of southern migrants, Lulu Belle underscored the uneasy, conflicted relationship of the rural working-class with middle-class norms through her musical enactments and parodies of southern culture and gender.

For an audience of southern migrants wrestling with their own subject positions, Lulu Belle's rube character encouraged a complex interplay of identification and disavowal.[56] Typical of the hillbilly archetype, she turned the anxieties of displacement into fodder for her buffoonery—a southern woman in the urban North who did not conform to normative definitions of respectability. Such antics could be appreciated as farcical representations to elicit the laughter of those southern or rural listeners who identified with Lulu Belle's outsider identity. While her audience embraced her lowbrow buffoonery, her old-fashioned dress and exaggerated manner further underscored the theatrical traditions that simultaneously engendered an imaginary South and a legacy of comediennes challenging and questioning social normativity. Henry Jenkins argues that the cultural work of the clown or comic stage figure is to exist "'betwixt and between' the normal structure of the social order" by "speaking to and for the under-culture at a time of a economic crisis, expressing a discontent with rigidity, hierarchy and emotional repression" and reveling in "the freedom that comes from straddling cultural categories."[57] Lulu Belle offered rustic masks that defied male authority and critiqued domesticity while she spoke to and for her audi-ence of southern migrants, rural dwellers, and women. Her listeners, in turn, could partake in a rural fantasy of alterity where the displaced, the midwestern farm wife, or the waitress or clerk in the service industry could find release from the prescriptions of middle-class norms, ideals that were difficult to maintain during the social and material crises of the Great Depression.

Yet her disruptive agency could also run the risk of reinscribing the physical and verbal excesses associated with rural southern women's bodies. Audiences had a choice of embracing Lulu Belle's regional and class persona or of dissociat-ing their own agrarian identities from her grotesque mimicry, which reminded them that she—and not they—was an outsider, a member of the underclass. In other words, Lulu Belle's parodies of southern music could be interpreted as cultural products of a benighted South, far removed from the ambitions of social mobility, including those of white migrants searching geographically for a better life in a modern industrialized Midwest.

Fan Reception of Lulu Belle

WLS's audience made clear how it interpreted Lulu Belle's rustic buffoonery. Like the fan letters in *Stand By!* that contested or heralded the aesthetic merits of comedic rubes (as discussed in chapter 1), appreciators of WLS perceived Lulu Belle's rube character as explicitly playing with the aesthetics of low culture. Indeed, those members of WLS's audience who forged a personal connection to Lulu Belle's plebeian act identified with her stage antics and took pleasure in how her rustic humor distanced itself from bourgeois aesthetics and taste. As Mrs. Maybelle Harvey of Michigan put it, "Lulu Belle may not be an opera star but she gives more pleasure and happiness to people than anyone else on the radio."[58] Similarly, Mr. and Mrs. Vail explained, "Lulu Belle is the only lady singer on the air that we listen to. When any other lady sings, we switch to another station, but she's clear and plain and, well, not so highfalutin'."[59] Another appreciator of Lulu Belle confirmed that the performer's talent had more to do with her comic antics than with her vocal abilities: "Lulu Belle isn't an accom-plished singer but she's an entertaining one."[60] A fan from Illinois welcomed Lulu Belle's burlesques: "Lulu Belle wouldn't be Lulu Belle without her giggling and side-splitting jokes."[61] Wanda of Indiana explained, "WLS has always been my favorite radio station because the characters act more like common people do. They aren't afraid to mix a little fun in. I like all the other WLS stars, too, but to me Lulu Belle is 'tops.'"[62]

But not every fan of WLS welcomed Lulu Belle's lowbrow parodies of southern music and humor. With a vested interest in the aesthetic symbols of respectability, several of WLS's listeners complained that her parodic singing style and overall stage manner fell below their standards of taste. A listener in Wisconsin asserted, "Lulu Belle isn't any better singer than lots of others and she's too silly for words. She has an idea she's awfully cute."[63] A woman from Illinois took issue with the comedienne's physical comedy of chewing large amounts of gum: "Lulu Belle would improve her appearance greatly if she would leave that big, ugly gob of 'chawin' hum' out of her mouth."[64] Those listeners who did gravitate toward the sentimental expressions, and not the buffoonery, of hillbilly music wished that Lulu Belle would conduct herself in a more respectable manner. Miss Wakeford of Michigan wondered, "If Scotty and Lulu Belle know so many old songs, as was said in a recent *Stand By!*, why don't they sing some of them on the Barn Dance instead of repeating the same silly songs every Saturday night. Our neighbors always turn their dials for that reason when they start to sing."[65] Another critic of Lulu Belle addressed her devoted followers with an explicitly condescending tone: "You give me a pain in the neck the way you praise Lulu Belle. The way you act, you'd think she was the only person on the air. How foolish those singers at your station, who know something about singing, must feel when they hear her sing all the time and forever the mention of her name being praised."[66] For this member of the WLS radio audience, Lulu Belle's vocal performances did not measure up to those of the Three Little Maids or Sophia Germanich, female performers whose vocal styles were more in line with mainstream or bel canto vocal techniques.

Lulu Belle's fans reacted against these criticisms and largely grounded their opinions in matters of musical hierarchy. To those listeners who did not appreciate Lulu Belle's humor and music, a fan retorted, "Why in the heck don't they tune in on some grand opera program and leave us simple folks to enjoy the type of program we appreciate? There are enough trained sopranos and baritones on any of the other stations, singing, their classical songs, surely to meet the needs of this class of listeners."[67] Even a devotee of Lulu Belle went as far as to question the morality of a listener who voiced her disdain of the comedienne: "When a person expresses her dislike of our own Lulu Belle we wonder just what sort of person she is."[68] In these heated debates that erupted in WLS fan letters, an appreciator of WLS acts wondered if his fellow listeners were failing "to understand the type of character Lulu Belle portray[ed]." Her defender had seen her in a live performance and explained that Lulu Belle's act involved displays of rustic buffoonery—"I smile now as I can see again how handy it was to wipe her shoes with the white hanky which the sedate Scotty had given her to wipe her nose on! Well, nobody slumped in their chairs that day!"[69] This fan of Lulu Belle understood that her comic antics involved highlighting the divide between respectable entertainment and lowbrow burlesque to mock social conventions.

Lulu Belle and Scotty's Sentimental and Romantic Duets

Though her role of the hillbilly clown was integral to her stage shows (as evident in the positive fan letter quoted above), the famous comedienne would slip in and out of roles. With her duet partner, Scotty, Lulu Belle would occasionally perform sentimental songs longing for an illusory South. Originally dubbed Skyland Scotty, Wiseman took on the performance identity of the stalwart guard of southern musical traditions, a version of the dignified mountaineer (an educated folklorist). As a duo, Lulu Belle and Scotty would perform a repertory pointing to an idyllic past. "Homecoming Time in Happy Valley," a song that Wiseman had popularized on radio and recording in the 1930s before teaming up with Lulu Belle, provided a comforting narrative of returning to one's country home of family and friends, fitting for an audience of displaced southerners.[70] Just as Tucker performed "My Yiddishe Momme," a sentimental piece that gestured to a Jewish tradition where women remained devoted mothers, Lulu Belle could also participate in the nostalgic tropes of the South.

"Homecoming Time in Happy Valley" opens to Lulu Belle singing a lyrical melodic line that is harmonized by Scotty's vocals.[71] In contrast to the rhythmically derived vocal parts of "Hi Rinktum Inktum" or "Wish I Was a Single Girl Again," the lyricism of the principle theme in "Homecoming Time in Happy Valley" encourages Lulu Belle's use of legato phrasing to smoothly transition from her head register to chest register. Lulu Belle sustains the opening melodic notes right above her vocal break in her head register to emphasize the words "its home."[72] The vocal line jumps down to the tessitura of the song and then returns to the sustained upper notes of the melody before descending in stepwise motion to give the impression of reaching for and securely arriving at this idyllic meeting ground of family and friends. Further adding to the lyrical flow of the song is the harmonic language of secondary harmonies (an unusual feature in Lulu Belle's comic repertory) that brings about a blissful conclusion—"calling home the good old friends I love."

But the tone of the song shifts in the bridge, where Scotty's and Lulu Belle's vocal parts become distinctly more emphatic and declamatory to emphasize that the subjects are returning to a community marked by the clamor and revelry of southern culture. Their rustic home is a place for "all day singin' and dinner on the ground," where "aunts and your uncles and your double first cousins gather around." In the 1950s radio transcription, Lulu Belle inflects nasally the declamatory vocal line in her chest register, producing a vocal tone of twangy patter to signal her southern home to which she is returning. After this lively moment, the main phrase returns and resumes its more lyrical melody, thereby encapsulating and mediating the rhythmically derived "noise" for listeners with a vested interest in sentimentality. The song still suggests that Lulu Belle and Scotty are rustic figures tied not only to the expressions of pastoral longing but also to the potentially unruly soundscapes of hillbilly music.

In addition to including nostalgic songs and comic narratives of courtship and marriage in their act, the duo started to sing romantic songs that incorporated the aesthetics of mainstream popular music. Scotty emerged as a prolific songwriter, composing notable country standards such as "Mountain Dew" (1939), adapted from the Bascom Lamar Lunsford version, and "Have I Told You Lately That I Love You?" (published in 1943).[73] Whereas "Mountain Dew" is replete with hillbilly imagery of buying and drinking moonshine—that "good old mountain dew"—"Have I Told You Lately That I Love You?" is a song about romantic love.

Lulu Belle's performance of a love ballad was not uncharacteristic of women of the popular stage. As mentioned earlier, the comedienne Brice would drop her Yiddish accent to sing the torch number "My Man," providing an aural version of Anglo femininity. In comparison, Lulu Belle does not perform with an explicit nasal-twang singing voice as in her earlier songs. No longer playing the part of the wench or giving the sonic impression of a naive country girl, she leaves behind her rustic enactments to render a song that addresses the poignancy of love in a musical setting that evokes the aesthetics of a love ballad. As Lulu Belle later stated, "I became a little more sophisticated after Scott and I got married. He got me out of that. He really made fun of me for singing like that; he didn't think it was natural."[74]

Lulu Belle first performed "Have I Told You Lately That I Love You?" in the film *Sing, Neighbor, Sing* (1944) before Scotty and she recorded the song in 1947. Starring in a film with other prominent radio stars, such as Roy Acuff and the Smokey Mountain Boys, Lulu Belle does not play her well-known rustic radio characters as she does in other films, such as *Shine On, Harvest Moon* (1938) and *Swing Your Partner* (1943). Though she is referred to by her stage name, Lulu Belle dresses in modern pants suits and wears glasses in order to play the part of a young, urban college student of phrenology. She appears as a serious-minded student and is devoted to her studies until she notices Scotty, part of Roy Acuff's ensemble. She finds her newfound emotions and affections for Scotty perplexing until one of the lead characters of the film (played by Stanley Brown) advises Lulu Belle to focus less on education and on more on romantic courtship: "You used to think that the skull was the most important part of the anatomy but now you have discovered it is the heart. . . . Up to now you have been an intellectual pill, now be a sugar coated one." Lulu Belle's classmate, Virginia (played by Ruth Terry), remakes Lulu Belle into an alluring woman by outfitting her in a form-fitting dress, flowers in her hair, and jewelry. Virginia then hands Lulu Belle a guitar and encourages her to pursue Scotty romantically. In response, Lulu Belle sings "Have I Told You Lately That I Love You?" in a crooning vocal style of rounded tones and smooth-sounding registral shifts.

The opening hook of "Have I Told You Lately that I Love You?" falls easily within the husky timbre of Lulu Belle's chest register. Without the use of nasality or vocal hiccups, she slides smoothly from her chest to her head voice to sing the first four bars of the second phrase, "Have I told with all my heart and soul how I adore you?" Her southern accent is minimal and only noticeable on the long *i*. More prominent is her use of legato phrasing, which helps render the arch-shaped melodic pattern with little strain. Each time she reaches the upper tessitura of the melody, the vocal line then requires Lulu Belle to return to the warm-sounding resonances of the chest register, providing a vocal tone of security. Like Brice's vocal performance in "My Man," Lulu Belle's rounded, smooth singing voice provides an aural impression of romantic love connected to the feminine ideals of the white middle class. In other words, Lulu Belle sounds like a "proper" woman, far removed from her musical enactments of rusticity. In response to her tendered-hearted serenade, Scotty whistles a countermelody and then joins her vocals in harmony to sing intimately about their love for each other.

While Lulu Belle is winning Scotty's heart, one of the other female students, Rachel (played by Rachel Veach), is watching in the bushes and takes note of the effect of Lulu Belle's singing. Rachel then sings the same song to Beecher Kirby, known as the comic character Bashful Brother Oswald in Roy Acuff's Smoky Mountain Boys, where he plays Rachel's brother. Those who follow Veach's and Kirby's career on the *Grand Ole Opry* realize the joke of Rachel's singing this romantic song to her stage brother. Moreover, Rachel's performance of "Have I Told You Lately That I Love You?" is noticeably different from Lulu Belle's. While Lulu Belle performed it "straight," Rachel sings the song in a deliberate rustic and comedic manner. She dramatically increases the tempo, turning the languid, daydreaming feel of the love ballad into a fast-paced number and sings in a style that signals her hillbilly character. Raising the key of the song by a whole step from Lulu Belle's performance, Rachel purposely strains to reach the upper notes of the melody in the chest voice, producing a piercing nasal-twang vocal tone. On top of this, she skips around Kirby while singing and playing the sped-up song on the guitar, making a farce out of the love ballad. Thus it is Rachel who provides the rustic parody, in this case, of Lulu Belle's performance by reminding appreciators how easy it is to slip from expressions of romantic love to comedy.

Deviating from her usual slapstick humor and the musical parodies that
defined her career in the 1930s, Lulu Belle's film performance of the love ballad
moved closer to the more "serious" aesthetics of the popular-music mainstream,
a sensibility cultivated by other WLS acts. Indeed, several of Lulu Belle's fans
seemed surprised that the comedienne could cross the divide between serious
and comic expressions. A woman in Chicago stated, "We never thought Lulu
Belle could be so serious as she is when she sings those beautiful duets with
Scotty."[75] Marie Hawks of Greenup, Illinois, was also surprised to hear Lulu
Belle's vocal renderings of romantic popular songs: "I guess Lulu Belle can be
just as serious as any one."[76] And another female fan of Lulu Belle embraced
the middle-class aesthetic of her love ballads: "We like Lulu Belle and Scotty,
especially their serious songs together."[77]

Lulu Belle and Scotty in Film

Lulu Belle and Scotty's repertory of longing for the bucolic southern home or
declaring their love for each other certainly helped mitigate elements of Lulu
Belle's unruly persona. At times, it appeared that Wiseman's more-sentimental
rustic persona had rubbed off on Lulu Belle and helped mold the performative mode of the husband-and-wife team into one of old-fashioned propriety
and domesticity. Their routines, however, persisted in highlighting Lulu Belle's
rustic caricatures and the gender strife inherited from the popular stage. Even
in his stalwart rustic persona, Wiseman did not challenge or undermine the
boldness of the comedienne in performances. Instead, by playing the straight
man, he often acted as a foil to highlight Lulu Belle's buffoonery, evident in their
film debut in the Republic western *Shine On, Harvest Moon* (1938)—starring
the singing cowboy Roy Rogers and the leading lady Mary Hart. Lulu Belle
and Scotty played the secondary comic couple (a convention in musicals and
in early films), bringing the slapstick buffoonery that made them famous in
radio to film.[78]

The musical numbers in which Lulu Belle plays the man-hungry rube or the
wench in duet with Scotty explicitly contrast in theme to the romantic Tin Pan
Alley love ballads that the singing cowboy crooned tenderly to his beloved. For
a local gathering, the "Fourth of July Celebration and Community Picnic," Lulu
Belle and Scotty provide the entertainment by performing "In the Dog House
Now," a song composed by Wiseman that evokes the well-known Jimmie Rodgers song "In the Jailhouse Now." Extending the imagery of imprisonment to
marital entrapment, the verse begins with Scotty reminiscing about his "single
life," which also recalls the themes of the well-known nineteenth-century song
"I Wish I Were Single Again." In response, Lulu Belle reminds him in her high,
thin, nasal-twang vocal patter that he had begged her to be his wife. In the

chorus, however, Lulu Belle's vocal part drops to provide a slightly deeper and more authoritative voice that criticizes and refuses to tolerate her husband's suggested sexual promiscuity, subtly expressed in the lyrics and the blues-inflected music. In particular, the opening phrase of the chorus includes the harmonic movement I-IV-I, typical of a blues progression, and Wiseman sings a bluesy melody to suggest that his extramarital pursuits are what led to his sentence in the proverbial doghouse: "I'm pettin' the dogs in little ole dog house now."

After their initial performance of the song, Lulu Belle and Scotty further highlight their conjugal strife in slapstick dialogue where Scotty accuses his wife of being a complaining shrew that continually "chirps."

> SCOTTY: "You know, Lily, after a few remarks like that I ought to know why some people call a woman a bird?"
> LULU BELLE: "Why?" (in a high nasal voice)
> SCOTTY: "'Cause you're always chirpin', that's why."
> LULU BELLE: "You know, I thought maybe it's 'cause we sometimes pick up a worm."

Though Scotty intends to keep his wife in her place with an insulting accusation, Lulu Belle outwits Scotty by turning the joke on him. The entire audience bursts into laughter, and the camera immediately pans to an older, respectable-looking couple exchanging surprised and amused looks (especially the woman) at Lulu Belle's audacity. Immediately following this shot, Lulu Belle launches into the chorus, "Oh, I'm telling you what, you're really in the doghouse now." The performance concludes with the hyperbolic movements of Lulu Belle's buffoonery. While exiting the stage, Lulu Belle collides with Scotty and trips across the platform, holding her head in confusion. She turns to the audience and takes a low, exaggerated bow after which Scotty grabs her arm to pull her off the stage before she embarrasses herself further. The scene ends with the audience laughing at Lulu Belle's kinetic comedy.

In another scene, Lulu Belle's musical role works as an entertaining ruse to distract the authorities from arresting the wrongly accused rancher Milt Brower for cattle theft. When the business leaders and the sheriff arrive at Brower's home, Lulu Belle (at Rogers's urging) distracts the men with a song so that Brower can safely escape from the false charges. In her attempts to serenade the sheriff, Lulu Belle sings "I'm Dying for Somebody to Love Me," in which she enacts the man-hungry rube. Comparable to her performance in "Hi Rinktum Inktum," Lulu Belle's vocal delivery aims at but fails to achieve a model of feminine deportment. With nasal-twang inflections, Lulu Belle begins the song in the lower range and then ascends above her vocal break to sing the line "I'm dying to get a nice fellar," giving the sonic impression of a rube chasing after eligible men. She ends the phrase, however, in her airy-sounding head voice by singing an ascending melody on the words "to get a nice beau," as if she were striving to impersonate a lilting soprano voice. In the refrain, though, Lulu Belle no longer feigns a genteel bearing and ends with an accentuated slide in her chest voice that exploits her nasal-twang vocal quality on the word "spurn" in "I'm dying, I'm sighing mere friendship I ever shall spurn." She thus dons the vocal mask of southern rube and sings in a purposely strident, nasal timbre.

Her aural enactment of a country rube trying to conceal her man-hungry ways with a thin veneer of feminine charm seems to work on the sheriff, who falls under her bewitching spell. "I'm Dying for Somebody to Love Me" is in triple meter, to which Lulu Belle waltzes around the room while singing and playing the guitar. With all eyes on the rustic buffoon, including those of Rogers and Wiseman (who exchange conspiratorial looks), her physical movements prove to be infectious, compelling the sheriff to dance in step with the comedienne, completely forgetting his official role in the attempted arrest of Brower. When more men show up at the door, Lulu Belle tries to distract the aging banker, the crooked ringleader among the business community, with her alluring tactics. She leans against him while she sings ironically, "I like a foolish young gun," which elicits an uncomfortable guffaw from the older man, whose corruption remains concealed by his middle-class standing at this point in the film. Unlike the rural sheriff, the banker appears slightly shocked at Lulu Belle's rustic attempts at seduction.

WLS's Publicity for Lulu Belle

How did the radio station WLS market its "Belle of the Barn Dance," who had a national and regional following not only in radio but also in film for her comic license? Lulu Belle's theatrical guises unfolded against WLS's publicity machine, which tried to provide a veneer of respectability for the station's various acts. At stake was Lulu Belle's position as the first southern female character to incorporate slapstick comedy into her stage performances on the *National Barn Dance*. Though she joined other buffoon figures, such as the Swedish rube Ole Yonson, the blackface character "Spareribs," and other white hayseeds, notably Arkie the Woodchopper and Pat Buttram, Lulu Belle's grotesque mimicry cast visions of rustic womanhood to the margins of society at a time when WLS paraded female performers as domestic icons of middle-class decorum in order to meet the demands of an emerging consumer ethos. As McCusker has argued, figures such as the "Little Sunbonnet Girl," enacted by Parker, conveyed a civilizing and respectable presence as the designated "girl singer" of the Cumberland Ridge Runners.[79] But Lulu Belle was not another genteel representation of mountain life. Rather, her mimicry of southern culture was a constant reminder that her rustic mask was one of the low Other.

In promoting the hillbilly comedienne, WLS initially highlighted Lulu Belle's kinetic energy and gum-chewing routines: she "parked her chewin' gum just before a split-second camera caught her actually still for an instant." The promotional material emphasized that Lulu Belle's stage antics were a natural extension of her real personality, as Myrtle Cooper, as if Lulu Belle was an "authentic" embodiment of rural southern culture.[80] "Lulu Belle's real name is Myrtle Cooper, and she was born in a little home in the South. Listeners love her as the noisy tomboy singer of funny songs."[81] In this description and accompanying photo, Lulu Belle is seen working hard at playing those boisterous songs on what looks like a homemade guitar straight from her mountain home (see figure 5).

In the write-up, however, the publicists of WLS tried to mitigate Lulu Belle's gross mimicry of rural womanhood and gender variance by separating the onstage character from a respectable private self. Though both Lulu Belle and Myrtle Cooper came from the South, Cooper could possess such a "genteel"

Figure 5. Lulu Belle. *WLS Family Album*, 1935.

manner "that you might think her an entirely different person" from the character heard over the radio and seen in the accompanying photo. According to the
WLS Family Album, "Whenever she approaches the microphone or appears on
stage, she chews gum with a vengeance, but offstage she scarcely ever touches
it."[82] By emphasizing that underneath Lulu Belle's comic persona, she was a
model of propriety, the writers were attempting to make her lowbrow mugging
palatable to the sensibilities of its middle-class audience while still reaching
those listeners drawn to the intriguing humor of Lulu Belle.

Pamela Fox has opined that Lulu Belle "played the independent hillbilly gal
buffoon to the hilt" until her 1934 marriage, at which time "her private identity
as conventional wife and mother increasingly blurred with this public persona to
produce a more temperate domestic image."[83] As mentioned at the beginning of
this chapter, WLS dubbed the duo the "Hayloft Sweethearts" to market them as
the ideal married couple who could counter the shifting, contested roles of men
and women during the Depression. Even over the airwaves, WLS transmitted the
duo's domestic felicity when the station announced the birth of Linda Lou, born
January 3, 1936, during NBC's national broadcast of the *National Barn Dance*.
Lulu Belle's female fans embraced the news by sending the Wisemans "literally a
hundred baby gifts" of "handmade quilts, handmade christening dresses, handmade sweaters" to celebrate the performer's newfound status as a mother.[84]

Though Lulu Belle's well-publicized marriage to Wiseman helped negotiate
her slapstick humor and vocal parodies of highbrow and lowbrow music, her
promotional material of the mid-1930s continued to wrestle with the marked
differences between her radio character and the ideals of middle-class propriety.
It was as if her radio persona as an audacious, outspoken female rube could not
be completely contained within the constructions of folk and domestic culture.
A 1937 *Stand By!* article, "Girl On the Cover," explained, "[The] gum-chewin'
mountain gal who plunks a 'git-tar' and sings hill-billy songs" is also the mother
to Linda Lou Wiseman. The same piece also emphasized that when Lulu Belle
returned home, she shed "the title of Radio Queen, bestowed upon her by the
vote of radio listeners, and [became] Mrs. Scott Wiseman, mother of Linda
Lou."[85] In other words, Lulu Belle simply sloughed her rustic mask and associated stardom once she entered the sanctity of her home, where she resumed
her domestic roles.

Another *Stand By!* article, "The Royal Family: Lulu Belle Winner of the Queen
Contest, Thanks Her Fans," also juxtaposed Lulu Belle's radio character and
success with the domestic details of her daily life. The article began with Lulu
Belle pointing to her southern rube character as she described her costume and
manner of verbal expression—"I haven't any crown to wear on my pigtails but
I sure feel like I'd thrown away my old high-top boots and been wearing glass
slippers ever since the editors of Radio Guide told me I was to be Radio Queen

of 1936. . . . It makes me truly 'as happy as a big sunflower.' . . . I didn't dream that an every day gal from the hills of Carolina would ever be given such an award." The article abruptly switched from Lulu Belle's hillbilly persona to the domestic sphere as Lulu Belle informed her devotees that she was home caring for her infant, "a-crawlin' around on the floor with Linda Lou," when she learned that she had won the title of "Radio Queen." She elaborated on this familial setting, remarking that she "almost let the pork chops burn" in the excitement of the news and that her new title as "Radio Queen" was not preventing her from caring for her family. The inverse was actually the case, according to the write-up. With her success, she could now be "settled in one place" and have a "real home," and "do [her] own cooking."[86] Although the article ostensibly proclaimed Lulu Belle's public title, it was mostly concerned with tempering her musical projections as a comedic rube with overdetermined descriptions of her roles as a traditional wife and mother.

Her publicity, however, could not completely disavow Lulu Belle's hillbilly charades after her marriage to Wiseman. A brief 1936 article about the coast-to-coast broadcast of the *National Barn Dance* at the Illinois State Fair with eighteen thousand people in the audience took pains to mention Lulu Belle's stage antics as a man-hungry rube. "Lulu Belle, always up to some mischief, almost wrecked the show when she ran up and kissed the Governor at the close of his brief speech."[87] Even in the 1950s, the *WLS Family Album* continued to market Lulu Belle as an "irrepressible comic on the stage and before the microphone."[88]

Though Lulu Belle's private self, as constructed by WLS, played an integral role in the domestic imagery that surrounded the Wiseman family, in performance she remained the hayseed buffoon, parodying southern culture, while Scotty appeared as the purveyor of southern tradition. Indeed, their very act presented the dialect of the comedic rube and the respectable mountaineer while gendering these stock characters. WLS often emphasized that Wiseman was the more serious of the two, a quiet, educated young man when he came to WLS. He soon "fell in the love with handsome laughing Lu."[89] Further elaborating on the differences between their radio personalities, an additional promotional blurb explained, "Lulu Belle was a young girl when she came to WLS, big, robust and good looking. She was something of a singer, with a big grin and gay chuckle. A little later the dignified young Scott Wiseman came from West Virginia, college trained."[90] Whereas Lulu Belle impersonated the "robust" clown, a bigger-than-life presence, Scotty played the part of the demure southern gentleman.

Conclusion

The Radio Queen of the 1930s was clearly part of a history of women vaudevillians taking over the caricatures of working-class women and immigrant women, and the comic styles of female impersonators. Through her stage and musical renderings, Lulu Belle participated in the theatric conventions of lowbrow humor by playing the part of a hillbilly buffoon largely through her parodies of southern vernacular music and stylized vocal idioms. Appearing as if she were aspiring but failing to achieve a level of cultural refinement, Lulu Belle could slip in and out of roles—the man-chasing rube fearful of turning into an old maid, the shrewish wife complaining about the responsibilities of domesticity, or the beguiled rustic maiden falling for the charms of debonair rogues.

What is significant is that her fans understood what was at stake culturally and aesthetically in Lulu Belle's performances. Her grotesque humor and comic songs played with the musical codes of taste during a period when those of the lower middle class and middle class clung to symbols of respectability, southern migrants wrestled with the hegemonic terms of acculturation, and women responded to the economic crisis of the 1930s by transgressing gender norms. In this historical context, Lulu Belle's comedic style offered symbolic protests against patriarchy, conventional understandings of bourgeois femininity, and the class politics of white southern migration. With her vocal parodies of southern culture and narratives of gender strife, she made it clear that she was playing a rustic role of Otherness that enabled palliative fantasies of rebellion, which her audience could identify with and delight in or completely repudiate in favor of cultural forms of gentility and refinement. The magnitude of Lulu Belle's cultural and musical significance, however, extends beyond the Depression era. By bringing a model of womanhood—the outlandish and unruly southern white woman—to the forefront of radio, Lulu Belle imparted a performative archetype to country music that would resonate in the stage buffoonery of Minnie Pearl and June Carter on the *Grand Ole Opry*, in Rose Maddox's musical parodies in California's honky-tonks, and in the feminist-themed music of Jean Shepard and Loretta Lynn. Thus Lulu Belle's acts of comedic rebellion that confronted and contested the paradoxes of class, region, and gender would remain foundational to the theatrical flair and gender dynamics of women's country music even after the *National Barn Dance* and the "Belle of the Barn Dance" had faded from the spotlight.

3 Gendering the Musical West

*Patsy Montana's Cowgirl Songs
of Tomboy Glamour*

While Lulu Belle had won the title "Radio Queen" for her uproari-
ous routines, comic songs, and romantic numbers with her duet partner and
husband, Scotty Wiseman, on Chicago's WLS, Patsy Montana had risen to the
top of the station's star-studded cast as a soloist of western-themed music. Her
"singing cowgirl" persona embodied the theatrical staging of barn-dance radio
and frontier culture that projected a mythological West as a place of individualism, rebellion, and hope. Singing of independent heroines whose pursuits of
social and material autonomy were comparable to those of the heroic cowboy,
Montana offered her listeners narratives in which she could ride her horse across
the western plains, tame wild stallions, display marksmanship skills, and end the
day yodeling by the fireside near a herd of cattle. In a sense, Montana's musical
imagery was not that far removed from Lulu Belle's portrayals of unruly women
challenging the confines of domesticity. And just as WLS's marketing strategies pulled Lulu Belle from the performative stage into the domestic sphere to
mitigate her unruly hillbilly persona, Montana's self-directedness and displays
of gender variance were often softened by her musical enactments of feminine
charm and gestures to heterosexual norms, all couched within the mythology
of the American West.

This chapter brings the romanticized western imagery of Montana into the
performative fold of WLS to connect the musical and cultural significance of
the singing cowgirl with the stark realities of WLS's audience during the Great
Depression. When referring to the economic and social upheavals of the 1930s,
scholars have recognized the general significance of the singing cowboy, but
few writers have acknowledged the importance of his counterpart, the singing
cowgirl.[1] Along with cowboy crooners such as Gene Autry, men who emerged
as heroes in Depression-era fantasies of the West, Montana not only offered

hope to those suffering from the devastating effects of rural poverty, urban unemployment, and displacement but also provided a model of independent womanhood that addressed the conflicted gender issues of the 1930s. While the singing cowgirl appeared capable and confident in managing the crises of the decade, she did not relinquish her feminine charm and affability. Montana thus simultaneously articulated and assuaged the era's concerns about class and the shifting roles of men and women by carefully combining gender conventions with musical imagery that called those models into question.

Montana could speak to Depression-era concerns with compelling musical narratives that stylized and authenticated her gendered illustrations of the West while drawing on the stylistic fluidity of barn-dance radio and early country music more generally. Her self-penned "I Want to Be a Cowboy's Sweetheart" (1935), for example, reflects a web of influences from early country music and Tin Pan Alley packaged in a dance-music arrangement in which she combined yodeling with a broadly appealing singing style that was often labeled "sweet." She could also remake folklike cowboy ballads into songs that juxtaposed the confines of female domesticity with the cowgirl's desire for the social freedoms associated with frontier culture, as she did in "The She Buckaroo" (1936). In so doing, Montana expanded on the conceptual and musical frame of performance and gender in early country music through her savvy use of musical style. As such, her actions helped mold sonic portraits of yodeling cowgirls on the open range who could sing "sweetly" about female autonomy.

The Making of Patsy Montana

Before Montana reached the apex of her success in the 1930s on WLS, she developed her musical talents as a singing cowgirl in Los Angeles, at a time when the city had begun to foster a country-music industry through radio, film, and recording. Montana (born Ruby Blevins in 1908) left her family home in what is now Hope, Arkansas (with one of her brothers and his wife) in the late 1920s to pursue a college education in California.[2] To support herself in California, she started to perform on radio shows in the Los Angeles area. Montana's musical background involved violin lessons as a child, teaching herself to play the guitar, and listening to a wide range of music on the family's wind-up Victrola, including the recordings of Jimmie Rodgers.[3] With an understanding of the fundamentals of music and an ear for vernacular idioms, she won a local talent contest by performing two songs by Rodgers, the cowboy song "Yodeling Cowboy" (replete with yodels) and the sentimental number "Whisper Your Mother's Name."[4] The award for the competition provided Montana the opportunity to appear regularly on KMTR's radio program the *Breakfast Club*, from which she emerged as the first solo cowgirl in Los Angeles radio.[5]

Montana's musical skills as a singer, yodeler, and instrumentalist soon attracted the attention of Stuart Hamblen, a key figure in the development of Southern California country music. Hamblen had started his own radio career in Los Angeles as one of the Beverly Hillbillies (initially a 1930s radio act), but he left behind the rustic mask of the comedic rube to cultivate a western persona as a songwriter and performer of cowboy songs, with his best-known hit being "Texas Plains" (1932). Impressed by Montana's talents, Hamblen hired her to perform with musicians Lorraine McIntire and Ruth DeMondrum. He christened the trio the Montana Cowgirls, and it was Hamblen who encouraged Ruby Blevins to take the stage name Patsy Montana. Broadcast over Hamblen's daily program on Inglewood's KMIC, the trio played an assortment of music, including the Tin Pan Alley song "When It's Night Time in Nevada" (1931) for their opening number. The ensemble's three-part harmony yodels and accompaniment of violin and guitar realized the nostalgic narrative of the open range, here acting as the ideal backdrop for recalling the sentimental pleasures of past love.[6]

As the first cowgirl ensemble on Los Angeles radio, the trio had few musical models to emulate apart from successful male acts. In fact, the Montana Cowgirls would often listen to the broadcasts of the Pioneer Trio (an early incarnation of the Sons of the Pioneers) or Elton Britt (the yodeling cowboy, who also got his start in radio with the Beverly Hillbillies) to learn new yodel melodies.[7] Britt, in particular, was in the midst of developing a reputation as the "Highest Yodeler" with his vocalizations soaring to the heights of his falsetto range. His style of yodeling must have influenced Montana's development as one of the most virtuosic yodeling cowgirls of the 1930s.[8]

The Montana Cowgirls' success continued to grow, as they toured with Monty Montana (the world champion roper) in live performances up and down the West Coast and became a regular feature of Hoot Gibson's rodeos on his ranch at Saugus, approximately thirty miles north of Los Angeles. In addition to their personal appearances and their continual radio work on Hamblen's program, the Montana Cowgirls could be heard on a number of radio stations in California and even in Oregon. They also crossed into the medium of film.[9] The group's growing fame, however, came to a sudden stop when both McIntire and DeMondrum chose marriage over their performance careers.

Determined not to let the breakup of the Montana Cowgirls deter her own ambitions, Montana landed a spot on Chicago's WLS as a singing cowgirl. While visiting her family home, she had tuned her radio to the *National Barn Dance* and listened to the "beautiful harmony" of the cowgirl sister duo the Girls of the Golden West, Dolly and Millie Good (originally their last name was Goad). As Montana remembered, "I wrote my first fan letter to them and told them I was going to be in Chicago and I was a singer of western songs from the West

Coast; I'd like to meet them."[10] Just as the Montana Cowgirls had dominated the airwaves of the West Coast in the early 1930s, the Girls of the Golden West had established themselves as a midwestern radio act first on St. Louis radio stations, the border station XER, and then on WLS.[11] In response to Montana's correspondence, the sister duo informed her that the string band the Prairie Ramblers (another WLS ensemble) were looking for a "girl" singer.[12] Influenced by the increased presence of cowboy and cowgirl performers on the radio station, the string ensemble had changed its name from the Kentucky Ramblers to the Prairie Ramblers and developed a style of playing that included the dance idioms of western swing to promote a western image instead of a southern one. When Montana auditioned for the part of lead vocalist, her talents in singing, yodeling, and songwriting made for a perfect fit for the ensemble.

Initially, Montana and the Prairie Ramblers were part of Gene Autry's road production, the *WLS Roundup Show*, which also included the Girls of the Golden West. Like other WLS troupes, they toured the Midwest playing in theaters and schoolhouses with other vaudevillian acts, and Montana quickly became one of the main stars, closing performances with her artful showmanship. She recalled how the theatricality of variety entertainment helped shape her vibrant stage presence: "We were given a half hour [in the State and Lake Theater in Chicago], our whole troupe, and that's vaudeville. . . . I was the last one on the show. I'd come blowing on the stage singing 'Texas Plains' . . . a real fast yodeling number, and I'd stop the show. . . . An old stage guy told me this, 'Patsy, always leave them wanting.'"[13] As the grand finale of the *WLS Roundup Show*, Montana (singing and yodeling Hamblen's "Texas Plains") quickly emerged as one of the most successful performers in Autry's troupe and also on the radio station WLS.

The Romance of the West on WLS

What Montana offered that differed from some of her western counterparts on WLS and in Autry's performance troupe was her dynamic stage presence, a result of her skill at combining various musical idioms, which projected the cowgirl's autonomy against the western landscape of romance and opportunity. When she started to perform on WLS in 1933, she joined a cast of western performers who had brought the imagery and music making of white rurality closer to the mainstream aesthetics of sentimentality and glamour. The primary example of this was Gene Autry. The first western singer on WLS, Autry started his radio career performing a repertory of maudlin songs, including "That Silver-Haired Daddy of Mine" (1931). Even his early western songs, like "Cowboy's Heaven" (1933), in which a lone cowhand yearns for an afterlife to escape his meager existence, carried sentimental themes to the western frontier. Yet as Autry continued to promote his western persona, he gravitated toward a more contemporary popular aesthetic in his cowboy repertory, singing Tin Pan Alley songs with a crooning voice cultivated by microphone technology. Now as a crooning cowboy, Autry specialized in creating dreamy landscapes of the West, unlike Montana, who would yodel to the top of her range and turn upbeat dance tunes into musical anthems for the cowgirl.

The Girls of the Golden West, the cowgirl duo who helped Montana secure a place on WLS, also had a sound that was completely different from Montana's. Like Autry in his early songs, the cowgirl duo brought sentimental-sounding tunes to the radio station. Their lilting vocal harmonies of rounded tones and softly crooned yodels accompanied by the quiet strumming of the guitar came to the forefront of their performance. Singing directly into the microphone without a multi-instrumental accompaniment, the duo's music created the aural effect of an intimate musical setting, in which the broadcasts of barn-dance radio could be heard as an extension of the home.[14] Even their cowgirl songs of self-determination sounded as if they came directly from the domestic parlor, an acceptable venue for female music making. In "I Want to Be a Real Cowboy Girl" (1935), for example, the Girls of the Golden West expanded on the subjectivity of the cowgirl within a musical context of sentimentality.[15] Lyrically, the cowgirl yearns to inhabit the cultural space of the western hero by literally putting on the garb or costume of the cowboy: "I want to be a real cowboy girl and wear all the buckles and straps . . . tote a six-shooter too, wear a belt that is four inches wide." Ironically, these desires of appropriating the dress and the masculine swagger of the cowboy incorporate the maudlin idioms of Autry's music by borrowing a musical phrase from "That Silver-Haired Daddy of Mine." They sing the lyrics, "And know how it feels to wear spurs on my heels then strut about in my chaps" to the music of Autry's bridge: "If I could erase those lines from your face and bring back the gold to your hair." Linking their performance identities to the music of the tenderhearted cowboy, the duet does not necessarily evoke the position and stance of the virile western protagonist. The cowgirl duo thus mediates a lyrical image of independence with music that recalls nineteenth-century sentimentality.

Unlike Autry and the Girls of the Golden West, the Westerners were a popular WLS dance band that offered upbeat swing renditions of western-themed songs such as "Bunkhouse Jamboree" (1939).[16] The Westerners first formed in 1928, when the Massey family patriarch, Henry Austin, started an ensemble that included three of his children (Louise, Curtiss "Dott," and Allen) as well as Milt Mabie (Louise Massey's husband) and later accordionist Larry Wellington.[17] The Westerners lent a polished sound to their dance numbers, which could be heard over the airwaves of WIBW in Topeka and on KMBC in Kansas City, at a time when the city had become a notable center of swing music. Dott Massey even led a dance orchestra at the Pla-Mor, Kansas City's largest ballroom.[18]

With the Westerners' growing prominence, WLS station managers took note of their appealing sound and by 1933 had hired the ensemble to occupy a central position among the lineup of radio acts.[19] On WLS, the Westerners had their own daily show, *The Westerners on Rhythm Range*, advertised as "one of the most tuneful shows of the morning."[20] During the afternoons, the Westerners could be heard on the well-known *Dinnerbell* program, which included Sophia Germanich's soprano renderings accompanied by the WLS Orchestra and the comedic routines of Arkie the Arkansas Woodchopper or the Hoosier Sod Busters.[21] The Westerners also performed on NBC's hour-long broadcast of the *National Barn Dance*, in which they appeared next to Lulu Belle and a range of other musicians.[22] By 1935, the radio trade journal *Stand By!* could report, "The group has become one of the most distinctive and popular acts in radio."[23]

Like Autry's crooning voice in his Tin Pan Alley songs, the lush-sounding popular music of the Westerners offered a middle ground between the rustic buffoonery of comic characters and the aesthetics of Western art music for WLS's heterogeneous audience. Dott Massey of the Westerners could sing, according to WLS publicity, with a "soft baritone voice" and could write "singly, or in collaboration, a score or more of tuneful numbers, ranging from the sweet ballad type to the prancing rhythms of such selections as 'Mexican Jumpin' Bean,' and the Westerners' famed whirlwind number, 'Benjamin's Nest.'"[24] In other words, Dott Massey could croon supple melodic lines, as did Autry, or compose swinging dance tunes to an orchestrated accompaniment. Like Dott, Louise Massey's singing style and songwriting abilities fit with the stylized swing idioms of the family band. She crooned western songs with a sonorous pop-inflected voice of rounded tones and composed with Lee Penny one of the Masseys' most successful songs, "My Adobe Hacienda" (1941), a Tin Pan Alley ballad invoking the romanticized Latino influence and presence in the American Southwest.[25] Yet Louise Massey did not channel her musical talents in the direction of writing songs about the cowgirl's subjectivity or offer performances that combined a range of vocal idioms as Montana did.

More than that of the other singing cowgirls on WLS, Montana's fame resided in her ability to negotiate heterosexual conventions with the cowgirl's desire for independence in performances that combined a competing range of popular and vernacular styles. On WLS, Montana largely sang with a pop-inflected vocal tone with some southern inflections of pronunciation, contrasting with the consistently smooth, mainstream vocal techniques of Louise Massey. Montana's vocal style was also unlike the Girls of the Golden West's sentimental, intimate vocal expressions. Unlike theirs, Montana's performances explicitly highlighted the vitality and energy of the singing cowgirl with upbeat music and a spirited stage presence that she had cultivated in live performance. She yodeled at the top of her range and wrote songs that showcased the independence of the cowgirl. Moreover, unlike Louise Massey, Montana was distinctly positioned as the lead singer of the Prairie Ramblers and performed songs that underscored her prominence as a soloist. Not until later in the 1930s when the Westerners changed their name to Louise Massey and the Westerners did Louise receive a similar top billing.[26]

Unlike the Westerners, though, Montana was not an established entertainer of the Alka-Seltzer-sponsored portion of the barn-dance broadcast by NBC.[27] However, she did appear as a guest on the network portion of the barn dance and regularly as a performer of the regional broadcasts of the *National Barn Dance*, for which she was billed as a soloist by WLS's publicity.[28] By October 1935, the growing prominence of Montana and the Prairie Ramblers was evident when they became a regular feature on the daily morning program *Smile-A-While*.[29] The sponsors of the show (Peruna tonic and Kolor-Bak hair dye) hired WLS announcer Hall O'Halloran to host a radio program on WOR in New York City. O'Halloran, in turn, enlisted the musical talents of Montana and the Prairie Ramblers, who became the first country act to appear on the New York radio station.[30] They were an immediate success, receiving more fan mail than any of the other radio acts. Though Montana had written her signature song, "I Want to Be a Cowboy's Sweetheart," in Chicago while performing on WLS, she and the Prairie Ramblers gave their first performance of the cowgirl tune on WOR. Montana later explained that she was successful with the song in part because it was a polka, a style that directly appealed to New York City's as well as Chicago's Irish and Polish radio listeners.[31] From these New York City broadcasts, Bob Miller, a song publisher, heard Montana's performance and offered to publish the song. With a vested interest in promoting Montana's cowgirl tune, Miller convinced Art Satherley (the artist and repertoire [A and R] man for American Records Company) that the song would reach a viable market.[32] A promoter of American vernacular music, Satherley recorded Gene Autry and the Western-ers. But he believed female soloists could not sell recordings.[33] Montana soon proved him wrong.

"I Want to Be a Cowboy's Sweetheart"

The title "I Want to Be a Cowboy's Sweetheart" appears to signal that the cow-girl's access to the symbolic advantages of the West might depend, in fact, on heterosexual romance.[34] The song's lyrics and Montana's musical performance, however, point in a different direction: toward the realization of a cowgirl's life in a realm not limited by the constraints of societal normativity. Though Montana opens and ends the first verse with the nominal phrase, she does not develop a narrative of romantic love in the interim. Rather, she elaborates on the cowgirl's longing for the metaphoric freedoms of frontier culture: rope and ride, yodel, and strum a guitar before retiring next to a sleeping herd of cattle. Thus Montana's cowboy serves less as an idealized sexual partner than as a conduit to all the promises of "the West."

What made Montana's song so compelling, however, was not just the lyrical narrative but also the ways her sonic portrait of autonomy was based on dance idioms of the 1930s. "I Want to Be a Cowboy's Sweetheart" is a swing-inflected polka. As Montana explained, "My songs had to have a definite beat or they didn't sell. Remember, that was the western-swing era. But there would be two mikes in the studio. I would be on one side with a bass fiddle, and Art [Satherley] would be on the other side of my mike. . . . If he couldn't feel that beat, the number was out."[35] In Montana's song, the fiddle plays syncopated melodic lines to the prominent string bass part that provides the typical oom-pah pattern of the polka. The string bass's steady rhythmic movement on the downbeats is reinforced by the guitar's bass notes alternating with full chords on the upbeats, providing a strong pulse that surely pleased Satherley.

As a songwriter, Montana also incorporated an intertextual web of song sources to place the heroine in a stylized western setting. Montana begins the opening hook of her song in a manner similar to Stuart Hamblen's "Texas Plains" from 1934, a song that portrays a cowboy's desires for a life free from societal constraints, while he drinks his coffee from an "old tin can" and listens to "the song of a whippoorwill" and "a coyote cry" (see Ex. 1 and Ex. 2). "Texas Plains" is also a polka with a harmonic progression (I–V7/V–V7–I) that Montana includes for the opening two phrases of her piece. As mentioned earlier, "Texas Plains" was integral to Montana's live performance repertory while she was touring and performing with Gene Autry's road production, the *WLS Roundup Show*, and it was the first song she had performed on the *National Barn Dance*.[36] She

Example 1. Measures 1–4 of "Texas Plains." Lyrics and music by Stuart Hamblen, 1934. Transposed from B-flat to G for ease of comparison.

Example 2. Measures 1–4 of "I Want to Be a Cowboy's Sweetheart." Lyrics and music by Patsy Montana, 1935.

had changed the lyric of "Texas Plains" to "Montana Plains" in her first guest performance on the NBC broadcast of the *National Barn Dance*, when she again brought the house down (even with Lulu Belle's mugging antics meant to detract from the cowgirl's performance).[37] Given her success with Hamblen's song, it makes sense that Montana looked to "Texas Plains" for musical inspiration for what would become her signature song about the cowgirl roping and riding "over the plains" and listening to the "coyotes howling."

Montana may have turned to an additional source to shape her musical narrative: the 1933 song "You Gotta Be a Football Hero (to Get Along with the Beautiful Girls)," written by Tin Pan Alley songwriters Al Sherman, Buddy Fields, and Al Lewis. Introduced on radio by Fred Waring and His Pennsylvanians, "You Gotta Be a Football Hero" became one of the most frequently heard football anthems at college games. The song was also used in a 1935 Popeye cartoon, in which Brutus shows off his skills as a football player to lure Olive Oyl away from Popeye. At the beginning of the game, Olive Oyl, dressed as a cheerleader, sings the last two phrases of the chorus, encouraging Popeye to join the opposing team and win back her affections.

The title phrase of Montana's cowgirl tune leads with the same hook as the chorus of "You Gotta Be a Football Hero" (see Ex. 3). For the concluding phrases, Montana departs from the harmonic design of "Texas Plains" and instead follows both the melodic contours and the harmonic pattern of the very phrases that Olive Oyl sings in the Popeye cartoon. Perhaps Montana was inspired by the feisty nature and performance of the cartoon heroine. Specifically, both songs include the return of the opening hook in the beginning of the penultimate A' phrase and a circle-of-fifths movement (common in Tin Pan Alley songs) in the conclusion, thereby ending with a musical affect of peroration. As in the football anthem, the cowgirl's desires seem to direct her audiences to rally behind the protagonist's wishes for the fictitious West, where female autonomy and gestures toward idealized love can easily coexist in a stylized portrait contingent on the idioms of popular music.

Montana's talent for drawing from a wide palate of musical idioms and interweaving them into a single song involved her skills not only as a songwriter but

Example 3. Measures 1–4 of the Chorus of "You Gotta Be a Football Hero." Words and music by Al Sherman, Buddy Fields, and Al Lewis. Published by Leo Frist, 1933. Transposed from C to G for ease of comparison.

also as a vocalist. The cowgirl's dynamic vocal performance brought together the yodel, as a sonic example of female agency, with a singing style that her audience considered sweet. In her lively polka, Montana swings a fast-paced major-mode yodel melody that clearly shows off her ability to switch back and forth quickly between registers while highlighting the bright timbre of her upper range. Yodeling is a vocalization that uses the larynx muscles and glottal stops to accentuate the abrupt change of vocal register between the chest and the head voice.[38] Even though women have distinct registers—chest, an extensive midrange, head, and whistle—the vocal break occurs between the chest and the head voice. As the vocal pedagogue Richard Miller explains, a woman singer "is capable of making a shift in registers from chest to head, in the lower range of her voice, but she cannot produce the marked transition from the middle voice to the head voice."[39] Even if a woman yodels from the midrange (where she can sing notes in either her chest or her head range), she is still featuring a break between the chest and the head voice.[40] Unlike many male vocalists who sing mainly in the chest register, women often yodel to vibrant-sounding head registers.

Though Montana claimed that she initially learned to yodel by listening to Jimmie Rodgers's recordings, her fast-paced yodeling passages and switching between registers contrast with the more relaxed yodel melodies typical of Rodgers. Like Rodgers's, though, Montana's yodel signals a range of yodeling practices introduced to the United States in the nineteenth century and worked into the American vernacular. Alpine yodeling, coming from an Austrian-Swiss folk tradition of communication and herding livestock, was first introduced to U.S. audiences in the 1820s by operatic female vocalists, such as Maria Malibran, Henriette Sontag, and Antoinette Otto, before yodeling families, such as the Rainer Family, traveled to the United States in 1839.[41] Timothy Wise's research on the repertory and critical reception of well-acclaimed sopranos embellishing their vocal lines with yodeling, such as Henrietta Sontag's performance of Carl Eckhart's well-known Swiss song "Er liebt nur mich allein," demonstrates that the yodel operated as an aural sign of nineteenth-century female vocal virtuosity and feminine charm in songs largely steeped in pastoral imagery.[42]

Yet as the nineteenth century continued, the yodel moved from art music to the vernacular in the United States, where it took on comedic and parodic tones. On the popular stage, blackface performance troupes, such as Rainer's Original Ethiopian Serenaders, incorporated Alpine-derived yodels in their caricatures of black culture.[43] In ethnic humor skits and plays, the bumbling Dutch (Deutsch) character, a German male immigrant, spoke and sang broken English with a strong German accent. One of the first successful singing actors of the Dutch character was J. K. Emmet, who composed several yodel songs, such as "Lullaby" and "Cuckoo Song," that evoked the feminine and the pastoral for his theatrical role, beginning in the 1870s, as "Fritz Van Vonderblinkinstoffen."[44] That the yodel was a vocal device of masculine parody in relation to theatrical caricatures of ethnicity and race was evident in the performative history of another well-known lullaby yodel song "Sleep, Baby, Sleep" (published by John Handley in 1885). The African American performer Charles Anderson, for example, often appeared as a mammy singing and yodeling in his countertenor range "Sleep, Baby, Sleep" (recorded in 1923).[45] Moreover, additional Dutch characters emphasized the feminized signification of the yodel in songs like "The Happy German Twins," recorded in 1906 by George P. Watson (who also recorded Emmet's "Lullaby" and "Sleep, Baby, Sleep") and Len Spencer. Watson yodels, and Spencer responds with, "Vat is this noise, this 'lay-ee-dee, lay-ee-dee'? Is that some voman lady or you start some female impersonation?"[46]

The vocal technique of yodeling also became a component of the blues and early country music.[47] Jimmie Rodgers began his recording career by also yodeling in "Sleep, Baby, Sleep" (1927) with the same yodel melody as his predecessors had in his first recording session with Columbia Records, linking masculine parodies of the stage to early country-music recordings.[48] In many of Rodgers's songs, including his blues songs, the vocal technique often transformed into a languid, loosely syncopated instrumental break, unfolding in a limited range of sequential sixths.[49] With the sonic impression of loneliness in his sentimental tunes or bravado in some of his blues songs, especially those that featured a blues-inflected yodel melody, Rodgers's vocalizations influenced his contemporaries and successors in country music, including the singing cowboy Gene Autry.[50] Like Rodgers, Autry usually featured a narrow range of sequential sixths in his vocalizations that reached to his thin-sounding falsetto range, complementing his sentimentalized depictions of frontier culture.

But some male yodelers of Montana's generation, including Elton Britt, could demonstrate the brilliance of Alpine yodeling practices while converting the yodel into an upbeat, syncopated, bluesy vocal device, as in "Patent Leather Boots" (1939) in which the cowboy dandy sings of putting on his stylized western wear—"patent leather boots," "silk and scarf," and "Stetson hat"—to ride out with his "lady love." As mentioned earlier, Britt started his career in California at the same time that Montana first appeared on radio in Los Angeles. She often tuned into his broadcasts to learn new yodel melodies, especially as he developed a reputation as the "World's Highest Yodeler," best demonstrated in his vocal performance in "Chime Bells" (1934). With "Chime Bells" (based on the Alpine-themed song "Mountain High" and recorded by Matt Keefe, a vaudevillian performer who played the theatrical part of the Dutch character), Britt alludes to the pastoral, feminized setting of the yodel: a mockingbird singing and a "maid" tucked away in a mountainous setting waiting for the male protagonist.[51] (Britt would later sing Paul Robert's "She Taught Me to Yodel"

[1938], which explains that he had learned to yodel from a "yodelin' gal up in a little Swiss chalet.") Britt's yodels recall the virtuosic techniques of the past while applying the vocalization to a 1930s popular-music context. Departing from the straight rhythms typical of Alpine yodeling, Britt swings his yodel melodies, varying the rhythmic language, then yodels in double time, continually speeding up his vocalizations until he leaps to a resounding high F_5, which he sustains impressively for a full minute.[52] Montana does not display the same level of vocal virtuosity and rhythmic dexterity heard in Britt's stellar yodeling performance. Like Britt, though, Montana swings her yodel melody while repeatedly reaching the upper range of her voice. In fact, she ends her yodel with a show-stopping octave leap to G_5, a step higher than Britt's concluding F_5.

If the yodel evoked a competing range of shifting and gendered meanings, Montana's vocal device, then, signaled the legacy of female virtuosity as the yodel was also deployed in sonic displays of masculine parody, cowboy sentimentality (as in Autry's maudlin cowboy songs), and even masculine bravado (as in Britt's "Patent Leather Boots"). Within this performative context, Montana promoted her own vocal abilities in a song concerning a woman's yearning for the societal freedoms usually reserved for the cowboy. Montana's yodeling thus exceeded the lyrical frame of "I Want to Be a Cowboy's Sweetheart." Carolyn Abbate has written about the power of the voice in opera, the way the voice "produces music that might itself be regarded as working against the story," even the one narrated by the singing subject.[53] This is certainly the case with Montana's yodel. It is the first vocalization one hears from Montana before she launches into the narrative of the song. She repeats her yodel melodies after each verse and ends the song not with a vision of heterosexual love but with her yodel challenging the cowboy's cultural power to claim the figurative open range as a solely masculinized space.

Montana, however, was not alone in recalling the connections between female vocal virtuosity and yodeling on WLS. Regularly featuring the show-stopping yodels of women vocalists, WLS's broadcasts included the DeZurik Sisters, a duo who evoked the nineteenth-century operatic diva as well as the image of the yodeling family. In performances, they appeared in traditional German dress to showcase their acrobatic yodeled harmonies, combined with tongue trills and other decorative vocal devices in their upper head register.[54] Moreover, the *WLS Family Album* billed Christine as its "little Swiss Miss with the clear, sweet voice" whose yodel songs could "go almost as high as the Swiss Alps where her ancestors used to live."[55] Like those of the DeZurik Sisters, Christine's vocalizations were meant to recall a Northern European musical tradition for WLS's listeners of German-Scandinavian descent. Usually dressed in a Swiss "velvet costume with a laced bodice and red blouse," Christine could sing with clear, rounded tones, a cultivated style that drew on bel canto vocal traditions, while yodeling in a manner that brought to mind the topography of the Swiss Alps.[56] Christine's performances thus recalled those nineteenth-century operatic divas yodeling in Swiss songs. Within this musical context of yodeling virtuosity, Montana could translate the vocalizations that represented the vastness of the Alps into a sonority that evoked the openness of the American western range, where a "singing cowgirl" like Montana could be free to roam.

In the same song, Montana combined her yodeling vocalizations with what was considered a "sweet" vocal timbre, comparable to the vocal production of Christine's "clear, sweet voice."[57] The tessitura of the melody in "I Want to Be a Cowboy's Sweetheart" falls within a range that continually crosses the alto's break between the chest register and the midrange. Montana sings with a relaxed open-throat tone in the chest voice for the first half of the phrase ("I want to be a cowboy's sweetheart"). In second half of the phrase ("I want to learn to rope and to ride"), Montana reaches for the melodic apex with a mix of chest and head to avoid pushing her chest voice to this higher range and producing a brash, loud sonority. Montana typically ends those phrases that fall above the break with a lilting sound produced in the head voice. Her diction is still inflected with southern pronunciations of certain words, such as pronouncing the long *i* of "ride" and "life" as "ah" and dropping the *g* in "howlin'."

Montana, however, would distance herself from the vocal expressions of a southern folk tradition by stating that she was not a hillbilly singer but rather a western performer influenced by popular artists. Kate Smith (1907–1988), who emerged in the 1930s as a popular singer of vaudeville, Broadway, and radio, was something of an "idol" for her in this regard.[58] Also an alto, Smith sang melodies in her resonant but bright-sounding chest voice. Yet she could seamlessly interweave the warm but bold-sounding tones of her chest register with a sonorous-sounding head voice, showcasing a vocal range of two and a half octaves. If Smith was one of Montana's favorite singers, it makes sense that Montana would also develop a voice of a two-octave range that showcased the rounded timbre of her chest voice and the vibrant sounds of her head voice in musical hybrids of popular and country music. Thus Montana's vocal performance brought together the cowgirl's virtuosic yodeling with a conventional singing style prevalent in popular music. In doing so, she could yodel to the heights of her range to symbolize the agency of the roaming cowgirl while still singing in a manner that realized the effective sonic codes of mainstream vocal practices.

Montana's Listening Audience Weighs In

Montana's listening audience repeatedly commented on her "sweet" vocal timbre that complemented the broadcasts of a diverse range of musical acts and singing styles. Mrs. Sanford of Wisconsin, for example, wrote, "We are indeed thankful for the splendid entertainment by first-class artists on the barn dance programs. The great artist, the sweet-voiced Patsy Montana, the ever pleasing, peppy Hot Shots, the lovable Lulu Belle and Scotty, and others."[59] Other appreciative listeners interpreted the cowgirl's vocal tone as one of sincerity that lent credibility to her musical depictions of the open range. A resident of Chicago who saw Montana perform at a rodeo in the city declared that she was the "highlight" of the day's entertainment, noting, "[Her] voice will be more sweet now than ever, for I know that the songs of the prairies and plains come right from her heart."[60]

For many fans of the singing cowgirl, Montana's sweetness of tone aligned her more with the vocal styling of popular singers such as Christine and the vaudevillian Grace Wilson than with rustic comic performers.[61] For example, Wilson's vocality was also described in similar terms as that of Montana's. Mrs. Small (also of Wisconsin) wrote pointedly, "I don't think anyone sings a song more sweetly than Grace Wilson."[62] Wilson, who had been with WLS since its first broadcast of the *National Barn Dance* in 1924, was one of the few solo female stars whose polished stage persona served as a model for Montana. As Montana later recalled, "I found myself always watching Grace Wilson. When she was on, I'd always get out on a front bale of hay where I could see her. . . . She was from the old vaudeville stage, and I learned a lot from her. . . . I would say she was almost my mentor when I . . . came to WLS."[63]

Wilson's ability to dominate the spotlight with her "sweet" renderings of popular tunes must have rubbed off on the singing cowgirl, for WLS listeners seemed to understand that the cowgirl's vocality had an effect similar to that of Wilson (a sweet vocal tone often implied for WLS listeners a sweet personality). A devotee of the cowgirl, Eleanor Hampton, declared that Montana had a voice that came from heaven, "sweet and unspoiled," and asked why WLS did not promote her as "the girl with a million dollar smile," a stage name similar to Wilson's, "The Girl with a Million Friends."[64] Another fan of Montana wrote, "I want to congratulate WLS for having that sweet little singer, Patsy Montana, with them. I agree with Eleanor Hampton that Patsy should be called 'The Girl With the Million Dollar Smile.'"[65]

Though many fans seemed delighted with Montana's singing voice, perceiving her singing style as an extension of her personality, some fans recognized the aesthetic play and differences between Montana's yodels that highlighted the break between the chest and the head voice and the rounded, smooth sounding tones of her singing voice. Mrs. Warren of Missouri worried that Montana's yodeling might actually ruin her ability to sing: "Oh, dear me, Readers of Matteson Illinois! I haven't anything against yodeling and I think Patsy's yodels are verr-e-e nice indeed. But she has such a sweet voice for *real* singing and I'm afraid yodeling will cause it to break in the middle like some cowboy yodelers I've heard."[66] For this admirer, Montana's yodels stood in contrast to "real singing" (or bel canto–like singing practices) and could possibly damage her vocal cords, making it impossible for the cowgirl to continue her radio career.

Plenty of listeners, however, readily accepted Montana's yodels alongside her manner of singing, while acknowledging the differences between the vocal techniques. As Mrs. Timm of Wisconsin opined, "There has been some discussion about sweet voiced little Patsy Montana. I think she is an expert on both her yodel and sweet singing."[67] Likewise, another fan stated, "I think her yodels are 50 percent of her sweet songs."[68] For these fans, Montana was able to combine two distinct vocal practices—one that possibly gestured to comedy or cowboy culture and the other that suggested a degree of vocal polish. Thus her sweet-sounding voice helped shape the imaginary West into a place where cowgirls could roam without relinquishing their feminine charm and style.

As a yodeling and sweet-singing cowgirl (who complemented the cowboy crooners of the time), Montana created music that could be interpreted as contributing to the glamorized settings of frontier culture. As Beverley Skeggs notes, "Glamour offers the ability to appear as something different from the mundane. It is an escape route."[69] Glamour has provided a means for working-class women to distance themselves from the stereotypes linking the lower classes with vulgarity, heightened sexuality, and tastelessness. For women wanting to "pass as feminine," style and attitude can be important outlets that disavow a low Other and transcend "the banalities of femininity which render women as passive objects." In this sense, "glamour is about a performance of femininity with strength."[70] In highlighting the allure and romance of the West, Montana's cowgirl songs could hold femininity and independence together in a respectable performance for her heterogeneous audience of women: farm women, urban working-class women, and former middle-class women having to confront the class and gendered politics of the 1930s.

As mentioned in the preceding chapters, the 1930s were an era of shifting gender roles, in which women's increased presence in the public sector challenged and questioned dominant concepts of gender normativity. Some social commentators were uneasy with women's increased presence in the labor market and vilified them for taking men's jobs, even though women typically found work in the "feminized" service sector. At the same time, midwestern farm women actively engaged in political debates about government policies that concerned the rapidly declining living conditions of the midwestern family farm. Within this environment, Virginia E. Jenckes became the first woman from Indiana to be elected to the U.S. House of Representatives in 1933, and she devoted her political career to feminist issues and agricultural matters.[71] Montana's sweet singing and yodeling abilities offered sonic models of female strength and style that resonated in an environment of visible women in political and social debates.

Montana's "The She Buckaroo" and the Gender Bending of the Rugged West

"I Want to Be a Cowboy's Sweetheart" established Montana's style of singing and writing upbeat dance songs about the cowgirl's desire for the romance and promises of the West. She later composed "Sweetheart of the Saddle" (recorded in 1936), "Ridin' the Sunset Trail" (recorded in 1937), "I Want to Be a Cowboy's Dream Cowgirl" (copyrighted 1941), as well as several derivatives of her original hit song, such as "I've Found My Cowboy Sweetheart" (recorded in 1937; copyrighted in 1941).[72] Satherly encouraged Montana to capitalize on the success of the original, and fans were eager to hear Montana's newest tunes, including the awkwardly titled, "The Answer to I Want to Be a Cowboy's Sweetheart."[73]

While she elaborated on the cowgirl's subjectivity and her possible romantic involvement with the cowboy in the imaginary West, Montana wrote several songs that largely drew on the image of the tomboy cowgirl figure, one that actively rejects heterosexual romance and contested feminine ideals. In these songs, Montana asserted a level of defiance in her cowgirl character that can be compared to Lulu Belle's rebellious versions of womanhood in her own adaptations of the wench figure (discussed in chapter 2). The theatrics of the Wild West show for the popular stage intertwined tomboy cowgirls with the thespian legacy of female performers taking over the masculinized wench role. For example, in her 1939 recording with the Prairie Ramblers, Montana's "A Rip Rip Snortin' Two Gun Gal" paints the cowgirl as a dangerous heroine who came of age with a "six gun in each hand" and warns men to keep their distance from her "corral" so they won't ignite her explosive temperament. She continues to elaborate on the identity of the singing cowgirl as a tough asexual heroine who explicitly challenges the West as a masculinized domain in some of her other self-penned songs, such as "Texas Tomboy" (1941) and "Wench from Wyoming" (1941).[74] In the latter, she sings that she is "a rootin' tootin' high faloutin' sorty gal," who sings "soprano" and "might even wear a shirt" (meaning a women's blouse or a loosely fitting dress) in her performance of a "a wench from Wyoming." Here she points to the theatrical tradition of the wench figure as a cross-dressed man impersonating a woman, combining a curious mix of masculine and feminine traits. In "Texas Tomboy" she continues to brag about her ranching abilities— "I can rope and shoot and throw with the best at the rodeo"—while she rejects outright various aspects of femininity: "I don't wear silk or calico, I can't bake or knit or sew; I quit long ago and went huntin' buffalo."

Montana's gender-bending songs recall the historical and stage settings of the American West as a cultural space of gender variance carved out by nineteenth-century depictions of frontier women and western heroines.[75] Literary protagonists of dime novels, such as Hurricane Nell, Wild Edna, and the historical figure

Calamity Jane were not the "genteel tamers" but instead were often the "wild cats" and "feral femmes" of the western frontier, known for their adventurous and courageous abilities to fight cattle wrestlers, rope wild mustangs, and even rescue cowboys who ran afoul of Native Americans.[76] In many of these tales, Calamity Jane appears as crossed-dressed military scout and Pony Express courier whose nonnormative image at times included same-sex desires, pointing to the intertwining imagery of rural working-class womanhood with "masculine or butch personas among queer women."[77] The sensationalized accounts of the dangerous outlaw Belle Starr and of the staged performances of the sharpshooter Annie Oakley in William Frederick "Wild Bill" Cody's international traveling show, Buffalo Bill's Wild West, further emphasized the ways in which the fictions of the West provided "some of the most fertile ground for sexual reversals" that extended to the western film genre, as Rebecca Bell-Metereau argues.[78] Once the Depression hit and audiences desired glamorized fantasies, Hollywood's productions of the western began to feature cowboys and cowgirls in glitzy attire and reconfigure the heroine, even the buckskin-wearing Calamity Jane, with a "mixture of tomboy features and stereotypically feminine attributes."[79]

In line with the historical images and themes of western heroines, Montana writes and performs "The She Buckeroo," a supposed autobiographical narrative about her own pursuits of a western life, in which she initially prefers taming wild horses and defeating cowboys at roping contests before deciding on domesticity.[80] Promoting a musical image of the valiant cowgirl on the open range, she begins the song in her chest register with the declamatory vocal line that she delivers with little vocal expression: "Some gals they like babies and houses and things." By using her chest voice in a neutral manner to state the assumed desires of women, Montana creates a distance between the usual constructions of femininity and her own self-fashioning. In contrast, when she voices her wish to participate in cowboy culture, she leaves behind her speech-like line to sing a more lyrical melody in her head voice: "But give me the feel of a horse that has wings, I'd ride him straight up like all cowboys do." As the ascending melody reaches its climax on the word "up," the music provides the image of Montana on a rearing horse, a musical enactment usually reserved to suggest a cowboy's virility. She uses her sonorous head voice, the location of her characteristic "sweet" tone, to simultaneously lay claim to a masculine position of bravado and mitigate the manly sonic appearance of the "she buckeroo." Montana continues to underscore the cowboy's incompetence as she plays the role of the audacious cowgirl who wins roping and riding competitions, leaving the cowboys to feel "blue." Certain of her talents as a "tough ridin'" horsewoman, Montana pines to tame the unruly stallion Strawberry Roan.

What makes the song about a "she buckeroo" convincing as a cowboy ballad is that Montana's musical and narrative source is a familiar cowboy song: "The

Strawberry Roan," written in 1915 by Curley Fletcher.[81] It tells a humorous tale of an experienced broncobuster's failed attempts to tame a wild stallion. This overly confident cowboy has never met a horse he couldn't tame until he attempts to break the Strawberry Roan, who bucks the cowboy into the stratosphere, leaving him "sitting on nothing way up in the sky." When the broncobuster eventually falls "back to earth," he declares, "I bet my money that a man ain't alive, that can stay with ole Strawberry 'til he makes his high dive." The tune emerged as a caricature of the cowboy hero, making its way into a variety of media. By the time Montana wrote and recorded her song, she must have heard at least one of the many renditions of "The Strawberry Roan." The Arizona Wranglers had performed the tune on radio in the late 1920s, Ken Maynard sang a version of it in the eponymous 1933 film, and it also appeared in Lynn Riggs's 1930 play *Green Grow the Lilacs*.

Montana, however, wasn't the only one to write a song relating to the parodic underpinnings of "The Strawberry Roan." A number of tunes, including "The Man Who Rode the Strawberry Roan," "Good-bye Old Strawberry Roan," and "The Fate of the Strawberry Roan," demonstrate a distinct preoccupation with Fletcher's humorous portrayal of the cowboy's impotency.[82] Further, Tin Pan Alley songwriters Fred Howard and Nat Vincent modified Fletcher's original ballad by adding a twenty-measure chorus in 1931. It was this rendition that appeared in the *Strawberry Roan* films starring Ken Maynard in 1933 and Gene Autry in 1948, where the themes of masculine anxiety illustrated in the song shaped the plots of these westerns.

Fletcher himself wrote three distinct songs in the 1930s and early 1940s that embellished the tale of the original with his "The Castration of the Strawberry Roan," explicitly realizing the theme of emasculation.[83] In this bawdy version, a penniless cowboy accepts an offer of employment from a rancher who owns the infamous Strawberry Roan and his progeny, which are proving to be just as difficult to ride as their sire. The rancher retaliates by convincing the cowhand to help him castrate the stallion. But during the cowboy's attempts, he suddenly hears "bloodcurdling squalls" and discerns that those cries are coming not from the horse but from the rancher: the Strawberry Roan "had the boss by the balls." The cowboy concludes, "The boss's voice changed, and I knew we was beat."

In borrowing from a song riddled with emasculated images to emphasize the prowess of the cowgirl, Montana magnifies the gender strife and anxieties of the 1930s. The cowgirl's desire to upstage the cowboy highlighted society's fears of capable women usurping men's cultural authority in the workplace as possible "breadwinners." Appearing as a swaggering broncobuster, Montana is confident that she will not suffer the cowboy's humiliating fate of failing to break the wild stallion. Indeed, the female protagonist even declares her disregard for men as a "man-hating lassie" in the refrain of the fourth verse. "The She Buckaroo" has much in common with the unruly roles of vaudevillian actresses who "took over male roles, sometimes dressing as men, and in other cases, gained control over men, assaulting husbands and mocking male authority figures."[84] Here Montana casts a critical eye on the cultural failings of masculinity while giving every indication that she wants no part of heterosexual love and domesticity.

But then the song takes a sudden turn in a different direction. In the last verse, Montana entertains the possibility of giving up her life as a cowgirl for domesticity with a worthy cowboy whose skills equal her own deftness in horsemanship. Once she finds that particular man, Montana will trade her western chaps for dresses, learn to cook, leave the western prairies for the city, and say goodbye to her performance identity as "Patsy." If this song is meant to be an autobiographical account of Patsy Montana, then the conclusion appears ironic in that it differs from her professional and personal life. Montana did not, in fact, end her singing cowgirl career even after she married Paul Rose in 1935. Though she lived in Chicago with her husband and daughters and likely learned to cook for her family (as mentioned in the song), the singing cowgirl continued to perform on WLS and wrote and recorded songs (fantasies at this point) about the autonomous western heroine. Thus the lyrics of this last section of "The She Buckaroo," where the cowgirl chooses a domestic life, seems to be a cursory nod of sorts to conventionality. Most of the strophic song with the same musical setting for each lyrical stanza shapes the cowgirl into an experienced wrangler. While the music remains the same, the lyrical narrative abruptly switches to the protagonist's consideration of marriage, leaving the listener wondering whether the "she buckaroo" could find contentment as a wife or mother.

Yet the song also does not end there. After Montana has sung the last verse declaring her desires for domesticity, she yodels the beginning of a well-known yodel melody, popularized by the theatrical Dutch character in performances of Septimus Winner's 1864 "Der Deitcher's Dog" ("Oh Where, Oh Where Has My Little Dog Gone").[85] This is a parodic song, based on the 1847 German waltz "Zu Lauterbach hab' ich mein Strumpf verloren," about the German male immigrant's love for beer and his search for his missing dog, which may have been used in the making of sausages.[86] Montana's concluding yodel in "The She Buckaroo" could therefore be heard as a sonic example of cross-dressing that alludes to the caricatures of popular theater. Thus she ends her song by assuming a male performative persona that once again underlines a thespian fluidity for playing the part of the defiant tomboy/cowgirl who considers, however ambiguously, domesticity.

Western and Domestic Myths: Montana's Multilayered Image

Comparable to the themes in her music, Montana's publicity highlighted her self-directed persona while trying to balance it with a sense of glamour and feminine allure. In a 1935 publicity shot, for example, Montana stands by a campfire, one foot hoisted up on a tree stump, her guitar resting against her leg. Montana's stance implies not merely that she takes pleasure in the freedoms of the far-reaching prairies but that her experience and inclination equip her to roam the plains on equal footing with the cowboy (see figure 6). As Montana stated in a 1984 interview, "I didn't want to look too sissy. To me a cowgirl wasn't supposed to look sissy. I'd roll my sleeves up . . . and I wore a gun."[87] With a gun strapped to her hip and her foot hoisted up on a tree stump, she appears as the quintessential tomboy cowgirl. The only thing that distinguished the cowgirl's look from the cowboy's was the skirt. To soften Montana's image, her publicity at times underscored her sense of fashion and style while she still freely roamed the frontier: "Sweeping in like a prairie breeze from the West, Patsy Montana arrived at WLS a couple of years ago, dressed in a fringed leather skirt, and

Figure 6. Patsy Montana, 1930s. Courtesy of Country Music Hall of Fame and Museum.

high-heeled boots."[88] In this particular description, Montana appeared as the glamorous cowgirl dressed in feminized western attire.

Throughout Montana's career on WLS, her publicity carefully broadened the gendered frame of the cowgirl by underlining the ways in which the western heroine's autonomy could reconfigure normative definitions of womanhood. WLS's trade magazines of other female performers, such as the Girls of the Golden West, often emphasized that their careers did not supersede their domestic responsibilities to their husbands and children, as demonstrated by Kristine McCusker.[89] Yet Montana's publicity did not fixate on her domestic life even when she married and started a family. Rather, her promotional material harmoniously commingled the divergent images of the cowgirl's pursuits on radio and the open range with her private domestic roles. Perhaps because Montana's big hits were not sentimental-sounding songs (as the music of the Girls of the Golden West was), her publicity did not market her as a "genteel tamer" of the frontier. For example, a close-up of Montana, replete in western wear with her left hand on the strings of her violin to show off her wedding ring, appeared on the cover of a 1935 issue of Stand By! Even with this clear visual image of her marital status, the accompanying "Girl on the Cover" article was largely a biographical account of Montana's successful career in California with the Montana Cowgirls, referring to their pivotal role in "coast radio" and experience as "expert riders and ropers," as well as her start with the Prairie Ramblers (referred to as her "best partners ever," a desexualized description). Toward the end of the write-up, it was briefly mentioned how she met her husband and that their newly arrived infant daughter took "after her mother. . . . She [did] plenty of yodeling." The final paragraph returned to Montana's cowgirl image with the statement that her favorite sport was riding—"or it would be, she [said], if she could locate a Western saddle in Chicago"—giving the distinct impression that this bone fide western figure did not quite fit with and was potentially restricted by her urban surroundings.[90]

Her publicity continually stressed her cowgirl life as just as important and essential to her private subjectivity as her roles as a wife and mother. The 1937 WLS Family Album, for instance, placed two photos one above the other. The one above featured Montana dressed in her western attire holding her then-toddler, and the one below showcased her buckaroo skills as she stood on a mule surrounded by the members of the Prairie Ramblers sitting and kneeling on theirs.[91] Montana's prowess in horseback riding—even though it was a mule on which she stood—seemed to suggest that the singing cowgirl did not have to relinquish her role as an accomplished wrangler for her domestic obligations as a mother. Similarly, in a 1938 write-up of Montana, the WLS Family Album gestured to her family—her husband, Paul, and daughter, Beverly—while also mentioning, "Patsy not only sings cowboy songs, but had done a great deal of riding in rodeos."[92] The continual references to Montana's western activities made it clear that her dynamic, convincing performances and stage persona could not be neatly contained within the domestic. Montana was still a "she buckaroo" who embraced the excitement of the open range even as she raised a family.

By synthesizing the illustrations of the Wild West with those of her domestic life, the promotional material emphasized the cowgirl's individualism even as a wife and mother. In a 1937 *Stand By!* article addressed to her fans, Montana wrote about a family vacation with her husband, daughter, and mother-in-law to California, "her home." She exclaimed: "It was a real thrill to all of us to arrive in California. To Paul it meant seeing the many things I had been raving about for the past three years. To Mother Rose, it meant the end of her longest journey. And to Beverly it meant she could be turned loose to run and play to her heart's content. To me it meant *home*."[93] Montana intertwined her family with her cowgirl persona: a trip out West, similar to all those pioneers venturing forth to make a life on the frontier. Though Montana was originally from Arkansas and did not relocate to California until she was college age, she claims the West as the place where she was raised. During the vacation, her family rode horses, explored the terrain of Nevada at Beaver Creek Canyon, and attended a rodeo where the Montana Cowgirls used to perform. Montana recounted, "One of the Sundays we spent at Hoot Gibson's ranch attending a rodeo. It was the same place where my two pals and I used to show off on our horses."[94] Not only did the article point to Montana's equestrian skills, but it also positioned her family within the grandeur of the western landscape. Even her daughter could be "turned loose" to enjoy the freedoms of frontier culture. To further cement this impression, Beverly began to appear in Montana's publicity photographs in her own western attire, "a fancy cowgirl outfit just like her mother's."[95] Montana acted as a role model to which young girls, including her own daughter, could aspire. Hence, the intoxicating romance surrounding Montana's imagery permeated all aspects of her life to even the most private, enabling the members of her family to participate in the myths of the West.[96]

Conclusion

For those listeners drawn to the romance of Montana's cowgirl persona, constructed through radio and recording and by WLS's trade magazines, they could appreciate the singing cowgirl through another medium, film. In 1938, she performed her hit song "I Want to Be a Cowboy's Sweetheart" in a Gene Autry western, *Colorado Sunset*.[97] The premise of this film involves Autry with his comedic sidekick Frog Millhouse (played by Smiley Burnette) and a posse (a string-band ensemble, the CBS-KMBC Texas Rangers) discovering and combating the corruption of the professional class in a rural community in California. As in many of his Republic westerns, Autry plays himself, a singing cowboy who croons his melodies about the open prairies while defending the economic interests of rural communities against the exploitation of the privileged. In *Colorado Sunset*, Montana plays a secondary role, a waitress of the local Lonestar Café, owned by the leading female character, Ginger, a strong-willed woman and the backbone of the community. While ordering a meal at the café, Millhouse and the Texas Rangers sidle up to the counter and ask the waitress Montana what she is doing in this part of the country. As a newcomer to the western frontier, Montana first responds with an eager question, "Do you really want to know?" and then somewhat improbably runs out from behind the counter, grabs her guitar, and launches into her song "I Want to Be a Cowboy's Sweetheart" to the instrumental and vocal accompaniment of the Texas Rangers.

To a Depression-era audience, Montana gave the impression that the symbolic freedoms of the expansive prairies could be the ideological place for working women of the service industry. Through a gender lens, she portrayed American migration to the West as a means to harness opportunity and to explore social freedoms. While Autry as the cowboy hero eventually succeeds in protecting rural communities from the fraudulent economic pursuits of the elite (the social class blamed for the economic collapse of the 1930s), Montana's film performance attempts to resolve the contradictions that surrounded workingwomen. The cowgirl was equipped to face the social changes of the Great Depression with a boldness that stretched the normative understanding of gender without explicitly violating its middle-class parameters. Thus her "performance of femininity with strength" did not explicitly threaten the social order of gender and bourgeoisie values. Instead, she helped manage the discord that surrounded working and public women during the 1930s by providing an image that cast capable women in a more flattering light. This balancing act of gender performance established the singing cowgirl archetype in western film narratives and continued developments of country music in California (as will be discussed in the following chapter). Patsy Montana therefore proved the singing cowgirl to be an effective performance model of womanhood, one that could offer the delicate solution of expanding the norms of gender in the mythologized West—a place where anything was possible.

PART TWO

California Country Music

4 Carolina Cotton

Yodeling Virtuosity and Theatricality
in California Country Music

My discussion of California country music begins with an examination of the musical career of Carolina Cotton (1925–1997) before turning to Rose Maddox in the following chapter. To better understand how each performer contributed to the emerging vibrancy of California country music and engaged with the concerns and circumstances of their regional and national audiences, I consider an area that has received little scholarly attention: the musical presence of female performers in the dance-hall environs of western swing, which extended into mass media. Cotton established herself in the live performative context of nightclubs and ballrooms and would appear in Hollywood films in the mid-1940s and early 1950s. She became a formidable vocalist in the leading western swing bands—Spade Cooley and His Orchestra, Hank Penny and His Orchestra, and Bob Wills and His Texas Playboys—in which her virtuosic yodeling style matched and enlivened the rhythmic language of this hybrid style. She was thus fundamental in placing the female voice at the center of a type of music commonly identified with male bandleaders and instrumentalists.[1]

Recent studies have explored how Los Angeles has served as a major production center for country music, rivaling Nashville's iconic status. For example, Gerald Haslam traces the developments of a distinct "California Sound" of rhythmic vitality and amplified instrumentation to the western swing style that dominated the 1940s.[2] Peter La Chapelle takes a more sociological perspective and connects the "live performance-oriented" dance style of western swing to the formation and transformation of 1940s Okie culture. The cosmopolitan sensibility of country jazz promoted in the dance hall, according to La Chapelle, "countered depictions of migrants as backward and parochial and allowed audiences to begin to view themselves as part of a dynamic, more pluralistic urban culture."[3] In other words, western swing provided a multicultural musical setting of urban sophistication and thereby served as a way for former rural inhabit-ants and migrants to distance themselves from the Depression-era stereotypes of dispossession. In considering the ways that Carolina Cotton's performances resonated in the popular-music industry and with fans of western swing, I describe how this particular singing cowgirl contributed to the glamour and pop sheen of country swing while recalling and reconceptualizing the rural white identities linked to hillbilly music and her audience of displaced white migrants, commonly referred to as Okies. As David Brackett has pointed out, the popular-music industry, though acknowledging the success of popular musi-cians' covers of country songs, still viewed western swing recordings as sonic exemplars of "corn."[4] With western swing's urban sophistication cultivated in California's dance halls standing in stark contrast to the popular-music industry's interpretation of this "folk" style, Cotton negotiated the aesthetic and cultural terrain of 1940s country music with thespian flair.

Like her predecessors and peers in barn-dance radio, Cotton contributed to California's theatrical staging of country music. Specifically, her vocal prowess, which included the virtuosic as well as the comedic elements associated with the yodel, enabled her to play the part of comic rural characters while still maintain-ing the command of a glamorous stage performer. In her recordings and film performances, she used the yodel's historical links to pastoralism, female vir-tuosity, and vaudeville slapstick to enact a variety of roles—the Alpine maiden, the hillbilly clown, the jazz soloist, and the tomboyish singing cowgirl. Cotton's theatrical incarnations of womanhood unfolded against a historical backdrop of migration and displacement, including the shifting social and material circum-stances of white transplants, in particular Okie women, many of whom were the riveters and welders of World War II. In this sociohistorical context, Cotton's rural and class images were contingent on the concept of virtuosic physicality. Carolina Cotton was a skillful performer whose stage imagery, even when it was sexualized, pushed domesticity to the side, as she sang and yodeled to swinging rhythms to which her audience of wartime women was dancing.

The Okie Migration and Country Music

Southern California, as a major center of popular music and entertainment, served as a dynamic place for the production and circulation of country music even before the Okie migration brought hundreds of thousands of white migrants from the Southwest and southern plains to the urban and rural regions of Cali-fornia. California's radio industry followed the national trends of barn-dance programming and included a range of country music styles replete with the usual stock characters, such as the romantic mountaineer, the rural maiden, the comedic hillbilly, and the singing cowboy and the singing cowgirl. In 1930, Glen

Rice, the manager of the Los Angeles station KMPC, for example, drew on the well-established hillbilly parodies of region and class and translated them for a California context when he claimed to have discovered a village of mountaineers in the hills of Malibu (instead of the hills of southern Appalachia) and decided to invite a few to come down to the station and perform on the air. What emerged from this tale was the successful radio act called the Beverly Hillbillies, which attracted several musicians who later became prominent figures of California country music, such as Elton Britt and Stuart Hamblen.[5]

Though hillbilly imagery permeated radio programming, California and Hollywood, in particular, seemed a natural fit for also producing the myths of the West that had circulated in nineteenth-century dime novels and traveling western troupes, such as William Frederick Cody's Buffalo Bill's Wild West, a stage show that had toured the United States and Europe. Alongside radio, the film industry drew on these earlier narrative tropes and stage spectacles to play up the action-packed fantasies of the West in its production of "horse operas" or inexpensive Republic B-westerns. The most prominent singing cowboy in these films in the 1930s, Gene Autry, established his western persona first on Chicago's radio station WLS before translating his radio identity to Hollywood's silver screen. Moreover, countless western acts rose to prominence in California. The Sons of the Pioneers were widely popular, glamorizing the West on their radio broadcasts on Hollywood's KFWB, recordings for Decca Records, and performing in many western films. The original members of the ensemble, Bob Nolan, Tim Spencer, and Leonard Slye (Hugh and Karl Farr would later join), blended their individual crooning voices in mellifluous harmonies, shaping the western frontier into a place of homosocial camaraderie. Nolan, the group's prolific songwriter, provided western singers for years to come with a repertory that included "Tumbling Tumbleweeds" (1934) and "Cool Water" (1936). Also from this ensemble, Roy Rogers (known as Slye) emerged as a baritone cowboy crooner who acted and sang with his duet partner (and later wife) Dale Evans in westerns throughout the 1940s and early 1950s.

In California country music, the singing cowgirl as a glamorous working-class heroine, first popularized by Patsy Montana, continued to be a performative archetype for female artists. Dorothy Page, a popular singer who performed with Paul Whiteman's band, starred as the leading character in Grand National Pictures' productions *The Singing Cowgirl* (1938), *Water Rustlers* (1939), and *Ride 'Em Cowgirl* (1939).[6] She crooned her melodies of the West while playing the part of the courageous western woman confronting the greed of elite landowners and businessmen (who symbolized the culprits largely responsible for the Great Depression) and defended the welfare of the rustic working class. Following Page onto the silver screen, Dale Evans, the "Queen of the Westerns," emerged as the quintessential singing cowgirl costarring with cowboy crooner Roy Rogers in western films. Hollywood's production of "horse operas" frequently featured Evans contesting heterosexual confines and the ideals of middle-class femininity in plots that often pitted her against Rogers. Yet the films usually relied on the "marriage trope," a conventional narrative device (commonly used in American musicals), in which marriage functions allegorically as a form of "resolution of seeming incompatible peoples or ideas into a stabilized partnership," as explained by musicologist Raymond Knapp.[7] However at odds symbolically or ideologically with each other, Evans and Rogers, by the end of the film, usually fell in love, echoing their real-life marital union.

Along with the production of western films, the singing cowgirl emerged as a vocalist to the swing rhythms of western swing bands. Bob Wills, for example, hired Laura Lee Owens McBride, a yodeling cowgirl, in 1944 to perform with his Texas Playboys. A year later, when McBride left the ensemble, he hired the cowgirl duo the McKinney Sisters, who sang and yodeled gently swung harmonies in a style reminiscent of the Girls of the Golden West, who had starred on Chicago's WLS. Within this performative context of Hollywood's stylized, talented cowgirls who could sing and act, Carolina Cotton would emerge as a western swing performer, a yodeling cowgirl, and an actress in westerns.

The popular-music and entertainment industries already present in Southern California expanded on the production of country music and its associated western imagery during the Okie migration, bringing fans and a number of important musicians to the West Coast. Country musicians such as Woody Guthrie, Patsy Montana, Bob Wills, Spade Cooley, Rose Maddox, and Cotton (born Helen Hagstrom) had left southern and southwestern homes for new opportunities in California. Whereas the popular-music industry had pulled Wills and Autry to the Golden State, the Maddox and the Hagstrom families had left due to the economic collapse of the regional agricultural industry. The ecological disasters of drought, dust storms, and floods, which contributed to the downfall of the cotton, wheat, and corn markets, pushed white tenant-farm families and landowners to the West Coast. Searching geographically for a means to survive the dire conditions of the 1930s, hundreds of thousands of white migrants made their way to California, where they found work in the rural agricultural regions of the state or in the metropolitan areas, notably Los Angeles and San Francisco.[8]

Carolina Cotton was born and raised in a farming community outside Cash, Arkansas, where her parents and maternal grandparents grew cotton and peanuts on their family farm. In addition to the collapse of the cotton industry, drought reached northeast Arkansas, convincing the Hagstroms to join one of the largest internal migrations in U.S. history.[9] Like many families leaving the Southwest and the southern plains, the Hagstroms (parents, Helen, and her sister, Winifred) traveled by car and stopped at various places along the way to earn money for their journey across the country. They had settled in San Francisco by late 1936 and early 1937.

Though plenty of migrants, including Cotton's father (who worked as a cook in a San Francisco restaurant), found employment in the industrial or service industries of large cities, it was the plight of those who had settled in the agrarian valleys of California that has come to characterize the Okie migration. John Steinbeck's *Grapes of Wrath* (1939) is only the best-known cultural product to describe the poignant struggles of a southwestern family migrating across the country only to find political and social oppression as farm laborers in California. In addition to this fictional account, the agricultural economist Paul Taylor (who was the first to publicize the massive influx of "drought refugees" to California) sounded the alarm for desperately needed state and federal aid for migrants trying to eke out an existence in the Central Valley of California.[10] The federal government responded, and the Farm Security Administration constructed livable communities (commonly referred to as farm labor camps) and established an emergency program of assistance and medical care for the disadvantaged.[11] Despite government assistance, however, many Californians viewed the Depression-era newcomers as unwanted intruders who confounded all notions of white middle-class codes of behavior. Originating from a region associated with the benighted South, white migrants were the tenant farmers of Erskine Caldwell's *Tobacco Road* (1932), living in squalor, disease, and ignorance and clinging to a rural mode of existence; they were also the southerners who put John Scopes on trial for teaching evolution in the infamous "Monkey Trial."[12] The displaced thus appeared to be moored to their regional culture. They worked in a stigmatized rural occupation (intended for Latinos and Asians, ethnic Others), depended on state and federal aid, and lived in separate, dismal communities (labor camps).

La Chapelle explains that the perceptions of middle-class Anglo Californians were strongly influenced by a contemporary discourse of eugenics that called into question the ethnicity of southwestern and southern plains migrants. Many believed that the rural poverty and isolation of the Dust Bowl region were responsible for their hereditary inferiority and degeneracy, even though many displaced Okies came from urban areas and were only slightly less educated than other recent newcomers to California. Based on the beliefs of white supremacy, eugenicists also proposed that people from the state of Oklahoma were likely of mixed race—Anglo-Saxon and Native American—because of the large settlements of Native Americans in the region.[13] Proponents of the antimigrant movement applied their racialized views to Okie women in particular, who labored in the fields next to their male relatives and were photographed in makeshift domestic settings, tents that could be transported easily to the next farm needing harvesters. The number of white migrant women toiling in California's fields nearly doubled in the 1930s, while the number of male farm laborers increased by only 7 percent.[14] The photographer Dorothea Lange recorded this phenomenon in a number of portraits, the best known being the "Migrant Mother" (1936). Here Lange has captured the desperation of the moment with her camera lens focused on Florence Owens, who sits in a dilapidated tent with two children, dressed in rags and clinging to her, and a baby sleeping in her lap. This visual image of an Anglo mother burdened by poverty became an iconic symbol of how migration and dispossession were attacking the basic principles of womanhood and maternity, and by extension the moral integrity of the family and the nation. Lange repeatedly presented photographs of poor white women attempting the rituals of domesticity (cooking and cleaning) in their ramshackle dwellings to underscore migrants' struggles to maintain some sense of social normalcy.[15] For white middle-class Californians, however, farm labor and the poverty of dislocation stripped Okie women of any vestiges of femininity.

Despite these perceptions, the outbreak of World War II and the United States' involvement lifted the country out of the Depression and dramatically shifted the social and economic conditions of these white transplants. Those from the southern plains, including those "Migrant Mothers," who labored in the fields of the Central Valley, could now relocate to Los Angeles, San Diego, and San Francisco and find employment offering higher wages in the plants producing artillery, airplanes, and ships. Wartime factories beckoned rural migrants from the San Joaquin Valley to California's urban centers and also encouraged a continued influx of migrants from the Southwest and the southern plains. As a result, by 1950 over a million white migrants lived in California.[16]

In this context of wartime production, migrant women responded to the government's Rosie the Riveter campaign, which encouraged women to fulfill their patriotic duties by helping produce the matériel the nation needed to fight in World War II. They joined the rank and file in places like Santa Monica's Douglas Aircraft, where 87 percent of the workers were women, and earned wages that could be spent not only on necessities but also on leisure activities. Aircraft manufacturers specifically sought young single women from the Southwest and the Midwest as employees, and by 1944, the majority of female defense workers had come from outside California.[17] These female transplants flooded the dance halls (strategically located next to the wartime production plants), where they screamed and danced to the music of Bob Wills and Spade Cooley and marveled at the physical virtuosity of Carolina Cotton.[18]

The demand for country music, the lure of Hollywood, and the production infrastructure of popular entertainment had pulled the western swing bands of the Southwest to the urban centers of Southern California, where country jazz joined the polished vocals of the cowboy crooner and the singing cowgirl. Western swing combined rural music making with popular-music idioms, which fit the developing trends of California country music performed in films and on radio. In Texas and Oklahoma, western swing came to fruition as an amalgamation of regional vernacular and popular musics. Fiddle tunes accompanied by guitar and other string instruments were popular in the Southwest, where dance numbers in fiddle contests were dynamic displays of virtuosity and innovation. In a string-band environment, western swing ensembles featured skilled instrumentalists who could play breakdown fiddle tunes in hoedowns and a variety of regional dance styles, including waltzes, polkas, and schottisches derived from Spanish, Mexican, Cajun, and German musics. Western swing also incorporated a wide range of vernacular idioms, such as ragtime, stomps, blues, swing, and boogie-woogie, as well as Tin Pan Alley song forms and arrangements.[19] In this lively mixture, the country jazz style retained its regional and agrarian identity while responding to the ebullient dance craze of swing music that had dominated the popular-music landscape of the 1930s and 1940s. With its insistent beat, jazzlike improvisations of amplified guitars, and heavily bowed fiddles, "it was a rhythmic, infectious music designed for dancing."[20] Just as swing music emerged as a sonic emblem of hope during the Great Depression, western swing was also experienced as a means to, in the words of a 1933 advertisement of Milton Brown and His Musical Brownies at the Crystal Springs dance hall in Fort Worth, Texas, "dance away your troubles, live and laugh as ne'er before."[21]

Western swing, then, traveling from the countryside to metropolitan areas, can be interpreted as a sonic emblem of migration, place, and mobility for its primary audience. As musicologist Travis Stimeling observes, "In its heyday in the 1930s and 1940s, western swing was primarily an urban music directed toward the thousands of rural émigrés who moved to Fort Worth, Tulsa, Los Angeles, and other major southwestern cities."[22] Like the mediating power of swing music, country swing could offer "listeners new ways to make sense of the changing spaces and places of American life" within a historical context of "large-scale migrations and new patterns of urbanization," as noted by Andrew Berish.[23] Western swing, reaching fans who were working through the complexities of leaving rural homes for industrial employment, encapsulated urban sensibilities without straying too far from the theatrical and musical tropes that had governed hillbilly music. Within this musical and historical context, Cotton emerged as one of the most prominent female performers of this southwestern country-jazz style, which not only entertained its fans but also helped listeners, specifically Okies and women, adapt to the opportunities and transformations arising from U.S. involvement in World War II.

Carolina Cotton: The Yodeling Cowgirl of Western Swing

Carolina Cotton, who began her musical career in San Francisco while still in high school, initially developed a performance persona that largely fit with the cultural associations of western swing, particularly the interplay between urban glamor and regional identity. After winning a local radio talent show in the early 1940s, she attracted the attention of bandleader Dude Martin and His Roundup Gang, a successful swing band in San Francisco. The Bay Area, with its shipyards and military bases, had by this time attracted a number of transplants who constituted a fan base for western swing. In 1944, Bob Wills and His Texas Playboys played in the Oakland Civic Auditorium to reported crowds of nineteen thousand. Moreover, many Bay Area country-swing bands such as Ray Wade and His Rhythm Riders, Elwin Cross and the Arizona Ramblers, and Dude Martin acquired a local following of teenagers, servicemen, women working in wartime factories, and southwestern and southern plains migrants.[24] In the music trade journal *Tophand*, critic C. Phil Henderson offered a picture of how western swing in the mid-1940s was a predominant mode of live music making that was intricately associated with jazz. Not only did western swing cross over into the performative space of small swing and jazz combos, but it was also considered "hip" or "hep," terms that denoted the musical style's urban credentials. As Henderson writes, "The entire bay area seemingly is hep to the western kind of jive and the crowds that attend the shindigs prove that the western beat is their fave. The most surprising (to me) thing is finding western and hillbilly trios, quartets and similar small groups holding forth in many of the local bistros that formerly featured jive and race music." One of the most prominent bands, noted by Henderson, was Dude Martin and His Roundup Gang. The only ensemble broadcasting live in the Bay Area, "Dude and his gang [were] doing two half hour shows daily on KYA, plus an ABC net[work] show on Sunday nights. . . . Dude's dance in Redwood City on Saturday nights ha[d] a packed house every week."[25] To radio listeners, Dude Martin's broadcasts captured the dynamism of live performances in the Bay Area's prominent nightspots and also reached a national audience through radio.

By the time Henderson had written about Dude Martin and his success, Carolina Cotton had already become an integral member of the ensemble. In 1942, Martin gave Cotton her big break as a professional musician and hired the young performer to play the string bass and the lap steel guitar, filling in for the male musicians who had been drafted overseas. As Cotton recalled, the draft provided her with a window of opportunity in western swing as it did for many other female swing musicians.[26] "'Nobody's going to draft me,'" she explained. "So I played bass; in fact I played bass for Spade Cooley for a while, until he got a real bass player. I played bass. I played guitar. I played steel guitar. I played drums for a very short time. And I played steel guitar for a very short time."[27] She also became friends with the lead singer and yodeler Arvada Miller, who taught Cotton many of her yodeling songs. When Miller left the ensemble, Cotton assumed the singer's lead role in the band and gained important performance experience as a singer who could yodel to dance rhythms. In a single week, the band would make seventeen radio appearances over the airwaves of San Francisco's KYA and perform five dance jobs in the local nightclubs. In addition to her performance schedule, Cotton also studied harmony and song arrangement and later wrote her own dance numbers and yodel songs.[28]

With Martin's band, Cotton started to develop a musical persona that would resonate with an audience of transplanted Okies, like many country music acts such as the 1940s female duo the Oklahoma Sweethearts. As part of that development, she adopted the stage name Carolina. Later, when performing with Spade Cooley, she also exchanged her last name, Hagstrom, for Cotton to give the impression she was a singing cowgirl with musical and cultural roots in the South. Ironically, her name may have reminded members of her target audience of the Depression-era's collapsed cotton market, which had pushed many to leave their homes for California. Yet her stage name evoked not the material conditions of the cotton industry but the idyllic and nostalgic setting of the antebellum South, lending an aura of romance to her performance persona and fitting with normative images of femininity located in the pastoral. Cotton was still a transplant who most definitely was not a southern belle but instead a singing cowgirl whose desires and subjectivity were projected against a western backdrop of glamour and fantasies. She thus helped distance Okie womanhood from the portraits of rural white dispossession so prevalent in the 1930s. Unlike the distraught figure of Lange's "Migrant Mother," the singing cowgirl transcended the economic worries that had brought migrants to the fields of California. The musical imagery of Cotton and her California cohorts, including Dale Evans and Laura Lee Owens McBride, did not suggest the burdens of rural poverty and the struggle to care for a family. Apart from Evans, these singers were not necessarily domestic figures but rather heroines of the West, whose feminine strength, linked to the dynamism of western swing, ushered in an era in which women, including those migrant mothers, could leave behind farm labor, poorly paid service positions, as well as the domestic sphere for wartime job opportunities.

After working two years with Dude Martin and His Roundup Gang, Cotton was drawn to the music scene of Southern California. She had been going back and forth between Cooley's orchestra in Los Angeles and Dude Martin's ensemble in San Francisco. By the summer of 1944, she had to choose between the two and decided to work with Cooley, right at the moment when he was emerging as the "King of Western Swing" (see figure 7). Cooley and his orchestra got their big break as the house band for the Venice Pier Ballroom, established by Bert "Foreman" Phillips in 1942. The following year, Cooley left Phillips to play in the larger Riverside Rancho Ballroom (managed by Bobbie Bennett, a promoter of western swing acts), which included a ten-thousand-square-foot dance floor, to meet the demands of his growing audience.[29] At this time, when

Figure 7. Carolina Cotton with Spade Cooley at the Riverside Rancho, ca. 1944–1945. Courtesy of Sharon Marie, estate of Carolina Cotton.

Cooley was regularly performing at the Riverside Ranch Ballroom (1943–1946), Carolina Cotton became a key soloist of his ensemble.

To fill the lavish ballrooms with a lush string sound, Cooley had built an orchestra of up to twenty performers and performed pieces that had been written and orchestrated by big-band arrangers. His band usually included three fiddles (in addition to Cooley on fiddle), three guitars, two string basses, electric steel guitar, accordion, piano, drums, vibraphone, and harp. Cooley projected an urbane musical image associated with jazz, even competing against the leading bandleaders of swing—such as Benny Goodman and Harry James—in popularity polls and acquiring the title "King of Western Swing" from a national fan club.[30] *Billboard* advertised Cooley's new moniker by reporting that he had "justified the regal title by smashing records every place he ha[d] played with his famed Western Dance Gang. While on NBC's Furlough Fun air show, the program jumped up 2½ points."[31] Cooley thus was a spectacular success in live performance and on recording and radio.

With this in mind, Cooley offered a brand of western swing that "remade the very meanings of 'Okie' itself, refashioning the onetime slur into a proud expression of migrants' modernity and sophistication," as La Chapelle argues.[32] Okies were no longer connected to the dismal circumstances of migration and rural poverty but were instead linked to the cosmopolitan and "hep" dance rhythms and multicultural expressions of western swing, which, as previously mentioned, attracted a wide-reaching audience in California. Yet at the same time, western swing bands still included imagery and music that made their rural and southwestern roots clear. Even Cooley and his orchestra still gestured to the Southwest and often negotiated competing notions of rusticity and urbanity in which his star yodeler, Carolina Cotton, was instrumental.

Nowhere is this more evident than in the film short titled *Spade Cooley: King of Western Swing* (1945), which paints a picture of the rural origins of this hybrid music style and its developments into a "hep" style, a marker of urban sophistication. The filmic narrative positions western swing as a catalyst for imposing civilization on the lawless frontier of "sudden death, overrun with warring redskins and ravaging whites," as the film's narrator intones. With the western frontier referring to the region west of the Mississippi, the Southwest— the regional home of western swing—is connected to the ideals of Manifest Destiny (masking the genocidal reality) rather than to the perceptions of the benighted South. In this telling, the musicians of western swing "are the sons of the old West." Cooley himself, so we are told, "descended from a long line of western wild cats" and was "fast to become one of the nation's leading hep cats," responsible for redirecting the brutality and danger of the frontier into "swaying strains of rock solid rhythm."[33]

Against this cinematic backdrop of dance bands simultaneously arising from and taming the wild frontier, Carolina Cotton emerged as a lead soloist during a performance of "Turkey in the Straw." Originally known as the blackface theater number "Zip Coon," "Turkey in the Straw" had become a well-known fiddle showpiece that fiddlers played to demonstrate melodic innovativeness and virtuosic bowing techniques in the fiddle contests of Texas and Oklahoma. The film's narrator cements this image of familiarity and rusticity by stating, "Folks were beginning to realize that there was nothing like an old-fashioned square dance." The staging of the scene features Cooley and his orchestra positioned among bales of hay in front of an outdoor dance floor of people square dancing. Yet like most swing ensembles that play standard fiddle tunes, "Spade gave it to them in suede," meaning Cooley offered a slicker swing arrangement of this rustic tune.

In this scene, while the dancers are swinging their partners, Cooley, on the fiddle, plays the verse and chorus of "Turkey in the Straw" at a fast tempo, demonstrating his fiddling virtuosity. Immediately following this performance, the orchestration increases and provides a background of syncopated dance rhythms while the steel guitar plays a short rhythmic riff and the fiddle trio offers a harmonized response. Within this swing context, Carolina Cotton demonstrates her own sense of rhythmic dexterity and vocal agility via a fast-paced yodel solo, which functions as an instrumental break. She introduces her yodel melody with an opening melodic ascent of a major sixth followed by a short syncopated pattern of the higher note (short, long, short) before returning to her lower range. She takes her yodel melody a step higher with the same rhythmic pattern and finishes the first phrase by rhythmically varying the opening melody. In the second phrase, she continues to elaborate rhythmically on the original melodic motif while still emphasizing the upper range of her vocal line by repeating the higher notes in syncopated rhythms. She finishes the second phrase with a bluesy melodic line in her lower range before yodeling to her higher register. It is as if she were a coloratura who floridly decorates her upper melody with syncopated rhythms and then switches to offer blues-inflected melodies in her lower range, demonstrating her musical versatility.

An even greater exhibition of virtuosity takes place in the latter two phrases of her proper vocal solo. Here, Cotton pauses for a moment after the second phrase before catapulting into another yodel melody of straight, fast-paced sixteenth notes. At first, she maintains the ascending sixth (E_4 to C_5) but then moves the interval up and down chromatically while increasing the tempo, thereby underlining her percussive use of glottal stops. She repeats this pattern in the final phrase. The sonic effect is one of sheer brilliance, stunning in its execution. In her concluding moment, she dramatically pauses, swings the chromatic melody in her lower range before leaping to the high G_5, demonstrating that not only can she yodel at breakneck speeds but she can also showcase the brilliant sound of her upper range.

In this film short, Cotton's yodeling voice is positioned in a way similar to the lead instrumentalists in a swing ensemble. Like a scat singer imitating the jazz instrumentalists, her vocalizations are part of the improvisatory and virtuosic fabric. She is not, however, the first vocalist to yodel bluesy syncopated rhythms in a virtuosic fashion. Musicologist Timothy Wise points to Elton Britt's blues-inflected yodel melody in "Patent Leather Boots" (1939) as an example of "bravura yodeling typical of the cowboy song."[34] Britt's yodels of syncopated rhythms unfold at a fast tempo and show off a wide vocal range. If the virtuosic yodel of the cowboy is an aural sign of masculine swagger, then Carolina Cotton's yodel is an example of the cowgirl strutting her stuff.[35]

As mentioned in the previous chapter, even though the yodel has been associated with the cowboy, it has a long history of being connected to the female voice and virtuosity. As noted, beginning in the 1820s, European operatic divas were the first to introduce the yodel to U.S. audiences. Sopranos Maria Malibran and Henriette Sontag, for example, included Alpine-themed pieces in their recitals in which their yodeled melodies presented vocal displays of ornamentation and virtuosity.[36] As the yodel was incorporated into nineteenth-century vaudevillian practices in the United States, the vocal device still alluded to the feminine in ethnic humor skits of the Deutsch or Dutch character. It assumed the aural sign of otherness as it was incorporated into blackface performance acts and ragtime songs to parody African Americans. Also from a vaudevillian context, performers of blues songs incorporated the vocal dynamism of yodel in their staged acts. All these assimilations carried over to early country music as an extension of the vocal theatrics of the popular stage. With Cooley's orchestra, Carolina Cotton's performance evokes a history of female virtuosity while contributing to the ways the yodel has been subsumed within the stylistic fabric of popular music, in this case, the urban and modern setting of western swing.[37]

Carolina Cotton's yodels were often the closing act of a string of soloists, acting as the grand finale in a live performance and thus underlining her significance in the ensemble. In the film *The Singing Sheriff* (1944), we get another glimpse of Cotton's vocal role in Cooley's group, and it is similar to the one in the film short *King of Western Swing*.[38] Spade Cooley and His Orchestra appeared in several shorts and feature-length western movies as Hollywood captured the vibrancy of Southern California's live music scene. Cooley's first film appearance was in Universal's *Singing Sheriff*, starring the crooning bandleader Bob Crosby as a Broadway singing cowboy impersonating a rugged sheriff who still manages to capture the ruffians responsible for a murder in a small western town. As in many Hollywood B-westerns, music is a key ingredient. The Gilded Lady (the community saloon), mostly frequented by rough working men and the town's villains, is a place of music making where the scantily clad chorus girl Lattie (played by Pat Starling) sings in a nasal, off-pitch manner and speaks with a New York accent coded as "working class."

Unlike the music and clientele of the Gilded Lady, Cooley and his orchestra provide an evening of entertainment at the "Annual Barbeque" for "All Good Neighbors and Law Abiding Citizens." For the occasion, the ensemble plays a jazzy version of "Ida Red," another well-known fiddle tune that gestures to southwestern and southern musical cultures. In this performance, Cotton does not appear to be the typical female singer. In fact, it is a trio of male vocalists who sing in harmony during the chorus following each instrumental rendition of the verse. As in "Turkey in the Straw," the fiddles introduce the song before the rest of the orchestra transforms the tune into a swing number. The accordion and piano play riff-based syncopated rhythms answered by the lush harmonies of the fiddle trio, and a series of take-off solos follow, first the electric steel guitar, then the electric guitar, and finally Cotton's yodel solo, which closes the show.

As in her performance of "Turkey in the Straw," Cotton demonstrates her ability to vary her yodel melodies rhythmically while still including her virtuosic trademark of yodeling in straight sixteenth notes at an incredibly fast tempo. In

"Ida Red," she begins the thirty-two-bar solo by repeating the lower pitch in a syncopated pattern that ascends a sixth on an upbeat as she holds the higher note of the yodel. She returns to her lower range to repeat the syncopated rhythms on the same lower note. In the latter two phrases, she magnifies the rhythmic intensity by rendering the yodel's ascending sixth pattern in sixteenth notes, moving up and down by step or half-step but always maintaining the ascending sixth. The power of Carolina Cotton's voice involves a pronounced level of physicality. As viewers and listeners, we are acutely aware of the level of skill located in the singer's throat. She rapidly closes and opens the vocal cords to interrupt the flow of air with glottal stops, underlining the physicality of her performance. As Andrew Davis notes in his work on opera, "The presence of the singer is suddenly more apparent than ever; the nature of the work as a physical act of performance—sometimes an obviously difficult one, when the singing is virtuosic—is explicit."[39] With all eyes and ears trained on Cotton's vocal and physical presence, her virtuosity and physicality take center stage.

In addition to her filmic performances with Cooley, print media reinforced Cotton's high profile in this successful swing band. *Billboard* announced Spade Cooley and His Orchestra's prominence in California's live-performance scene by listing all the different venues in which the ensemble appeared and by naming the soloists with the band: "Jack (Tex) Williams, Smokey (Okie) Rogers, Duce (Ark) Spriggins, Carolina Cotton."[40] From 1944 to 1945, Cotton appeared with Cooley in a number of performance venues and B-westerns, in which she would yodel to the rhythms of western swing. When she left Cooley's band for first Deuce Spriggins and His Orchestra in 1945 and then Hank Penny and His Orchestra in 1946, *Billboard* referred to her as the "top yodeling cowgirl," and *Tophand* announced her appearances at the Riverside Ranch with Hank Penny's orchestra: the "Riverside Rancho opened its doors again to the dancing public" with "Hank Penny" fronting the band that featured "The Rancherita Carolina Cotton."[41] The write-up also pointed to the role of Cotton's manager, Bobbie Bennett, who also oversaw the careers of Penny and Cooley, in cultivating the glamorous image of western swing.[42] "The Western Trail-blazer, Bobbie Bennett, is managing the ballroom—and there's a gal with vision and the Pioneering spirit!" the article proclaimed. "Ever since Spade Cooley started the Rancho off on the western trails under her tutelage . . . she's been handling the top names and organizations in the field—and now she's out in front in the new trend (if I may coin a phrase) glamourizing the sagebrushers for the carriage trade."[43] Cotton was part of Bennett's enterprise shaping western swing into a dance style of musical sophistication for not only southwestern transplants but also mainstream, middle-class fans, in *Tophand*'s conception, the "carriage trade" (see figure 8).

In the dance halls and ballrooms of California, Carolina Cotton's vocal power and dynamism helped glamorize country swing, imbuing it with a stage presence

Figure 8. Carolina Cotton with Hank Penny and His Orchestra at the Riverside Rancho, 1946. Courtesy of Sharon Marie, estate of Carolina Cotton.

that must have also resonated with women working in wartime industries. With the Second World War offering opportunities for women in male-dominated vocations, women were no longer vilified for working outside the home as they had been in the previous decade. Indeed, society continually emphasized that it was women's patriotic duty to assume "men's jobs" in order to maintain the wartime economy. Instead of working as a store clerk, a waitress, or a secretary, women now could earn more money in aircraft manufacturing plants or ammunition factories. In particular, women who had migrated to California's urban areas and worked as riveters and welders not only danced to the swing music of Wills and Cooley but also must have appreciated the prominence of Carolina Cotton and her aural image of physical skill and power, the very qualities that working women were encouraged to embody. At the same time, however, conservative social commentators grew increasingly wary of the newfound independence of women, afraid that their cultural autonomy would unleash an excessive, dangerous sexuality, destabilizing the social ordering of patriarchal society.

These concerns about women's sexuality extended to Cotton's image. In one breath, she could be marketed as an independent ranch woman at home on the range with Cooley and his band and in the next billed as the "Western Bombshell."[44] By 1946, she would even be referred to as the "Yodeling Blonde Bombshell," conflating her vocal power with an image of explosive sexuality.[45]

The publicity that was shaping Cotton into a yodeling sex symbol had much in common with the World War II–era iconography of scantily clad women straddling bombs painted on U.S. fighter planes, making a clear link between sexualized images of womanhood and aggressive military power. Lurking within the shadows of these sexualized depictions was the fear, according to historian Elaine Tyler May, that "if such erotic force were unleashed within the nation (rather than against its enemies), the results could be disastrous."[46]

This image of Cotton as a "Yodeling Blonde Bombshell" was one of the many examples of the eroticization of women during World War II. The anxiety in some quarters of society about the destructive power of unleashed female sexuality grew out of a rhetorical climate that intertwined notions of women's sexual allure to the ideals of patriotism. In rallying women to fulfill their patriotic duties, society not only encouraged them to work in male-defined factory positions but also to participate in the military's strategies for offering companionship. Historian Marilyn Hegarty explains how women wrote servicemen letters and visited them at their military bases, where they played cards and danced with them.[47] The military would bus in hostesses (typically young white middle-class women, who were perceived as respectable) to offer servicemen an evening of entertainment and companionship on military bases as a means to contain their sexuality. There was grave concern about servicemen contracting and spreading venereal diseases, and wartime hostesses were the means to keep men out of brothels. In this campaign to make women available in public places, such as a dance hall located near the military base, military policies attempted simultaneously and paradoxically "to mobilize and contain female sexuality" and "attitudes toward male and female sexuality."[48]

Yet the dance hall could also be a place of liberation for women, especially for those female defense workers who extended their homosocial relationships of the factory floor to the dance floor in nightclubs and ballrooms, which were often located next to wartime production plants. Women who labored in the factories explored the terrain of sexualized dancing and the politics of pleasure without the availability of many male partners.[49] At the same time, they screamed to the performative male bodies of Bob Wills, Tex Williams, and Spade Cooley, displaying their sexual yearning and desire while dancing together and socializing. With the security of female friends, the dance floor could be a place where the "pleasures of the [female] body are embraced and privileged."[50]

Indeed, as the "Yodeling Blonde Bombshell," Carolina Cotton negotiated this same complex dance of female sexuality and autonomy in her performances. She often wore glamorous stylized western wear that softened the explicit sexual allure ascribed to her by her publicity. As the sociologist Beverley Skeggs has argued, glamour has been a powerful trope for women to use in taking control of their image so that they do not appear as objects of sexual passivity.[51] Cotton's combination of style and yodeling demonstrated authority and control, forever reminding her audiences of her vocal virtuosity. Moreover, Cotton did not necessarily appear as a domestic figure. Unlike Evans, Cotton wasn't coupled with one particular cowboy performer. Her distinct persona, whether in front of the microphone or in film, was markedly independent and could intertwine glamour with vocal virtuosity in a way that signaled her musical and physical prowess, a package that could be socially destructive to gender norms.

Carolina Cotton and Theatrics of the Yodel

Along with her charisma and vocal talents, Carolina Cotton's appearances in film undercut any sort of static image. Like many women of early country music, she could play a variety of rural roles—a hillbilly gal, a rustic maiden, or a singing cowgirl—and more modern parts, such as a jazzy chanteuse or an urban college student. At the beginning of her marketing as Cooley's "warbler," for example, *Billboard* announced that she would have a part in Roy Acuff's 1944 film *Sing, Neighbor, Sing*, which also starred Lulu Belle and Scotty.[52] As previously mentioned, Lulu Belle did not play her well-known radio role as a hillbilly clown or sentimental mountaineer maiden in this film. Instead she was cast as a college-age woman studying phrenology. To play the part of a young, enthusiastic, urban woman driven by her academic studies, Lulu Belle delivered her lines and sang "Have I Told You Lately That I Love You?" to Wiseman without much trace of her rural southern accent and nasal-twang singing style that she used in performance of her Lulu Belle roles over the airwaves and on the silver screen. In the film, Carolina Cotton also played a young college student but without a key part in the plot. Nevertheless, she may have come to understand how country performers can fluidly move in and out of theatrical roles.

Her use of the yodel's multivalent connections to nineteenth-century female virtuosity and pastoralism, gendered links to ethnic humor, and swing-inflected cowboy songs were instrumental in her fluid transformations of womanhood in recording and in film. While she was performing with Cooley's orchestra, Cotton composed one of her signature songs, "I Love to Yodel" (1944), which combined vocal virtuosity with the comic legacy of the yodel. She did not record it until 1946, when she was performing with Hank Penny and His Orchestra and made a number of recordings, including her self-penned "Three Miles South of Cash (in Arkansas)" with King Records. Yet in several film performances, beginning as early as 1944, she performed "I Love to Yodel" in a variety of narrative contexts that continually underlined the comic tone, theatricality, and virtuosity of her vocal abilities.

Cotton's earlier and later filmic performances largely reiterated the yodel melodies and vocal performances of the 1946 recording of "I Love to Yodel."[53]

From the beginning of this fast-paced song, her vocal delivery of clear chest vocal tones produced in a declamatory, clipped manner gives the impression of a singer carefully articulating the lyrics to create a scenario. She does not necessarily sing in a pushed, nasally inflected chest voice, and her southern accent of twangy brightness is still audible but not overly emphasized. Similar in timbre to Patsy Montana's singing voice (described as "sweet" by her fan base), Cotton's open vocal tone is more aligned with the aesthetics of 1940s popular music sung by women to jazz-inflected soundscapes than with what was considered "hillbilly" or "mountain" music. Also, like Montana and other virtuosic yodelers such as Rosalie Allen, Cotton's vocal talents are demonstrated in the ways her yodel shapes the very narrative of her song.

Throughout "I Love to Yodel," Carolina Cotton draws on the usual tropes associated with the yodel and turns them into caricatures. The song begins with a narrative that connects the yodel to the picturesque countryside by inserting a short yodel melody in the opening line, "I love to yodel, high-yip-tiddle-ee air-ree dee, all the songs of romance of the spring." We have the impression of the female protagonist rejoicing in the blooming foliage of spring by yodeling within this scenic environment. In the following phrase, however, she begins to upturn her idyllic tale through buffoonery that involves farm animals and romance. Her love interest appears to be a pony that she would serenade with her yodels, but it won't lead to "matrimony, 'cause he can't buy a golden wedding ring." She elaborates on the yodel's connection to western images by directing her affections to a "handsome cowboy." But we soon learn that he is not an attainable love interest but rather a film actor, and we understand that Cotton is invoking the fabricated images of Hollywood's western fantasies. In the last verse, she sings of how nobody wants to listen to her yodels, apart from the cows to which she will "yodel lullabies" and "gaze into their eyes." Here, she points to the changing meaning of the yodel. Initially, invoking the stylized folk elements of the yodel in Alpine work songs, Cotton appears to be in charge of a herd of cows to which she will yodel. Yet by yodeling a lullaby to the farm animals, she recalls the theatrical tradition of Dutch characters yodeling lullabies in parodic performance of German immigrants and masculinity.[54] In essence, she appropriates the theatrical incarnations of male ethnic humor to caricaturize the western male figure who supposedly lulled cattle to repose through song and yodeling. Here the cowgirl uses a feminized vocalization linked to masculine parody to soothe her own bovines.

Carolina Cotton's protean use of the yodel continues via her extensive vocal passages after each verse. At first, she decorates the end of her yodeling passages with tongue trills in her higher range, creating the sonic picture of birdcalls and nature, similar in effect to the yodel melodies of the DeZurik Sisters, who could also evoke the pastoral and virtuosic ideals that feminized the yodel in the first half of the nineteenth century. Yet Cotton also makes it clear that she can infuse her yodels with blues notes and syncopated rhythms, and she concludes her song with her usual dynamic flair as she did in performances with Cooley's orchestra. She follows by launching into a similarly fast-paced sixteenth-note pattern of ascending sixths, as in songs discussed previously in this chapter, thus connecting her showmanship to the theatrical comedy of the yodel. Drawing and elaborating on the variety of sonic and thematic tropes associated with the yodel, Carolina Cotton often performed "I Love to Yodel" in many of her filmic performances, making the song part of her comedic and stage persona that offered contrasting versions of womanhood. It is as if Cotton had shifted the meaning of her yodeling to help her move in and out of character. In this way, Cotton's vocal skill complicated and expanded on the conventions of rustic humor that were linked to the staging of country music. Even the mainstream popular-music industry, which often referred to western swing songs and other country styles as "corny," could not help but acknowledge Cotton's talents. In the dance hall and on the silver screen, Cotton reminded her audience that she was a singing actress of theatrical transformations ever intertwining comedy with performative agency.

In her first film performance of "I Love to Yodel," Carolina Cotton played the part of Abigail "Abby" Alden, a hillbilly maiden who lives with Ma Alden in Pitchfork, Arkansas, in *I'm from Arkansas* (1944).[55] From the beginning of the film, the narrative combines the diverse strands of country music with a depiction of an Ozark community of hillbillies who have come to national recognition because their prized pig, Esmeralda, has produced a record-breaking number of piglets in her latest litter. The town of Pitchfork, associated with barnyard fecundity, is characterized in exaggerated stereotype as a rural southern locale with customs that stand in stark contrast to those of the citified interlopers. The male manager of a Broadway troupe of pushy urban women decides that they will travel to Pitchfork to entertain the thousands who will be flocking to this Ozark area to see the famous sow.

As the film hyperbolizes the differences between the snobby city slickers and the so-called local yokels, the main character, Bob Hamline (played by Bruce Bennett), hoodwinks the seemingly urban sophisticates by playing to their preconceived notions of southern rusticity. He exaggerates his rural roots and feigns a hillbilly identity when in actuality he is the talented leader of a swing band that includes the crooner Jimmy Wakely. By extension, Pitchfork turns out (rather implausibly) to be an entire community of musicians who can perform an impressive range of musics. Indeed, the point of this film seems merely to be a vehicle for introducing and showcasing the latest country music talent. Wakely, to the orchestral accompaniment of Bennett's band, croons love songs such as "Don't Turn Me Down Little Darlin'" and joins the vocal trio the Sunshine

Girls (who include Mary Ford) to render "You Are My Sunshine" in mellifluous harmonies. The country vocal duo the Milo Twins perform old hillbilly hits, and the popular vocal quartet the Pied Pipers sing swung harmonies in their performance of "You're the Hit of the Season." Against this multifarious musical backdrop, Cotton's shy Abby entertains the urban visitors in her family's board-inghouse with a rendition of "Yodel Mountain," a song about traveling west to a mythical Yodel Mountain, applying the Alpine-influenced yodel to the western landscape of the United States. Initially the talent manager jumps in surprise when Abby launches into her yodel, which highlights the vocal break between registers with percussive glottal stops at a fast tempo. But as the song continues and she yodels in her trademark fashion of vocal trills, syncopated rhythms, followed by her sixteenth-note yodel runs, the manager and his lead singer are more impressed, as if her vocal abilities pull the yodel from its pejorative comic associations and return it to its former standing as female virtuosity. Following her yodeling performance, the audience erupts in applause as the bashful Abby flees the room.

Later in the film, Cotton sings and yodels her signature song, "I Love to Yodel," in a performance that is being broadcast from Pitchfork. Here she appears in an embroidered dress and a blouse with puffed sleeves with her hair in braids and decorated with flowers. In a costume that resembles traditional (in the eyes of American audiences) Swiss female garb, Cotton gives the impression that she is straight from the idyllic countryside and again underscores the yodel's association with the Alpine regions. While she performs this comic song, which interlaces virtuosity with satire, Abby transforms into a performer who is just as savvy as the other artists featured in the film and in the town. No longer the shy hillbilly maiden who has a talent for yodeling, Abby, in front of the micro-phone accompanied by a swing band, acts out the lyrics of her song: she makes a mournful face to sing of how only the cows want to hear her yodel and gives the bandleader a coquettish smile when she mentions a "handsome cowboy." In her pastoral costume playing the part of a hillbilly maiden, Cotton transforms into a stage performer whose vocal abilities and slapstick humor exceed the role in which she herself was cast. In its review of the music in *I'm from Arkansas*, Nat Green of *Billboard* focused solely on the musical performances of all the artists and exclaimed, "Singing honors go to Carolina Cotton, who goes to town on *Yodel Mountain* and *I Love to Yodel*."[56]

In contrast to playing the part of the hillbilly maiden in *I'm from Arkansas*, Cotton takes on the role of the gun-toting western heroine in *Apache Country* (1952), starring the well-known singing cowboy Gene Autry, accompanied by his comic sidekick Pat Buttram.[57] Again, she performs her song "I Love to Yodel." Yet in an interesting twist given Cotton's prominent role in the film's narra-tive, she is not the love interest of Autry, who typically croons his way into the hearts of his leading ladies. Rather, she appears as a rustic tomboy or an asexual cowgirl, a queer identity, in her masculine pursuits. The historical and fictional accounts of the western heroine, appearing in men's clothing and participating in "masculinized" activities of rounding up cattle and bronco riding, have been part of the gender-bending stage of the American West since its inception. The singing cowgirl Patsy Montana, as discussed in chapter 3, purposely modeled her western look on the tomboy version of the working-class western heroine to offer a visual account that gestured to a legacy of nineteenth-century frontier women, such as the buckskin-clad military scout and outlaw Calamity Jane and the sharpshooter Annie Oakley.

Similarly, in *Apache Country* Carolina Cotton is an embodiment of the cowgirl who is at home on the frontier and can match the heroism of the cowboy. Her skills with firearms (at times outshooting many of the other cowboys, including Autry) and in cultivating friendships with the local Native Americans make her an invaluable peer on the western range instead of just an object of desire. But this is still a film tinged with rustic humor, and Cotton's asexual frontier persona often resembles the goofy tomboy, "the most popular masculine heroine of the fifties," according to film scholar Rebecca Bell-Metereau.[58] With her exaggerated rustic accent, strong presence, and, at times, kinetic humor, Cotton comes across as the gregarious rural woman who in her masculinized demeanor appears oblivious to the societal niceties of femininity.

The rustic humor of the film largely arises from the incongruities of Cotton's gender-variance performance. Her rural tomboy image, for example, stands in stark contrast to the explicit refinement and femininity of the only other female character in the film, Laura Rayburn (played by Mary Scott), an urbane upper-class woman. Typical of Hollywood's portrayals of manly western heroines—such as the character Calamity Jane, played by Jean Arthur in *The Plainsman* (1937) and Doris Day in *Calamity Jane* (1953)—the unruly cowgirl is often juxtaposed with a female character who embodies the ideals of gentility. The Calamity Jane in both of those films, Bell-Metereau argues, appears "awkward and ignorant of the household and fashion secrets that all women supposedly know."[59] Cotton is also completely unaware of how to be a genteel "lady." Yet, unlike these Calamity Jane characters, Carolina Cotton isn't taken under the wing of a middle-class woman to learn how to behave as a "proper" lady. Rather, the story line of *Apache Country* is class based and equates feminine gentility with uppity corruption by making Rayburn part of the scheming elite. Typical in Autry's western films, the individuals of the communal rural working class appear trustworthy, sincere, and authentic in character, populist ideals that further accentuate the ways in which Cotton's plebeian, tomboy image clashes with the monetary greed of the upper class, whose refined manners mask their corruption. Autry, in typical fashion, as the male hero, uncovers the crimes of the local ruling class but not without the help of Cotton.

From the beginning of the film, when Cotton first meets Autry, Buttram, and Rayburn in a stagecoach ride, she intertwines her musical and yodeling talents with her sharpshooting skills. To musically set the scene, they (apart from Rayburn) sing "The Covered Wagon Rolled Right Along" with Cotton inserting a yodel melody into her vocal line. Soon thereafter, the evildoers launch an attack on the stagecoach, and Cotton, Autry, and Buttram defend themselves by shooting back. When Autry shoots one of the villains, Cotton exclaims that she could use him in her act. (We later learn that she is the master of ceremonies and a performer in her own traveling medicine show.) Autry asks what she does in her performances, and she responds by yodeling. Buttram immediately evokes the comic legacy of the yodel as a vocal device of humor and aesthetic derision by interpreting her yodel as a cry of pain—"Where did they get you, Miz Carolina?" Clearly annoyed, Cotton shouts back, "I ain't hit, you big baboon; I was jist yodelin'." Misinterpreting what the film will later present as an aural signifier of female autonomy and virtuosity for a cry of pain, Buttram concludes, "No wonder I am scared of women." Following this remark, Buttram exclaims that he has run out of bullets for his gun, and Cotton offers her extra bullets (while she continues to shoot and hit the evil pursuers), making it clear that she is a valiant yodeling heroine.

Cotton's abilities to handle a gun and yodel while facing the perils of frontier culture extend to her theatrical role in her traveling medicine show, a vestige of the nineteenth-century Wild West show, initially developed by "Wild Bill" Cody (1846–1917). Cody's hyperbolized and romanticized stage settings of Buffalo Bill's Wild West included "real" American Indians by the 1870s. His intention was to play on the noble-savage stereotype to market his action-packed dramas to nineteenth-century middle-class audiences concerned about the plight of Native Americans and the industrial transformation and destruction of the perceived Edenic frontier.[60] Like Buffalo Bill, Cotton, as the proprietor of her own show, includes Tony White Cloud's performance troupe of Jemez Indians, demonstrating that the cowgirl, similar to the frontier hero, is a romantic, noble figure who can coexist peacefully and harmoniously with Native Americans.[61] Cotton induces the Jemez Indians "to do some of their native dances, which are more sacred to their tribe and people." The film score and the plot, however, still underline the musical and cultural stereotypes of Indian culture, while the individual scenes of the Jemez Indians try to present Native American culture in a way that educates 1950s audiences.[62]

In the staging of her medicine show, Carolina Cotton, however, masks her asexual, working-class image by donning stylized, form-fitting western wear, including a skirt, a fringed vest, and a western blouse, with flowers decorating her pin-curled hairstyle, in keeping with Hollywood's glamorous production of manly cowgirls. Beginning her own staged performance by yodeling and then listening for the response, she gives the impression that she is on an Alpine hilltop. But she is standing in front of a stage setting of the western plains of the United States, conjuring up images of the yodel being used as a means of communication on the open range. Buttram reacts with "here she goes again" as he is about to plug his ears, pointing away from the yodel's pastoral association to its history of "corny" comedy and parody. Autry tells him, "Shut up, that girl can sing," defending Carolina Cotton's vocal talents by equating the act of yodeling with that of singing. She performs "I Love to Yodel" and repeats the yodel melodies of her 1946 recording. For her closing yodel, she again showcases her sixteenth-note yodel passage during which she physically demonstrates the effort it takes to yodel at breakneck speeds. At the end, she acts as the bandleader of the accompanying instrumental trio, conducting the ensemble as she vocally engages in a call-and-response pattern with the instrumentalists and then concludes with an octave leap to her upper range. In all aspects of this performance, Cotton is the one who is musically in control, employing the vocal device as a means to assert the cowgirl's autonomy in the Wild West.

In addition to her asexual roles as the rustic maiden in *I'm from Arkansas* and the tomboy cowgirl in *Apache Country*, Cotton could lay claim to female sexuality through her rural codes of womanhood. As in her other films, Cotton did a number of costume changes in the lead female role in the western *Hoedown* (1950), also starring Eddy Arnold.[63] Cast as Arnold's cousin, Cotton initially appears as a comic character, attired in gingham dresses as well as western shirts and denim pants, who chases after a handsome singing cowboy. Yet for a musical performance, she does a quick costume change from a hypersexual rube to a seductive cowgirl attired in stylized, glitzy western wear and croons the number "I Betcha I Getcha" (which she recorded for MGM in 1950). While she voices an explicit desire for her love interest ("Now I'm no Venus, I'll admit, but what I want I always get") and dances suggestively to the syncopated rhythms, Cotton begins to attract the amorous attention of the handsome cowboy while another male admirer, the farmhand referred to as Small Potatoes, grows jealous.

After her song-and-dance number, the local sheriff asks her to "do some fancy yodeling." Moving away from her seductive performance, Cotton provides a spectacular yodel performance in "Oh Where, Oh Where Has My Little Dog Gone," the nineteenth-century comic song originally known as "Der Deitcher's Dog" and recorded by George Watson in his Dutch comedic role in the early twentieth century.[64] She even opens with a yodel melody that closely resembles Winner's melody and Watson's yodel. Though she is alluding to the role of the male Dutch character, Cotton's performance does not preclude the cowboy's developing interest in her. Indeed, his admiration seems to grow the more she yodels, causing the farmhand to erupt in jealousy and engage in a slapstick fistfight followed by other humorous mishaps.

As I have observed previously, the yodel's historical and dualistic relationship to virtuosity and comedy extended to a number of Cotton's performances in film and in recording. Even when she recorded what could be a straightforward song of the singing cowgirl pursuing romantic love on the open range, fitting with conventional understandings of femininity, Cotton used the yodel as a comic device that turns the narrative slightly on its head. For example, her 1946 recording of "Singing on the Trail," accompanied by the swing arrangement of Hank Penny's orchestra, is a comic song that parodies the cowgirl's self-determination in matters of the heart.[65] She attempts to win over the cowboy with her yodel melodies, but she ultimately fails to get him in front of a minister so that she can pin him down in marriage. Cotton, still encouraged, ends the song by singing of her plans to slip a "halter" on him "at the altar," thereby taming the cowboy into domestic submission.

In its review of "Singing on the Trail," *Billboard* acknowledged Cotton's vocal talents: "Carolina Cotton has a good, pleasant, warm voice, which she uses in a Western style of vocalizing, and then embellishes the melody here and there with some fancy yodeling." Yet the review begins by stating that this song is an example of "peppy corn music," typical of the trade magazine's view of the various styles of country music recorded during the 1940s. Nevertheless, *Billboard* could not overlook Cotton's talents, which she first displayed in the dance hall and now had extended to recordings. The popular-music trade magazine repeatedly praised her vocal talents with comments such as, "This girl might come to the big town and show the city slickers a thing or two. This is the better brand of folk music and interesting."[66] In other words, Carolina Cotton was a vocal force whose "fancy yodels" and "pleasant voice" could mediate the "corn" imagery tied to country music. In film and recording, Cotton may have played a range of rustic comic roles that embodied and continued the slapstick buffoonery of barn-dance radio. However, like the 1930s "Queen of Radio," Lulu Belle, she could combine humor with other performative traditions in her acting and vocal abilities. Though the popular-music industry recognized Cotton's yodeling as a form of artistry, her thespian range as a singing actress constituted creative skill, including her theatrical flair for corn.

Conclusion

By the late 1940s, Carolina Cotton's success as a recording artist and actress started to rival the popularity of the "Queen of the Western," Dale Evans. As stated in a 1948 issue of *Billboard*, "Carolina Cotton looks like the next big cowgirl in pictures with the imminent retirement of Mrs. Roy Rogers (Dale Evans). Carolina will be queen of the rodeo at the Sunset Ranch Ninth Annual Rodeo, Gilmore Stadium, Los Angeles, and will act in the same capacity at the Coliseum rodeo later. She will also represent the Cowgirl of Today in the Easter parade in Hollywood. Carolina starts her next movie April 1."[67] Her filmic roles and presence in the dance halls of the 1940s extended to other live performative events—such as parades and rodeos—in Southern California, making her an icon of the region (see figure 9).

Cotton's live performances and recording and film career continued to flourish into the 1950s. Apart from her well-known song "I Love to Yodel," she also wrote "Three Miles South of Cash," which she recorded with Bob Wills and His Texas Playboys for MGM records in 1952. Here, Cotton appears as an Arkansas transplant in a comic narrative that offers many stereotypes of southern rusticity. As *Billboard* insinuated in its review, both Wills and Cotton hammed it up in their performance of a song that is about home, having "a ball on this infectious novelty with cute lyrics, as they hand it a fine warble."[68] Yet just as in her film performances, Carolina Cotton could switch from playing the hillbilly transplant to the assertive cowgirl in her recordings. In "You Gotta Get a Guy with a Gun," performed in the film *The Rough, Tough West* (1952), Cotton sings with tongue in cheek of securing a domestic mate through force. She cowrote "You Always Keep Me in Hot Water" (1951) and "Yodel, Yodel, Yodel" (1952), a virtuosic yodel number that she performed in *Blue Canadian Rockies* (1952), starring Gene Autry.[69] She also toured with leading acts of California country

Figure 9. Carolina Cotton publicity photograph. Courtesy of Sharon Marie, estate of Carolina Cotton.

music, including Merle Travis, the Sons of the Pioneers, and Bob Wills and the Texas Playboys during the 1940s and 1950s.[70]

Cotton proceeded to take on male-defined roles by becoming one of the first women disc jockeys in country music, promoting country hits over the airwaves of Los Angeles KGER beginning in 1948.[71] For the New York publication *Rustic Rhythm*, Cotton wrote about Los Angeles country music in the column "Bits 'n' Pieces from Carolina Cotton's West Coast Treasure Chest!"[72] Moreover, Cotton had her own radio program, *Carolina Cotton Calls* (1952–1954), for the Armed Forces Radio Services that featured well-known country musicians, including Joe Maphis (who played in Cotton's band) and guest artists Rose Lee Maphis, Bob Wills, Patsy Montana, Little Jimmy Dickens, and Skeets McDonald.[73] She was even scheduled to have her own television program, titled *Queen of the Range*, beginning in 1950. It would have been an action series with Cotton playing the western heroine, who gallantly rides off into the sunset in each episode. Unfortunately, the program never came to be, as the era of the singing cowgirl was coming to end.

Though Carolina Cotton does not usually come to mind when music historians recount the vibrancy of the western-swing era in the dance halls of California, she was a key participant in the musical landscape of 1940s Los Angeles. Like many of her contemporaries in western swing, she performed to a distinct audience of transplanted Okies and women working in wartime industries. Right at the time when society started to become concerned about women's growing independence and autonomy, Cotton's musical renderings and glamorous but variant image could be an example of how to assert female agency and showcase physical skill in a variety of rural roles.

If she helped glamorize the "sagebrushers" for an Okie audience as well as a mainstream one, she also continued the theatricality of rustic humor that had extended from barn-dance radio to film and even to live performances in California's dance halls (as seen with Rose Maddox and the Maddox Brothers, the topic of the following chapter). Cotton extended her yodeling showmanship to her self-penned songs and filmic performances, which underscored her vocal talents in a range of thespian roles. Her yodeling could be a pyrotechnical display, a vocal mode of comedy, or a combination of the two that simultaneously mediated, hyperbolized, and disavowed the "corn" perceptions of country music promoted by mass media. As a consummate performer of thespian fluidity, she undercut and complicated static categories that extended from the stage to her audience of working-class women, notably transplants from the Southwest and the southern plains, who were in the midst of remaking their own visions of themselves within the gendered reconfigurations prompted by wartime growth and opportunities in 1940s California.

5 Rose Maddox

Roadhouse Singing and Hillbilly Theatrics

From the dance hall, the same venue that launched Carolina Cotton's illustrious career, Rose Maddox emerged as a significant performer of California country music. With her family band, the Maddox Brothers and Rose, she honed her performative and vocal talents first over the airwaves of local radio stations in Modesto, Stockton, and Sacramento, and then in the 1940s and 1950s roadhouses and nightclubs located in the Central Valley and the southern region of the state. Drawing from the theatrical and musical conventions of barn-dance radio that had shaped California country music, Maddox initially played the part of the singing cowgirl performing the very repertory that Patsy Montana had made famous. Yet unlike Montana and Cotton, Maddox did not excel in building her persona around the vocal tropes of glamour associated with the cosmopolitan strands of western swing that so compellingly mediated the Depression-era stereotypes of Okie culture. Instead, Maddox, with her family band, blended the theatrics of the nineteenth-century saloon with the grotesque humor of the hillbilly buffoon to exaggerate the stereotypes of southern plains migrants to the point of comic disbelief.

The Maddoxes' parodic performances of well-known country songs (like Hank Williams's "Honky-Tonkin'" or Woody Guthrie's "Philadelphia Lawyer") underlined the sexual codes and subversive nature commonly attributed to Okie working-class men and women. Using unruly humor, they simultaneously created a distance from and flouted the prevalent perceptions of regional, class, and gendered deviance. The kinetic energy, spilling forth from Rose Maddox's dynamic performances, fueled the family band's fluid blending of western swing idioms with the emerging stylistic traits of rockabilly in songs like "George's Playhouse Boogie" (1949) and "(Pay Me) Alimony" (1951). In these performances, the Maddox ensemble also highlighted the carnivalesque revelry of the roadhouse and the historical incongruities of gender roles that had emerged during and after World War II. With Rose as the lead singer, the music reminded women in particular of the social and physical freedoms of the dance hall, a predominantly homosocial site during the era of "Rosie the Riveter."

In addition to her parodic and boisterous performances, Maddox cultivated a singing style that could resonate within the architectural and sonic environments of California's nightspots. Her belting voice combined a chest-dominant vocal technique with vernacular southern idioms in what I term a "roadhouse vocality." She could thus vocally transport the aural vestiges of southern culture to her homesick audiences in the roadhouse or dance hall, places of leisure that simultaneously acted as a cultural buffer to and an avenue for coming to terms with the shifting geographical, social, and cultural terrain. In addition to connecting with her audience of displaced whites, the expressive power of Maddox's voice and her bold stage persona helped carve out performance spaces for female artists in honky-tonk and rockabilly. Jean Shepard and Rose Lee Maphis, in particular, cultivated a full-sounding voice (similar to that of Maddox) in their honky-tonk ballads, while Wanda Jackson's rockabilly hits, such as "Fujiyama Mama" (1957), displayed a heightened female sexuality influenced by Maddox's rockabilly-like performances. Maddox not only created sonic versions of womanhood that questioned 1950s gendered and class norms, but she also provided a model for female performers of California country music.

The Maddox Brothers and Rose: Dangerous Okie Outlaws

Like many of the rural dispossessed, the Maddox family tried to forge a livelihood first as sharecroppers in a farming community outside Boaz, Alabama, and later as itinerant farm laborers in Depression-era California. Sharecropping depended on the labor of the rural poor and could hardly support its workers with a decent wage in the best of times let alone during the Depression, when the price of cotton plummeted.[1] As Rose Maddox stated in a 1985 interview, "When we got down so poor and everything 'till there was nothing to do and the Depression was on," Lulu Maddox (Rose's mother) decided it was time to leave the South.[2] The mythological frontier culture promoted in dime novels, barn-dance radio programs (notably WLS's *National Barn Dance*), and Hollywood films depicting the western United States as a land of "milk and honey" contrasted dramatically with the poverty and backbreaking work of tenancy. Convinced of the imagined possibilities linked to the West, Lulu Maddox (a matriarchal force) persuaded her family of seven to make the long trek from Alabama to California when Rose was only seven years old. Unlike those migrants who had loaded their possessions on top of their cars and driven across the country, the Maddoxes hitchhiked, walked, and rode the rails in a cross-country journey that took three months.[3] After their arrival in California, their dramatic tale made the *Oakland Tribune*, which featured the headline "Family Roams US for Work" with an accompanying photo of a tired-looking Maddox family.[4]

Once in California, the Maddoxes became familiar with the exploitative system of the agricultural industry, identifying strongly with what later would initially become their fan base, displaced whites searching desperately for a means of survival. Like so many Okies, the Maddoxes worked alongside immigrant farm laborers as itinerant farmhands, known as "fruit tramps."[5] They followed the harvest season of different crops throughout the state: peas in the Imperial Valley, apricots in the Salinas and Santa Clara Valleys, fruit in the Sacramento Valley, and potatoes, grapes, and cotton in the San Joaquin Valley.[6] White migrants, competing against one another for farm jobs, flooded the employment market, of which the agribusiness greedily took advantage by paying the newcomers incredibly low wages for their labor.

Initially, landowners welcomed the surplus of cheap labor until it appeared that those so-called fruit tramps were capable of unionizing to protect themselves from economic exploitation. The conservative organization the Associated Farmers, representing the interests of the agribusiness, intended "to get laws passed that [would] protect them against Communists, and see that these laws [were] rigidly enforced," as reported by the agricultural economist Paul Taylor.[7] White southern plains migrants thus were viewed as either intruders in desperate need of economic support, draining the state of its few resources, or as communists plotting to destroy the economic foundation of the agribusiness. In turn, middle-class residents of California grew increasingly wary of white transplants and joined the leaders of the agricultural industry in fueling an antimigrant campaign to close the state's borders to any newcomers.[8]

Searching for opportunities beyond the backbreaking work and sordid conditions of farm labor, Fred Maddox pursued a career in country music. Through radio, film, and live performance, country music was a vital form of music making in both Central and Southern California with a growing audience of displaced whites from the southern United States. For a performance spot on Modesto's KTRB, Fred secured a sponsor, Rice Furniture Store (located in Modesto, California), whose owner was impressed with Fred's verbal persuasiveness and insisted that he be the announcer of the group and that the ensemble feature a girl singer. At this time, in 1937, Rose was eleven years old, and she started her career in country music as the lead singer of the Maddox Brothers and Rose.[9] A female singer, even a young one, could bring a sense of propriety to the band's musical image and appeal to a radio audience of women, viable consumers of household items, like furniture.[10] In their performances, the Maddox family band, however, was far from projecting a consistent image of respectability. Rather, the band featured a constellation of musical representations of rural culture by playing the role of the rebellious hillbilly—derived from the rube humor of barn-dance radio and the stage settings of minstrelsy and vaudeville—while also exploiting the more romanticized tropes of the West.

Their 1940 broadcast on radio station KFBK in Sacramento, California, drawing from dualistic performative images of country music, began with Fred and Cal's boisterous rendition of their theme song, "Oh! Susanna," originally a blackface song, composed by Stephen Foster.[11] The Maddoxes' version of the song also recalls a later incarnation titled "Oh, California." Continuing the theme of migration, "Oh, California" became a protest song against the economic conditions that drove westward expansion. For the working class and the working poor, nineteenth-century industrialism in the North and the Midwest offered low factory wages and terrible working conditions. In contrast, the West was considered a place where landownership and material means were within the grasp of the industrial dispossessed. According to Eric Lott, white men of the popular classes frequently performed "Oh, California" in blackface in the nineteenth-century saloons of California as a means to call "on current (racial) languages of social division to manifest their distaste for the class-riven realities that going west was meant to redress."[12]

The Maddox brothers did not use the visual stereotypes of blackness to represent the relationship between social class and dislocation. Instead, their musical satire translated this blackface song into a hillbilly tune to underline the subject position of the uprooted white southerner.[13] Though they were playing the guitar and the harmonica, Fred and Cal verbally presented themselves as disruptive hillbillies playing the noisy banjo during their travels from Alabama to California. Indeed, after their opening duet, Rose's introduction elaborated on the band's itinerant and dangerous identity: "Yes, sir, folks. And this is my famous outlaws the Maddox Brothers and Rose, straight from the hills of Alabama. We're goin' try to 'tain you here for a little while and we do hope you like it." From the mountainous region of Alabama, the band was presented as a group of outlaws, possibly dangerous subversive hillbillies, who lived outside "civilization" and posed likely threats to the social and political order of California.

In the same broadcast, Rose Maddox took on the role of the singing cowgirl to enact a romantic vision of the West, softening the class and regional origins of the Maddox family. She thus moved the listener's imagination from the southern hills to the western prairies of the United States. Fittingly, she performed a cowgirl song written by Patsy Montana (who had become a radio star on Chicago's WLS). In "Ridin' the Sunset Trail," Maddox followed Montana's narrative and sang of how the western heroine balances her pursuits of the symbolic freedoms of the open range with the rituals of romantic courtship: "Let me ride my pony down the sunset trail" and "sing a song to the one I love while he's ridin' by my side." Like many cowgirl songs written by Montana, the fantasies of western expansion from a woman's perspective included tales of self-directed cowgirls often framed within heterosexual narratives. In this song, the western heroine pursues the affections of the cowboy, a romantic partner of equal standing who will roam the prairies on horseback by *her* side. Yet while Rose performed this cowgirl number, Fred interjected a number of whoops and hollers, and at one point he even imitated the sounds of a howling coyote. His vocalizations were meant to depict the wildness of the West and instill a riotous tone in the musical backdrop of Rose's performance, potentially stripping the cowgirl of her polished image. In other words, Fred gave the marked impression of how easily the ensemble could turn the cultural myths of the West into an actual parody of those very desires for autonomy and individualism. An audience of transplants knew firsthand the distance between the realities of westward migration and the fantasies of Manifest Destiny.

Despite Fred's disruptive comedic role in the broadcast, Rose seemed earnest in her attempts to play the part of the singing cowgirl. She had learned a number of Montana's songs, including her signature hit, "I Want to Be a Cowboy's Sweetheart," and greatly admired western acts, especially the Sons of the Pioneers, for their mellifluous singing style.[14] In her performance of "Ridin' the Sunset Trail," Maddox attempted to model her performance after Montana's by singing the song in its original key and imitating her yodel melody. For all her attempts, however, Maddox did not fully inhabit the aesthetic space of the singing cowgirl, who often was a proficient singer in both her chest and head registers while yodeling to the heights of her range with virtuosic brilliance. In "Ridin' the Sunset Trail," Montana, for example, sang the melody with a degree of effortlessness in her fluid transitions from the chest to the head voice. The young Maddox, on the other hand, struggled to project a clear and well-supported head tone. Her airy, light timbre (with little diaphragm support) in the higher range was likely because her vocal folds were not fully developed at her young age, making it difficult for her to transition smoothly from the low to the high register.[15] Moreover, her weak and quiet-sounding head voice extended to her yodel melody. Unlike Montana, who soared repeatedly to the high E_5 in her yodel, Maddox could reach only a flat-sounding C-sharp$_5$, even with her brother Fred's encouraging comment, "Oh, get that note."

"Ridin' down the Sunset Trail" was Maddox's only solo number in the band's 1940 radio broadcast. The song, with a convincing performance, would have helped temper the family band's emerging outlaw identity. Maddox would have distanced herself not only from portrayals of the unruly Okie but also from a historical narrative that marked southern plains migrants as threats to the morality of the middle class and the political power of agribusiness. Instead, she was subsumed within the family band's outlaw imagery that purposely exaggerated Depression-era stereotypes of white migrants—those dangerous ruffians from the South invading the social and cultural landscape of California with their noisy hillbilly music. Within a familial performing context that explored the subaltern, Rose Maddox would offer models of womanhood that challenged gendered norms. Indeed, the family ensemble's riotous character and Maddox's brazen stage presence would persist at the height of their success after World War II and help lay the musical foundation for the emerging expressions of rockabilly.

Rose Maddox's "Roadhouse" Vocality

The Maddox Brothers and Rose temporarily disbanded when the brothers of the group—Fred, Cal, and Don (who joined the ensemble as a fiddle player in 1940)—were drafted and sent overseas to fight in the Second World War. Though Rose was a prominent member of the ensemble, she had difficulty continuing her career without the performative support of her family. She tried to join well-established ensembles, like Roy Acuff's Smoky Mountain Boys and Bob Wills's Texas Playboys, during the war years, but neither hired her. According to Rose Maddox, Acuff already had a female singer, and Wills did not even bother to audition Rose even though his female vocalist had just left the ensemble. The common story is that he did not want to work with Rose's domineering mother, Lulu Maddox, who managed the bookings, finances, and careers of the family band.[16] Yet maybe Wills's decision had less to do with Lulu's reputation and more with the fact that Rose Maddox did not aesthetically fit the singing cowgirl's performance style of vocal decorum combined with yodeling virtuosity. In response to Wills's rejection, Maddox angrily threatened to put him and his band out of business when her brothers returned from the war. According to Wills, they nearly did.[17]

By 1945, the Maddox Brothers and Rose re-formed and gradually included additional players to fit with the western swing soundscape that had come to dominate the dance halls and radio broadcasts of California. Initially, Fred (bass), Cal (rhythm guitar and harmonica), Henry (mandolin), and Rose (lead singer) appeared on Stockton's KGDM, and during the following year, they returned to Modesto's KTRB.[18] By early 1946, Don Maddox had returned from the war and rejoined the family ensemble on fiddle. With their growing popularity on radio, the Maddox Brothers and Rose started to appear in dance halls but soon realized that they needed a bigger and lusher sound to compete against Bob Wills's and Spade Cooley's swing bands. In the spring of 1946, the Maddoxes employed a couple of "hired hands": Bub Duncan on electric steel guitar and Jimmy Winkle on lead electric guitar. After Winkle's tenure, the band hired guitarists Gene LeMasters (1948), Roy Nichols (1949–1950)—who would later play with Merle Haggard and the Strangers—and Gene Breeden (1950–1953). With a larger sound, the band could fill dance halls and ballrooms alike with its riveting amplified music that highlighted the theatrics of hillbilly music and the kinetic rhythms of western swing, jump blues, and boogie-woogie. Galvanized by the family's musical fluidity, Rose Maddox wielded various vocal performance modes that deviated from the vocal styling of the singing cowgirl. Though Carolina Cotton had helped establish female performers in the live music scene of Los Angeles, Maddox had moved in a different direction aesthetically. She could evoke southern vernacular expressions in earnest renditions of gospel or folk tunes, offer vocal parodies of prominent country performers, and sing with a strong, chest-dominant belting voice.

The Maddox Brothers and Rose's recordings with Four Star Records from 1947 to 1952 capture the dynamics of their live performances during the era.[19] Don Pierce, the A and R man for the independent recording company, provided little guidance or criticism of the Maddoxes' performance styles. He simply encouraged the ensemble to record the songs that they had been playing in roadhouses and dance halls. Maddox explained that Pierce "never did tell [them] what to do," unlike Don Law, the A and R man for Columbia Records, with whom they would later work in the recording studio.[20] Law "tried to subdue us," Maddox said, taking "a lot away from our records. . . . It just wasn't the rambunctious Maddox Brothers and Rose like it was with Four Star."[21] To get a better understanding of what the Maddox Brothers and Rose sounded like in live performance and the musical significance of Rose Maddox's voice, I initially turn to the Four Star recordings of the Maddox Brothers and Rose.

Their spirited and upbeat songs of the late 1940s and early 1950s were integral to the transition from western swing and honky-tonk to rockabilly, continually blending all these musical styles. Maddox recalled, "We were doing what they called nowadays rockabilly. . . . We are basically the ones—Elvis told me one time, when we was working a show with him, he said, 'You guys are basically what got me into this.' He said, 'I loved your rockin' songs.' Of course, we didn't know they were rockin' songs. We was just singing, you know, and playing, but we had so much life and feeling in the stuff."[22]

Influencing the aesthetic direction of Elvis Presley, the performances of the Maddox Brothers and Rose were part of a longtime trend of country musicians including blues material (such as subject matter, song form, rhythmic language, vocal styling, and instrumental techniques). Jimmie Rodgers's blue yodels, Bob Wills's western swing numbers, and Hank Williams's blues-derived honky-tonk songs all demonstrate the centrality of the blues to various country styles.[23] As a musical hybrid that crossed racialized lines, rockabilly was largely an extension of the ways in which white southern culture had historically appropriated, borrowed from, and engaged with black music making. The music of rockabilly artists—Elvis, Wanda Jackson, Carl Perkins, and Buddy Holly, to name a few—highlighted the rhythmic language of jump blues with swing rhythms, boogie-woogie patterns, and riff-based solos and included honky-tonk's guitar-laden textures of electric lead guitar, rhythm guitar, upright bass, and (after 1956) drum kit. Also, rockabilly artists vocally deviated from the nasal-twang singing of honky-tonk singers and the smooth-sounding vocals of western swing crooners to feature extreme uses of vocal range exploited by an array of vocal devices—growls, throat vibrato, and hiccups, for example. The heightened musical language of driving syncopated riffs and vocal excesses was essential to rockabilly's dynamism of corporeal pleasures and hedonistic pursuits, which offered white youth a means to rebel against the conservative social mores of the Cold War era.[24]

Transitional figures in the development of rockabilly, the Maddox Brothers and Rose cultivated an act that grew out of a performative engagement with the sonic and social space of the roadhouse or the more-upscale dance hall. In either place, they offered parodies of the juke joint, captured the rhythmic energy of dancing bodies, and illustrated the gendered and regional dynamics of nightspots for displaced white migrants. At the same time, their radio work and performance tours of the West Coast, the Southwest, and the South would reach audiences throughout the country. By 1946, the Maddox Brothers and Rose had started to perform in the California Ballroom in Modesto and a year later in George's Playhouse, a rowdy nightspot in Stockton. As the guitarist Jimmie Winkle later told biographer Johnny Whiteside: "We'd play at George's Playhouse and the House of Blue Lights out on the Waterloo Road . . . and they got pretty rough sometimes. One time, I don't remember which club it was, we had a stabbing on the floor, right in front of the bandstand."[25]

As evidenced in *Billboard*'s announcement of the band celebrating "its first anniversary at George's Playhouse, Stockton, Calif.," George's Playhouse was a regular venue for the Maddox Brothers and Rose.[26] Indeed the band's 1949 self-referential song, "George's Playhouse Boogie," evokes the Saturday-evening revelry typical of the roadhouse by drawing on the excitement and vitality of rhythm and blues. *Billboard* aptly described the recording of this tune as a "romping boogie-woogie jump blues in the 'Tennessee Saturday Night' groove" that got "a superlative swing job from Rose and a jumping string ork (orchestra)."[27] In other words, the Maddox Brothers and Rose's "George's Playhouse Boogie" is a remake of the blues-derived country song "Tennessee Saturday Night" (written by Billy Hughes and recorded by Red Foley in 1947) and relates the revelry and hedonism of Saturday evening in the South to a California roadhouse. Henry Maddox on the electric mandolin begins the twelve-bar blues song with a riff-based introduction that explores the different registers of the instruments and sets the stage for the rhythmic intensity of the song. Launching into and repeating a three-note blues riff, Henry creates a musical momentum on which he elaborates by climbing an octave before descending to its lower range to elaborate on the original riff. Then he jumps to an even higher range on the mandolin to syncopate and fixate on limited pitch material (the first and fifth scale degrees), before dropping to the lower register and repeating the original bluesy riff. Above his playing, Fred yells, "Let's all go to George's Playhouse," offering a sense of community to an audience of white migrants. Fred then introduces Henry as "the working girl's friend" (the epithet that Fred gave Henry), suggesting that the sexualized encounters between working girls and paying men are par for the course in George's Playhouse.[28]

In addition to the electric mandolin's rhythmic licks, the instrumentalists continue to include the stylistic markers of rockabilly, combining them with those of western swing. At the first instrumental break (after Rose's first sung verse), Jimmy Winkle on lead electric guitar first swings the melody and then proceeds to break down the melodic contours of his solo into smaller riffs, to which Fred cries out, "Stop it, I can't stand it. It's driving me insane." Common to the performance practices of western swing, Don Maddox follows with his longbow fiddle style, and Bud Duncan's steel guitar enters the texture in a call-and-response section with the fiddle. The ensemble also included Fred and Rose each playing an upright string bass in the slap-bass style.[29] Contributing to the percussive pulse, Cal plays closed chords on the guitar, known as "sock" rhythm (typical of the rhythm guitar in a variety of country styles—western swing, rockabilly, and honky-tonk).

The building of rhythmic energy heralds Rose's dynamic vocals, adding to the boogie rhythms and riff-based music of the band. From this performance, we can hear that Rose has left behind her earlier attempts to sound like a singing cowgirl and instead has developed a strong chest voice supported by an open-throat technique. She can carry her chest voice well above the usual break between registers as well as demonstrate a flexible approach to tone with the larynx rising and falling with the contours of the melody. Gone are the days when she attempted to sing with a light, airy head register. Instead, she has developed a roadhouse vocality that brings the elements of southern singing into an environment of displacement for her live audience of Okies.

Even though this recording demonstrates that Maddox was a mature singer with a developed chest voice, it is important to keep in mind that she would have been unable to develop her vocal techniques without the use of microphone technology. To be heard in those rowdy roadhouses and large ballrooms—which could house up to five thousand patrons—Maddox relied on amplification, especially when she sang in the lower and, hence, quieter range of the chest voice.

Even when she employed a belting technique of singing melodies of a higher range in her chest voice, she would still need amplification. With an open-throat approach, Maddox also included elements of nasal twang in her vocal delivery to carry the voice to those seats in the back of the dance hall or roadhouse.[30] As noted, nasal-twang timbres produce bright, brassy, and high-frequency vocal tones. In a high-volume, live context, Maddox had to learn how to sing loudly and somewhat aggressively even with the microphone. Before World War II, the family band had only one speaker and a microphone. When the ensemble expanded to include additional players, they added two more microphones and pickups for the guitars, fiddle, and mandolin so they could be heard in the large dance halls.[31] Sonically rivaling the electric string instruments of the ensemble, Maddox cultivated a vibrant, resonant, and brassy chest voice intended for amplification as well as the architectural space of the roadhouse.

On the recording Maddox describes the relationship between music and place: "There's a real hot spot on the Waterloo Road, got a hillbilly band called Maddox and Rose." She sings the vocal melody, which lies comfortably in her chest range, in a fast, clipped manner while articulating crisp consonants and speech-like vowels indicative of her southern accent. Keeping pace with the upbeat tempo of the band and competing against a soundscape of thumping and amplified string instruments, she projects loudly and produces a brassy, ringing tone. Moreover, her flexible approach enables her to employ a range of vocal devices such as hiccups (on the second syllable of "woogie" of "boogie-woogie") and slides to create an impression of musical excess and elation. For example, she embellishes the conclusion of the first verse by stretching out the first syllable of "Friday" with a vocal slide of twangy brightness, underlining the fact that the end of the work week is a moment of celebration for her target audience in George's Playhouse.

For those melodies that extend to her higher range, Maddox's belting technique is evident. In the second phrase of the song, which describes how the Maddoxes' boogie-woogie "will wiggle your toes," Maddox belts an ascending line that climbs to the highest note (the blue note B-flat$_4$) located in the upper middle range of the alto voice. However, she does not tighten the throat to the point of producing an overly strained or nasal tone, like Kitty Wells or Hank Williams, in order to reach the higher note. Though some strain nonetheless results from a raised larynx and ascending to the highest note of the melody, Maddox resorts to almost shouting the lyrics. The singer continued to project her characteristic roadhouse vocality in a number of blues and rockabilly tunes and later in honky-tonk songs. As discussed later in the chapter, her vocal style of belting combined with the brassy timbres of nasal twang had a lasting influence on women in honky-tonk and rockabilly in the California music scene.

The Theatrics of the Dance Hall

As evident in their recording of "George's Playhouse Boogie," the Maddox Brothers and Rose developed a lasting reputation for their riveting, highly energized stage shows, which recalled the musical and theatrical legacy of the nineteenth-century saloon.[32] Providing an escape from the rigidity of industrial modernity and the concerns of dislocation, the saloon has historically fostered a festive atmosphere of drinking and music for a newly emerging working-class clientele in urban areas and small western towns. The nineteenth-century saloon keeper typically acted as the host by leading his drinking patrons in song and revelry and by hiring musicians to contribute to the merriment. Some saloons expanded to include concert rooms to entertain large crowds in what would become the concert saloon. "The lines between a small convivial gathering of workingmen and other theatrical enterprises such as minstrelsy and museum shows," according to Gillian Rodger, "began to blur as saloonkeepers moved into larger venues and presented daily shows on a raised stage."[33] Influenced by British music hall and Parisian musical taverns, the concert saloon provided an assortment of instrumental and vocal entertainment that drew on lowbrow humor, burlesque, and nostalgic sentiments: blackface skits and songs, ethnic numbers, prurient displays of scantily clad chorus girls, and female and male singers performing maudlin ballads about home and loss. After the end of Prohibition in 1933, the working class and the displaced would again gravitate toward communal meeting places like the honky-tonk or roadhouse, successors of the saloon.

The Maddox Brothers and Rose's stage shows incorporated the theatrical traditions of the nineteenth-century concert saloon in parodic and outrageous performances of well-known country songs, leaving their audience mesmerized. As Maddox explained, "We had more people come just stand and watch us than ever had to dance. The dance halls would be packed halfway back, at least halfway, and you get three, four, and 5,000 people in those dance halls . . . just standing and watching us, because we had a show of some kind going on on every single song."[34] One of the most famous examples is their stage performance of "Philadelphia Lawyer," Woody Guthrie's 1930s ballad. Guthrie helped radicalize a white migrant identity in Southern California with songs like "Philadelphia Lawyer" that served as political warnings to the elite who preyed on the disadvantaged.[35] A big-city lawyer attempts to lure a "Hollywood maid" (perhaps a displaced southern woman working in the service industry) away from her marriage to a gun-toting, "wild cowboy" named Bill (possibly a dangerous Okie). Before the lawyer is successful in his seduction, the menacing western character puts a punitive end to the exploitative designs of this upper-middle-class figure. As implied in the last verse, the cowboy shoots and kills the lawyer—"There's one less Philadelphia lawyer in old Philadelphia tonight."[36]

The Maddoxes' performance bursts into comic incongruity—histrionics combined with vocal practices that capture the familiarity of home—in painting a picture of exploitation and class division.[37] Rose, narrating the tale, draws explicitly on the conventions of southern vernacular singing.[38] Unlike her more relaxed approach and belting style in "George's Playhouse," she inflects her vocal tone with a strained nasal-twang timbre in the higher range of her chest voice. Throughout her singing career, Maddox could modify her use of twang in respect to brightness of tone and nasal inflections. Here she constricts her throat muscles, raises and tightens the larynx, and keeps the tongue in a high, flat position, all of which propel the sound to vibrate in the nose.[39] With physical strain, she infuses her melodic lines with acoustic tension and underlines the narrative of the ballad, making clear the narrator's southern origins.

Against Maddox's traditional manner of performance, the members of the band dramatized the plot with thespian flare before a live audience. Don, wearing a stovetop hat, played the part of the lawyer in pantomime. In the role of the gun-toting cowboy, Henry tried to shoot the "lawyer" with a water pistol, causing Don to jump into Bud Duncan's arms. But the water from the fake gun accidentally hit Fred, who fell to his death. Fred immediately arose and rushed to the microphone with Cal and Rose to sing the closing verse that declared the death of the lawyer in three-part harmony.[40] Rose's strident-sounding vocal timbre combined with the harmony singing of Cal's high tenor voice of noticeable nasal strain and Fred's bass vocal part. The family ensemble thus combined the sonic codes of country traditionalism with the staged theatrics of saloon culture in their rendition of "Philadelphia Lawyer" to reach their target audience of southern plains migrants, who were most likely enthralled by the entire performance.

The pronounced hyperbole in their stage shows often extended to Rose Maddox's performative caricatures of prominent country entertainers. Vocally, she would magnify the buffoonery of the rube by bringing the singing practices of the hillbilly developed in barn-dance radio to an Okie audience. Her vocal caricatures of prominent performers included Hank Williams, Hank Thompson, and Lulu Belle. Susan A. Glenn has argued that mimetic humor, especially the impersonations of well-known performers, has long been the province of female comics of the popular stage. Incorporating an eclectic array of music in her imitative parodies, Maddox moved in and out of character in a "fantasy of the fluid self."[41] She could forge versions of womanhood that flouted social normativity by questioning the gender norms of domesticity and by highlighting the ways in which Okie women and migrant culture still maintained their outsider status even after World War II.

Unlike in the Depression years, white migrants who had left the agricultural industry to serve in World War II or work in wartime production plants were thought of no longer as unwanted introducers but as valuable laborers. They thus came out of the Second World War with money in their pockets and the economic means to make California into a stable home. But they did not immediately relinquish their transplanted identities and assimilate into the middle-class culture. As La Chapelle mentions, after World War II, Okie musicians and fans were intent on maintaining "a more cohesive sense of working-class community" largely "because of their experience in California as scapegoats."[42] At this time, the Maddox Brothers and Rose continued to perform music that not only resonated with their audience of transplanted whites in California and likely elsewhere but also exaggerated the social and gendered politics of the roadhouse's live-performative context.

The Maddoxes' cover of Hank Williams's "Honky-Tonkin'" (1948) is a parody that magnifies the sexual metaphors that are often used to define the working class, in this case, those who frequent the honky-tonk, a site known for drinking, dancing, and momentary sexual encounters.[43] In the original, Williams plays the role of a gigolo who attempts to lure a woman away from her potentially unhappy relationship to the licentious honky-tonk.[44] When she is "sad and lonely," Williams promises to be her sexual escort for an evening of "honky-tonkin'." He explains that the evening's pleasures will be at her monetary expense, underlining the fact that the honky-tonk can serve as a marketplace where pleasures can be bought and sold. In the refrain, Williams's vocal performance highlights the sexual atmosphere of the juke joint: "We'll go honky-tonkin', honky-tonkin', honky-tonkin', honey baby." He emphatically sings "honky-tonkin'" with a vocal ascent that showcases his vocal break between his chest register and falsetto, a sonic device that can represent the libidinal cries of pleasure.[45] Butting against prevalent models of masculinity, such as the 1950s images of men as the family breadwinners, Williams enacts the part of the philanderer who offers fleeting sexual retreats from the middle-class mores of the era.

The Maddox Brothers and Rose released their cover in 1949, which became one of their most successful recordings, likely for the ways they offer an inside joke about the honky-tonk's sexual excesses. In assuming the vocal role of the protagonist, Maddox simply does not play the part of the honky-tonk angel, the alluring but wanton woman promising an evening of corporeal pleasure. Instead, her use of grotesque humor lampoons the heterosexual rituals within the honky-tonk itself. In the song's refrain, Maddox underlines the repeated usage of the word "honky-tonkin'" with a magnified use of nasality combined with vocal growls, vocal hiccups, and whistles. Maddox nasally growls out the first syllable of "honky" and imitates Williams's vocal break on the second syllable, accompanied by the whistles of another band member. Taken together, the family ensemble turns the word "honky-tonkin'" into the sound of a braying donkey, thereby infusing the sexual atmosphere of the juke joint with comic displays of barnyard noises that suggest animalistic desire.

The Maddoxes' performance makes the very act of "honky-tonkin'" into a satiric show of the sexual codes that are often mapped onto the bodies of the working class. As Sherry Ortner and Beverley Skeggs have each argued, exaggerated examples of carnal desire were thought to belong to the uncontrolled, undisciplined bodies of the low Other in American society. In particular, working-class women have been cast as the bearers of a heightened sexuality positioned against the expectations of middle-class respectability and bodily restraint.[46] In this context, Maddox overstates the sexual yearnings of those patrons of the working-class tavern in a musical burlesque that inflates the stereotypes of white migrants to the point of rupture, making the assumptions about Okie and working-class women and men unbelievable and unconvincing. She invites her audience members to join in this rebellious humor, which can help shake off the Depression-era perceptions of class dispossession and shame and, at the same time, assert a southern presence that middle-class Californians would recognize. In other words, Maddox makes it clear that the cultural noises of the southern displaced were not going to fade into the backdrop of suburban upward mobility but rather retain the distinct markers of class politics and dislocation.

Rose Maddox Plays the Wench in the Dance Hall

In addition to her parody of Hank Williams's "Honky-Tonkin'," Maddox offered a 1951 rendition of Lulu Belle's "Wish I Was a Single Girl Again," a song that had become popular in the 1930s. As discussed in chapter 2, Lulu Belle played the part of the unruly hillbilly comedienne who challenged the dictates of normativity. Her performance of this well-known number derived from James Cox Beckel's nineteenth-century wench-like song "I Wish I Were Single Again," designed for the popular stage. Maddox, in her imitation of Lulu Belle, participated in the long history of women assuming the wench role and, in that process, enacting models of womanhood that contest gender conventions.

Maddox's rendition of "I Wish I Was a Single Girl Again" recalls Lulu Belle's use of humor including her pronounced nasality, regional accent, and hillbilly dialect. But there are some significant differences between the two singers' individual approaches to singing. Whereas Lulu Belle's vocal technique combines head and chest resonances throughout the song, Maddox projects a predominant strong chest that works to amplify the song's parodic tone. Since Maddox sings the song in a slightly higher key than Lulu Belle does, we hear the effort it takes for the singer to push the chest voice well above the vocal break. For the opening line, "when I was single," Maddox wails the higher-pitched melody, producing a loud, strident tone. Similar to Lulu Belle's phrasing, however, Maddox drops to a lower range to sing a descending slide on the word "single," underlining her regional pronunciation by elongating a long *a* vowel followed by a pronounced nasal *n*. From the start, she, like Lulu Belle, highlights the gendered binds of a southern woman who cannot envision an escape from the restrictions of marriage and domesticity.

Along with her belting cry and distinct nasal-twang timbre, she uses word painting by means of vocal register to call attention to the comic tone of the narrative. In the opening line, where she explains that she was "afraid" she wouldn't find a husband, Maddox depicts vocally the meaning of the lyrics. For the word "afraid," she quickly sings the first syllable in a quieter head voice in her higher range and lingers on the second syllable in her lower range with a tremolo to give the impression that she is shaking with fear. Moreover, she calls attention to the actions of the uncaring and uncouth husband who "chaws tobacco" and "snores in his sleep" by breaking to her head voice on the word "tobacco," decorating the word "snore" with a descending nasal slide in her chest voice, and increasing the volume on the elongated *e* of "sleep." Fred also interjects his usual witty remarks to underline further the tone of marital strife. After Rose sings, "I wish I was a single girl again," he responds with "I wish I was a single boy again" and takes the side of the husband with the comment, "Good for him," when Rose complains that her husband insists she do the household chores. The deployment of these vocal devices enables Maddox to put on a rural and regional mask of theatricality, a "hick face," to challenge the gendered strictures of dominant society. For unruly hillbilly women of the stage, marriage and domesticity are not sacred arenas of idealized femininity. Rather they are cultural forms of contestation that highlight gender strife and conflict.

The band's instrumental accompaniment not only adds to Maddox's comedic performance of "I Wish I Was a Single Girl Again" but also helps make the song relevant to a 1950s audience of women. From the moment that Cal's harmonica playing introduces the melody, the ensemble highlights the conviviality of string-band music. Handclaps or knee slaps can be heard in time to the music, suggesting the bodily engagement and fun of perhaps a square dance or hoedown, thereby turning the dance hall into a barn dance. The fiddle—the primary instrument of square dances—cements this musical image by joining the acoustic texture and playing melodic fragments that complement the vocal line. For the first instrumental verse, Henry's tremolo picking on the unplugged mandolin purposely evokes the southern roots of the family band.

Yet as the tune unfolds, the music pulls the piece from the southern barn dance to the West Coast dance hall, thereby encapsulating the sonic experience of migration for its displaced audience. For the second instrumental verse, the electric steel guitar plays a syncopated blues-inflected melody, and the electric guitar supplants the fiddle part to play single-line runs to Rose's vocal part for the following the verse. The particular soundscape of blending a hillbilly string-band aesthetic with the stylistic idioms of western swing helps direct Maddox's parodic performance of gender and region to her 1950s audience of women, including transplants, who must have been feeling the ideological pressures of domesticity.

In this musical arrangement, Maddox exaggerates her rendition of the uncouth yet purposefully defiant southern woman, thereby underlining the uneasy relationship between Okie women and middle-class codes of decorum. As M. Alison Kibler has argued, "comic women who violate gender codes call attention to the artificiality of femininity but are also open to attack for their deviation from the norm."[47] For dominant society, Maddox's performances confirmed the lingering Depression-era perceptions of the displaced: depraved Okies who failed to leave behind their stigmatized southern roots to embrace the taste, manners, and ambitions of white middle-class Californians. Yet her hyperbolic illustrations of southern and gendered rebellion could offer an important counterpoint to the social marginalization of white migrant culture. As in her performance of "Honky-Tonkin'," audience members could understand Maddox's performance not as a realistic portrait of displaced migrants from the southern plains but as an exaggerated version blown up beyond belief. The heightened depictions helped create distance between the lived, personal experiences of migration and the caricatures of rural transplants from a premodern and backward culture unable to adapt to modern urbanity and industrialism. By extension, women who had worked in wartime industries (many of whom were white migrants from the southern plains and the Midwest) could find Maddox's musical acts of comic rebellion a necessary form of subversion against the emerging social confines of the post–World War II era.

The same year that Maddox released "I Wish I Was a Single Girl Again" she recorded "(Pay Me) Alimony" (1951), another song with roots in the theatrical traditions of the nineteenth-century popular stage.[48] The Maddox family reworks Bill Cox's 1934 song "Alimony Woman," an advice song to unsuspecting men whose wives had apparently turned into wretched shrews demanding divorce and alimony.[49] Even on her deathbed and beyond, the ex-wife haunts the male protagonist in her pursuit of court-ordered provisions. Besides "Alimony Woman," Cox wrote a number of songs—including "Rollin' Pin Woman" (1935) and the "Jailer's Daughter" (1934)—that featured themes of marital strife and discord, tropes that date back to blackface wench songs.[50]

Maddox's performance turns the wench-like song into an anthem of independence for women of the post–World War II era. Though the government had ended its Rosie the Riveter campaign and insisted that women relinquish their industrial and manufacturing positions, the majority of workingwomen were not eager to give up their well-paying jobs. As Elaine Tyler May demonstrates, "three out of four employed women hoped to keep working after the war, including 69 percent of the working wives."[51] Dominant society's insistence that women return to the domestic sphere overlooked the long history of women's work outside the home. Defense factory jobs had offered women higher wages in occupations usually reserved for men, unlike the gender-stratified positions (such as waitress, store clerk, and telephone operator) that women had occupied during the previous decade. Just as urban, working-class women left their low-wage and service positions for jobs as welders and riveters, white southern plains migrant women, who had worked as "fruit tramps" in the Central Valley, flocked to the shipyards and aviation factories of California's coastal cities to earn higher wages. Middle-class women were likely the ones who had left the domestic sphere to fulfill their patriotic roles during World War II. Yet even they were not convinced that they should return to the home after the war. "By the early 1950s," according to Ruth Milkman, "the number of gainfully employed women exceeded the highest wartime level," and "the rise in female employment, especially for married women, would continue throughout the postwar period."[52] Thus working-class and middle-class single and married women pushed against the ideological veneer of 1950s domestic femininity. Social commentators, in turn, grew increasingly alarmed over the desires of women to remain in the labor market. Many feared that men would return to domineering and demanding wives who would resist the social ordering of middle-class patriarchy and domesticity.[53] By exposing the social anxieties and incongruities of the years immediately following the war, Maddox's song suggests that married women need not succumb to the domestic terms of the 1950s. Unlike the complaining tone of "I Wish I Was a Single Girl Again," Maddox's performance of "(Pay Me) Alimony" offers a solution: divorce and sue for alimony.

In an arrangement that includes swing rhythms and riff-based instrumental solos, the Maddox Brothers and Rose's version of "(Pay Me) Alimony" evokes the dance hall, which, in many cases, was a homosocial place where women who worked in wartime production factories could spend their leisure time dancing to their favorite western swing band.[54] Emphasizing the dance rhythms, "(Pay Me) Alimony" opens to Gene Breeden's electric guitar, embellishing the melody with syncopated rhythms over the steady pulse of the rhythm guitar and upright bass. For the first instrumental verse, the lead electric guitar returns with the fiddle in duet, followed by the riff-based playing of the electric mandolin, punctuating the musical texture with rhythmically displaced blues notes connected by short, syncopated, scalar passages. Like so many of their performances, the heightened rhythmic language of the band not only recalls the physical abandonment of the 1940s dance hall but also pushes the music in the direction of rockabilly, a style of music that flouted social and musical boundaries, by which Maddox encourages her female audience to defy the 1950s gendered concept of domesticity.

Maddox begins the song by beckoning her audience of "single girls" to listen to her story about the travails of marriage. From the beginning, she inflects her melodic line with nasal twang and regional pronunciations similar in tone to "I Wish I Was a Single Girl Again." In the refrain, however, she belts the vocal line and showcases her characteristic roadhouse singing style. Maddox accentuates the repeated octave ascent on the words "to pay" by first stressing the upbeat with a percussive *t* consonant (in "to") and then leaping an octave and sustaining the word "pay" on the downbeat. Even though Maddox sings an open vowel, she still raises the larynx to hold on to that note. But she doesn't completely tighten the throat and loudly projects her vocal sound from the front of her mouth, producing a brassy, loud tone. Her singing style helps depict the narrator as a self-assertive woman who makes it clear to her female audience that they can leave their marriages with their economic standing intact. To a riveting soundscape that contributed to the emergence of rockabilly, Rose places models of Okie womanhood within the liminal site of the roadhouse, offering her listeners a musical means to resist or at least question the conventional definitions of domestic femininity that had arisen during the postwar era.

The Most Colorful Hillbilly Band in America

With their entertaining stage shows that offered vignettes of satire and critiques of gender and class norms and underscored the pleasures of dancing, the Maddox Brothers and Rose emerged as not only a prominent regional act but also a national phenomenon as the "Most Colorful Hillbilly Band in America." After establishing themselves in the San Joaquin Valley, the Maddox ensemble moved to Hollywood in 1949 to perform in luxurious dance halls, including the Riverside Rancho, and on leading television programs, such as *Town Hall Party* and *Hometown Jamboree*. Country music fans of various backgrounds, not just Okies in California, appreciated their lively, boisterous acts. They joined a community of country performers in Southern California that included Merle Travis, Tex Ritter, Ferlin Husky, Joe and Rose Lee Maphis, Carolina Cotton, and Spade Cooley. The family band also established itself outside the region on prominent radio programs such as Shreveport's *Louisiana Hayride* on KWKH, which had launched the careers of many country stars, notably Hank Williams and Elvis Presley.[55] In addition, the family band made transcriptions of a radio show that KWKH would broadcast at 6:45 a.m. and at 12:05 a.m. each morning and night. The broadcast, reaching the South and the Midwest, would advertise their live performance dates throughout these regions. After their Saturday-night appearance on *Louisiana Hayride* and Sunday taping sessions for KWKH, the ensemble would perform live for the rest of the week throughout Texas, Alabama, and Mississippi and up to Washington, D.C., expanding their audience.

For two years (beginning in 1952), the Maddox Brothers and Rose would appear on KWKH and tour the nightclubs and dance halls of the South for four months out of the year, and then return to California to appear on television broadcasts and in dance halls, exposure that contributed to their growing reputation.[56] As the trade magazine *Hillbilly & Western Hoedown* proclaimed, "The 'Hayride' boasts a talent roster that reads like the 'Who's Who' in country music." And the Maddox Brothers and Rose were well-known regulars, billed as "one of the most colorful hillbilly bands in America."[57]

In addition to their dynamic, theatrical performances, their newly donned matching western-style costumes helped cement their national reputation. Created by Nathan Turk, the brightly colored creations were embroidered with ornate patterns of vines, flowers, and cactuses that predated Nudie Cohn's rhinestone-studded suits, which characterized the ostentatious and also androgynous look of popular artists like Elvis and many male country performers such as Webb Pierce and Porter Wagoner. But at this time, it was unusual to see a country act appear in flashy stage wear. In fact, the country music industry appeared shocked at the ways in which the Maddoxes' attire made a spectacle of their growing success (see figure 10).

Figure 10. The Maddox Brothers and Rose. Four Star Records publicity photograph, 1947.

When the management of the Grand Ole Opry invited the Maddox Brothers and Rose to appear on Nashville's barn-dance program in 1949, their stage costumes seemed to outshine their actual musical performance. For their southeastern audience, Rose, Cal, and Fred sang in three-part harmony the gospel song "Gathering Flowers for the Master's Bouquet," offering a performance connected to southern vernacular tradition and devoid of their usual theatrics. Yet the master of ceremonies, Red Foley, and his comic sidekick Rod Brasfield fixated on the band's over-the-top glitzy wear instead of the performers' rendition of a solemn hymn. After the performance, Brasfield exclaimed: "Ain't they the dressed-uppest bunch of folks you ever seen? Look at them grapes on them britches." Foley, appearing dumbfounded by the dress of the family band and hardly able to comment on the actual music, simply murmured in response to Brasfield's exclamations, "They got grapes and vines and flowers all over."[58]

Their ornate attire came to signal the conspicuous consumption of the working class and contrasted not only with the somber gray suits and muted pastel dresses of the middle class but also with the country music industry's pursuit of respectability in the 1950s.[59] While the country music business (especially in Nashville) strove to shed its lowbrow status in the mass-mediated popular-music market, it attempted to shape its female and male musicians into individuals who adhered to the social values and appearances of dominant society (further discussed in chapter 7). Even when Webb Pierce started to wear the ostentatious costumes of Nudie Cohn in the mid-1950s, the country music trade press tried to pull the performer into the aesthetic realm of bourgeois moderation and taste.

In a similar strategy, the country music industry attempted to downplay the flamboyant presence of the Maddox Brothers and Rose by locating their commercial success in a narrative of propriety and social and geographical mobility. *Country Song Roundup*'s article "From Southern Rags to Western Riches" encapsulated these dueling tensions of simultaneously marketing and taming the Maddoxes' performative image. The article unequivocally stated, "A true 'rags-to-riches' story is the history of the Maddox Bros. and Rose—one of the most colorful, and certainly the most unusual of the Western and hillbilly bands in America!" Their singularity involved their personal story of migration and escape from laboring in California's agribusiness by breaking into the country music business and becoming one of "the highest paid Western and hillbilly bands in the U.S." The article stressed the dramatic tale of the Maddoxes' economic mobility, noting that they toured the country in "their own Cadillacs instead of ancient Fords. And instead of their once patched-up clothes, each ha[d] over 25 complete changes of wardrobe with a total value of $15,000."

The article continued by explaining that the ensemble's impressive and striking accomplishments were linked to their moral character grounded in "perseverance, hard work, loyalty to Mom, and to music." These admirable traits, noted in the unflashy terms of diligence and propriety, provided a contrast to the family band's theatrical stage antics and personas. The article thus suggested that their success had little to do with their riveting shows, which blended different styles of popular music with stagy flair and drew thousands to their performances. Rather, "all their success [was] due to Mom's coaching and advising on their every move." With "Mom Maddox" looming "in the background," the image of the Maddox Brothers and Rose was pulled from a live-performance context of working-class honky-tonks and roadhouses to a familial setting of togetherness and steadfastness in the face of grave challenges—a respectable account of achievement.[60]

Despite the country music industry's ambition to elevate and sanitize the sound and look of the family ensemble, the Maddox band still reminded its audience of its class and regional identity in California and emphasized its material success. The Maddoxes' glitzy appearance, theatrics, and rhythmically driven music that accompanied Rose's distinct singing voice clearly announced that they, along with their Okie audience, had not only survived the geographical and economic hardships of the Depression era but also found their economic and social footing. Instead of going back home or quietly accepting the social and aesthetic tropes of the middle class, the Maddox Brothers and Rose flaunted their newly acquired standing not only within the social fabric of California but also in the country music industry.

The Influence of Rose Maddox

Rose Maddox's career, however, came to surpass the theatrics of her family band as she became a solo singer. During the 1950s, in general, the country music industry as well as the popular-music industry moved away from producing and marketing ensembles to focusing on solo performers. In 1952, when the Maddox ensemble left Four Star Records for a recording contract with Columbia Records, Rose also signed with the record company as a solo artist capable of recording in a range of styles, including gospel, honky-tonk, rockabilly, and rhythm and blues. With her growing reputation in the 1950s, the country music industry not only singled Rose out as the star of the Maddox Family and Rose but also considered her one of the most successful female soloists in country music. In 1954, the regular column "Women in the News" in the country music trade magazine *Cowboy Songs* reported, "Rose Maddox, talented-young singing star, is one of the top female vocalists in the Country entertainment world" as well as the "featured vocalist with the popular group known as the 'Maddox Brothers and Rose.'" The article continued by focusing on Maddox's solo recordings: "Besides recording with her brothers, Rose has a contract with Columbia

Records by herself and has cut such numbers as 'I'd Rather Die Young,' 'I'm a Little Red Caboose,' 'Kiss Me Like Crazy,' 'Just One More Time' and her latest, 'The Birthday Card Song,' backed with 'Breathless Love.'"[61]

By the mid 1950s, Maddox had left the family band, and the country music industry continued to embrace her as a major soloist. In 1956, *Country & Western Jamboree* declared that Maddox was one of the "best female singer(s)," ranking number six (after Kitty Wells, Jean Shepard, Wanda Jackson, Anita Carter, and June Carter) and rising to number three in the category of "best female sacred singer" (after Martha Carson and Kitty Wells).[62] While announcing her "split" with "her brothers," the trade magazine declared, "Rose has a great poignancy in her voice, not quite evident in her work with the former group."[63]

The noted poignancy in Maddox's vocal deliveries was most evident in her honky-tonk ballads, such as "I'd Rather Die Young (1953)," that focused on matters of the heart.[64] Unlike the theatrical performances of the family band, in the recording Rose renders the song in a slow tempo to an understated instrumental accompaniment. The drums, rhythm guitar, and bass softly emphasize the triple pulse, the piano embellishes the opening hook with tremolos, and the electric steel guitar and lead electric guitar quietly take turns commenting on the vocal line. In this musical context of restraint, Maddox could mediate her belting vocality with a crooning style of singing, demonstrating a marked shift from the roadhouse to the recording studio. Singing right into the microphone, Maddox begins each of the four-bar segments in her upper middle range, where she projects a chest-dominant voice with less nasal inflection in her use of twang than in her Four Star recordings with the family band. Realizing the emotional urgency of the opening lyrics, "I'd rather die young than grow old without you," Maddox's voice swells in volume as she slides up to her higher register, where a twang singing technique briefly colors the vocal timbre on the word "rather" before dropping back down to sing a hard consonant on "die" to stress the singer's commitment to her beloved. She renders the rest of the passage in her relaxed-sounding lower range, elaborating on her vocal line with languid slides and elongated vibratos. Maddox's vocal approach is consistent throughout the song: her legato phrasing continually juxtaposes an impassioned belting voice against a soft crooning one that utters the last note of the verse in a quiet, lilting head voice. With an artful use of timbre, range, and register, Maddox underscores an expressive range of emotion: the intensity and tender sentiments that represent love.

Maddox's performance career in the dance halls of California, on radio, and as a recording artist had a bearing on the musical directions of West Coast country music, specifically for women performers. Following the release of Maddox's "I'd Rather Die Young," Jean Shepard released the same song for Capitol Records, demonstrating the influence of Maddox's singing style.

Shepard, originally from Oklahoma, migrated with her large family (parents and ten siblings) to Visalia, California, in 1943. At the beginning of her career in country music, she performed with an all-female western swing band, the Melody Ranch Girls, in which she played drums, string bass, and guitar, and also developed a resonant vocal style. According to *Country & Western Jamboree*, the Melody Ranch Girls were known for their riveting shows: "The musical femmes, to the envy of many a male maestro, soon had dance halls filled to overflowing with terpsichoreans who stepped it up to the girls' breezy Western swing."[65] As a successful western swing ensemble, the Melody Ranch Girls appeared on the radio and played for dances in various nightspots while sharing billings with other well-known country bands. On one such occasion, they "played on the same bill as Hank Thompson and his Brazos Valley Boys who had already made a name for themselves on the West coast," as reported in *Country Music People*. Thompson took note of Shepard's "clear, rich voice" and introduced the young performer to Ken Nelson, the head of the country music division of Los Angeles–based Capitol Records, the same label that had signed Thompson and would continue to produce important California country acts.[66] By 1953, Shepard had emerged as a recording artist at the same time that Maddox was establishing herself as a solo artist with Columbia Records in Los Angeles.

One of Shepard's initial successful recordings is her duet with Ferlin Husky, "A Dear John Letter," backed by her solo number "I'd Rather Die Young."[67] In comparison to Maddox's rendition of the same song, Shepard lowers the key of the song to make the most of her characteristic resonant tone in the lower range of her alto voice. The singer opens each four-bar segment with a broad sound combined with nasal-twang timbres in her chest voice, which she likely cultivated in the dance hall. Though her vocal manner points to that of Maddox, Shepard does not include Maddox's artful legato phrasing of contrasting the first half of the opening segment with that of the second half through shifts in register and timbre. Moreover, Shepard's use of nasality is heard throughout the song. She accentuates nasal consonants, such as *n* (as in "young" of the eponymous phrase) and vowels, such as the long *oo* (as in "you" and "do" at the end of phrases). When she belts the line "so don't ever leave me," she reaches for the higher range of the melody on the words "don't" and "ever" by maximizing the projection of her voice using nasal-twang techniques.

Like Maddox, Shepard learned how to combine belting and twang techniques to project the upper range of her chest voice while relying on microphone technology to amplify the lower and quieter tones of her register. With a flexible larynx, her singing voice was one of clarity and resonance, as evidenced from the repeated comments on Shepard's voice by the country music trade press. *Country & Western Jamboree* stated, "On-stage the capable young blonde reaches out magnificently over an entire audience with a surprisingly resonant voice," despite her small physical stature of five feet and weight of ninety-nine pounds.[68] *Country Song Roundup* declared that Shepard had "one of the biggest and best voices ever to sing on [the] stage of the world famous Grand Ole Opry."[69] *Folk and Country Songs* went into even more detail about the effects of her "full, rich voice," noting, "[It's] bound to reach—and touch—the listener. Tunes like 'Crying Steel Guitar Waltz' and 'I'd Rather Die Young' show Jean's vocal qualities to their fullest."[70]

As a promising young recording artist, Shepard joined Red Foley's *Ozark Jubilee* in Springfield, Missouri, a radio program that rivaled the success of the *Grand Ole Opry*. Soon afterward, Shepard (at the age of nineteen) also appeared on the *Opry*, and she eventually became a regular performer. Thus by 1955, she had joined Kitty Wells and Goldie Hill in establishing women's honky-tonk in Nashville (further discussed in chapter 6). In contrast to Wells's strained and constricted vocality in the upper chest range, Shepard wielded a broader sounding voice. Yet Shepard's vocal diction still underlined southern idioms of nasal-twang timbres and pronunciations, making it clear that her narratives about the contradictions and complexities of female sexual desire and agency in the modern style of honky-tonk were from the perspective of a southern white working-class woman.

Apart from Maddox and Shepard, Rose Lee Maphis was a recording artist and performer with a style of singing that resembled Maddox's belting roadhouse style and Shepard's resonant chest voice. Maphis, however, started her career singing in barn-dance radio in the late 1930s. When she moved to Southern California with her husband, guitarist Joe Maphis, they performed in the local dance halls and on Los Angeles television shows, notably *Town Hall Party*. With the Maddox Brothers and Rose also performing in Los Angeles, Rose Maddox and Rose Lee Maphis appeared in the same venues. Joe Maphis even played guitar on some of the Maddoxes' recordings for Columbia Records.

The Maphises signed with Capitol Records and recorded in a variety of country styles that typically showcased Joe's instrumental virtuosity on the guitar and other string instruments in narratives about the ideals and discord of romantic love. Just as the Maddox Brothers and Rose acted with theatrical flair in the roadhouse, Joe and Rose Lee often played the part of the vaudevillian husband-and-wife team and inflected a number of their duets with humor and slapstick conventions. But their most successful song was the 1953 honky-tonk ballad "Dim Lights, Thick Smoke (and Loud, Loud Music)," a dramatic tale of the honky-tonk angel as a wanton woman of sexual excess who stood in stark contrast to the 1950s ideal of domestic femininity. Rose Lee also recorded, as a soloist, songs in the honky-tonk ballad style, such as "Your Old Love Letters" (previously recorded by Jim Reeves) and "I'm Willin' to Try" (written by Joe Maphis for Rose Lee).

In "I'm Willin' to Try," for example, Maphis vocally portrays a female subject in the process of deciding whether to end a romantic entanglement. Maphis, like her California peers, has a resonant, full-bodied alto voice.[71] From the beginning of the song, she vocally depicts the protagonist's emotional angst with an expressive chest voice as she wails in its upper register, slides to and from notes, inflects the melodic line with vocal tears or glottal stops, and ends phrases with the use of vibrato, giving the sonic impression of weeping. Since Maphis's song is pitched higher than Shepard's "I'd Rather Die Young," she at times strains for the higher notes of the melody and employs vocal slides of stepwise motion to propel her voice to and from the melodic apexes. Though she still incorporates twangy timbres in her higher chest register, Maphis's resonant vocal tone includes less nasal twang than Shepard's and even Maddox's.

Contrasting with the previously edgy vocal tones in her higher register, Maphis sings comfortably in her lower range the concluding line, "I don't know what I'll do without you, but I'm willin' to try," thereby projecting a warm tone of ease that underlines the subject's emotional resilience. By the end of the verse, the subject decides that she will be the one who leaves the relationship. Even if Maddox did not directly influence Maphis's aesthetic and vocal choices, it can be said that a distinct vocal style emerged in California country music. In the 1950s, women country performers sang with resonant chest timbres and belting voices that signified a level of strength and power in their depictions of female subjects negotiating the terms and conditions of patriarchy and adult love.

Maddox's success as a performer of a range of styles also played a part in the emerging commercial visibility of female rockabilly artists. Coming from a blues-inflected background, Maddox persisted in establishing herself within the musical landscape of rockabilly right before 1950s California music erupted with a community of female rockabilly artists, such as Laura Lee Perkins, Lorrie Collins, Jackie DeShannon, and Wanda Jackson.[72] Beyond the California scene, Janis Martin and Brenda Lee were also stars of this southern blues-based style. Among her female peers, however, Maddox was one of the first to record rockabilly tunes as a solo artist in 1955 and 1956 with songs like "Wild, Wild Young Men," "Hey Little Dreamboat," "Looky There Over There," and "Old Man Blues."[73] Brenda Lee, for example, did not make a name for herself in rockabilly until her 1957 hit "Dynamite." Moreover, unlike Lee and others, Maddox didn't sound like a teenage girl rebelling against an older generation. Instead, her mature singing voice offered the sonic impression of an adult woman embracing the sexual frankness and pleasures associated with the hybrid style—an image that stood in stark contrast to dominant definitions of 1950s womanhood.

Maddox, for example, recorded Ruth Brown's rhythm-and-blues number "Wild, Wild Young Men" as a soloist in 1955 for Columbia Records.[74] In her version of the song, she projects her characteristic resonant voice and makes use of the vocal techniques associated with rockabilly—hiccups, growls, vibrato, and slides—to underscore the fevered context of female desire for young men who drink and dance to the grooves of rhythm and blues. The basic melodic contour of each phrase follows a typical blues pattern of descending from the highest note to the lowest, encouraging Maddox to punctuate the beginning of her vocal passages with loud, open-throat cries in her upper midrange, which reaches to B-flat$_4$. Launching into the song without instrumental accompaniment, Maddox makes the most of her vocal delivery by stretching and embellishing the title words with a pronounced descending slide on the word "wild," emphasizing the objects of desire, attractive young men.

The blues number continually rises in intensity with Maddox singing of how the bodily displays of these wild young men unleash a deep level of carnal yearning in the female protagonist. Taking her voice to new heights to describe the men's dance movements—"they can romp and stomp . . . they can do the bop"—Maddox punctuates the end of the short vocal passages with an ascending vocal slide from B-flat$_4$ to D$_5$. In so doing, she practically shouts the words "stomp" and "bop," as if she has lost all vocal composure in her rapturous state. She continues to sing in her higher range to describe the delirious setting of intoxicated male bodies that beckon the female narrator. In the closing line, "Well, mercy, mercy ain't that a shame, wild, wild young men scandalize my name," she repeats her ascending vocal slides to the higher range to underline the words "shame" and "scandalize." Her irrepressible vocals emphasize the fact that her lustful longing far outweighs any consideration of maintaining female respectability and restraint. She thus embraces the scandalous pleasures that have marred her reputation.

Maddox's vocal nuances and sexually explicit songs had a significant bearing on the dynamic vocals and song material of Wanda Jackson in particular.[75] Jackson, who migrated from Oklahoma to California in the 1940s with her family, fell under the spell of western swing and admired its woman performers. As she herself proclaimed, "It was in Los Angeles that I was introduced to western swing music. . . . As I watched the female singers in their shiny clothes, I knew at the age of six that I was going to be a 'girl singer.'"[76] Specifically, she recalled seeing the Maddox Brothers and Rose in performance, recalling, "They were so energetic; for those days it was very unusual." But mostly Jackson was impressed with Rose: "I learned all of her songs. She was very instrumental in my career, my singing style, because I liked her feistiness."[77]

Admiring the performative style of Maddox, Jackson started to pursue her musical interests after World War II, when her family had returned to Oklahoma.

While still a teenager, she had her own radio show on KPLR in Oklahoma City.[78] As with Shepard, Hank Thompson took note of Jackson's singing voice, invited her to perform with his western swing band, and helped her secure a recording contract with Decca in 1954. She soon gained national recognition, toured with Elvis Presley in 1955, and became a regular on Red Foley's prominent ABC network TV program *Ozark Jubilee* from 1954 to 1957. Her manager, Jim Halsey, then steered her away from Decca Records to Capitol Records, a recording label known for its recording and promotion of California's country music.[79] She thus joined Shepard and Maphis on the Los Angeles label, recording both rockabilly and honky-tonk songs. (In 1959, Maddox also signed with Capitol Records.) By 1956, the trade magazine *Country & Western Jamboree* reported that Jackson was number one for "Best New Female Singer" in country music and came in third place for "Best Female Singer," after Kitty Wells and Jean Shepard.[80]

With the support of Ken Nelson at Capitol Records, Jackson recorded her rockabilly hits, such as "Hot Dog! That Made Him Mad" (1957) and "Fujiyama Mama" (1957). The latter explicitly likens female sexuality to Japan's explosive volcanoes and the atom bombs the United States had dropped on Nagasaki and Hiroshima during World War II. While depicting the dangers of a volatile female libido, Jackson's performance refers to the nuclear destruction of the past and magnifies the current core anxieties and fears of the new Cold War era, otherwise known as the Atomic Age, a period of grave anxiety fueled by the threats of political and social disorder and nuclear annihilation. Dwight Eisenhower's militaristic strategies of political "containment," according to historian Michael Kimmel, translated into an ethos of social containment that enforced normality "with a desperate passion."[81] With sexuality and Communism linked to each other, any transgressive sexualities—such as female promiscuity or homosexuality—would somehow weaken the moral composition of the nation, making the United States easy prey for Communist plots. At a time when Americans were building bomb shelters in their suburban backyards, Jackson connects her licentious displays to the perils of the Atomic Age, implying that nobody is safe from the eruption of sexual chaos. She, in turn, could easily unleash the contagion of Communism and nuclear warfare. What she claims to have done in Nagasaki and Hiroshima, she can do to you, and once she starts erupting, nothing can stop her.

Like Maddox's performance of "Wild, Wild Young Men," Jackson uses the nuances of her singing voice to realize the narrative of "Fujiyama Mama."[82] From the beginning of "Fujiyama Mama," Jackson's voice takes center stage as she launches into her higher range. The instrumental ensemble of guitars and drums alternates between stop-time rhythms and punctuated riffs that respond to the singer's growling and aggressive vocals. Similar to Maddox's vocal approach, Jackson sings with a chest-dominant technique even in the upper middle range. Jackson, however, does not necessarily wield the broad-sounding, belting voice that Maddox had popularized in a variety of country styles. Rather, Jackson raises and pushes the larynx to an elevated position while, at the same time, closing the throat muscles, creating a raspy, distorted vocal tone. She, in turn, projects the voice from the front of the mouth with a tight larynx position that cuts off the resonances of the chest voice, similar to the technique of many rockabilly artists like Brenda Lee.[83] In contrast, Maddox usually sings with more lung and diaphragm support, presenting a fuller-bodied sonority. But when she makes the declaration "I'm a Fujiyama Mama," Jackson relaxes the throat muscles and projects a resonant sounding timbre in her lower range. Here Jackson makes use of an agile larynx to sing wide vocal leaps accentuated by hiccups or glottal stops, illustrating the eruptive powers of female desire. She concludes the verse with an aggressive singing style that includes growls and swoops, examples of vocal excesses that signal female eroticism.

The sexually charged performances of both Maddox and Jackson did not go unnoticed by the country music industry. In fact, both performers had to deal with the conservative performance culture of the *Grand Ole Opry*, in particular. During her solo career, Maddox returned to the *Opry* in 1956 as a guest performer. In one of her performances, she sang "Tall Men," while wearing a scanty costume (by *Opry* standards): a top that revealed her midriff, a short skirt, boots, and a cowboy hat. As she performed the song, the executives of the radio program came running to the sidelines of the stage demanding to know why nobody had insisted that she change her clothes. Brasfield, the comedian of the *Opry*, once again took delight in describing and humorously commenting on Maddox's costume for the live and radio audiences. As Maddox stated, "The audience just ate it up the way he [Brasfield] picked it up, because Red Foley didn't know what to say. . . . Women didn't do that on the Grand Ole Opry."[84] In the 1950s, Jackson also shocked the executives and the regular performers of the *Opry* with her dress of thin spaghetti straps that revealed her bare shoulders. While she was waiting backstage before her performance, Ernst Tubb insisted that Jackson change her costume for her performance. In response, she quickly threw a leather jacket over her dress so that she could still appear on the stage of the *Opry*.[85] Both women continually pushed against notions of respectability, offering models of womanhood that breached the gendered boundaries of propriety for female country performers and reminded their audiences of the bodily energy of female desire in rockabilly—a style too often thought of as masculine.

Conclusion

Rose Maddox was a key figure in the transition from the performance archetypes of barn-dance radio to dance hall culture. As she moved away from the singing cowgirl's vocal stylings to a more chest-dominant belting technique, Maddox developed a vocal style and a persona that influenced the musical directions of honky-tonk and rockabilly in the 1950s. She crafted a singing style designed to resonate in the architectural space of the juke joint or the dance hall, while she still recalled various musical idioms of the past for her audience of displaced whites. She thus not only opened up sonic and cultural possibilities for 1950s female performers in Los Angeles's country music industry, but she also contributed to some of the major developments in 1950s popular music.

Moreover, Maddox, initially with her family band, combined the fictional masks of rube buffoonery with the emerging rhythmic language and vocal idioms of rockabilly, helping forge the relationship between the rebellious hillbilly and rock 'n' roll. The dangerous southern rebel embodied by Wanda Jackson, Elvis, and Jerry Lee Lewis had its roots in the live musical productions of the Maddox Brothers and Rose. Maddox also was instrumental in the success of other key artists, notably Buck Owens, who would become the architect of the country music industry in Bakersfield. Owens not only recorded his first hits with the experienced singer ("Mental Cruelty" and "Loose Talk"); in 1969 he would also launch the television program *Hee Haw*, highlighting the grotesque humor that the Maddox Brothers and Rose had made famous in their stage shows decades earlier and which had entertained and impressed a young Owens. With these contributions to a distinct California soundscape of honky-tonk and rockabilly grounded in rube theatrics, Maddox emerged as an innovator on the performative stage and in the recording studio.

PART THREE

Nashville's Honky-Tonk and Country Music Industry

6   Voices of Angels

Kitty Wells and the Emergence of Women's Honky-Tonk

Kitty Wells burst on the country music scene in 1952 with "It Wasn't God Who Made Honky-Tonk Angels," the first song recorded by a woman to hit *Billboard*'s country music charts since its inception in 1944. An "answer song" to Hank Thompson's "Wild Side of Life" (1951), Wells's popular honky-tonk tune brought a solo woman's voice into the style's tropes of loss and desire.[1] In "Wild Side of Life," the male subject, unable to secure the promises of domesticity, ascribes the undoing of heterosexual unions to the honky-tonk angel: a sexualized woman who discards the ideals of femininity by spending her evenings in the local roadhouse. Shocked that women would prefer the convivial pleasures of nightlife to marriage and children, the protagonist bemoans the very existence of such women—"I didn't know God made honky-tonk angels." In response to Thompson's moralistic song, Wells's performance of "It Wasn't God Who Made Honky-Tonk Angels" enacts the fallen woman: a once-respectable wife who has turned into a honky-tonk angel.[2] From this subject position, Wells contends that women would be content in their domestic roles if men would only remain faithful. The infidelities of husbands, according to Wells, have driven wives away from the sanctity of marriage and to the licentious juke joint. But regardless of who is to blame for disrupting the domestic order of the 1950s, the carousing husband or the honky-tonk strumpet, the musical dialogue between Thompson and Wells makes it clear that neither protagonist can achieve domestic stability and respectability. That is, the honky-tonk itself is a symbol of the emotional and material deprivations of the working class.[3]

This chapter continues to explore country music's gendered responses to the concerns of class intersecting with those of migration. In the preceding chapter, I suggest that the performances of Rose Maddox asserted an unruly Okie identity for a displaced audience of white migrants and women in 1940s and early

1950s California. Her performative persona and vocal styling, both of which were developed in the roadhouse, helped pave the way for female honky-tonk artists to place representations of gender in the figurative working-class juke joint. In the discussion that follows, I examine the development of honky-tonk as a distinct style of music that emerged in the late 1930s and 1940s with the music of Al Dexter, Ernest Tubb, and Hank Williams. It remained a predominant form of country music after World War II, right when female artists began making recordings that drew on the honky-tonk style to voice the concerns of working-class women.

In the popular imagination, the post–World War II era was a time of economic mobility represented by domestic suburbia, where the nuclear family came to symbolize a newfound prosperity. However, despite these prominent ideologies, the United States did not quietly fall into a tranquil suburban repose, with women leaving the workforce to create a domestic haven for their war-veteran husbands. Instead, the politico-social climate of mass production and consumerism engendered great upheaval and uncertainty. For example, the working class "launched the largest strike wave in history" to challenge the emerging control of corporate liberalism; more women, including married women, entered the paid labor force than ever before; and one-quarter to one-third of the marriages contracted in the 1950s ended in divorce.[4] In the midst of these reconfigurations of class and gender, industrialism spurred massive migrations from rural areas to urban centers—in particular, the exodus out of the South to the Midwest—which would forever alter the cultural and social landscape of the United States.

To a listening audience composed of rural white transplants and a newly founded working class facing shifting gender roles, honky-tonk, I argue, disclosed the anxieties of class and displacement and undermined the basic premises of normative culture largely through metaphors of sexuality and domesticity. Of particular interest in the context of this study is the ways that women's honky-tonk of the 1950s engaged with the themes of male honky-tonk and brought representations of working-class womanhood into the style's sonic experience. Wells and her peers, Goldie Hill and Jean Shepard, contributed to a musical discourse that not only destabilized the ideals of the private sphere but also voiced the yearnings of working-class women and the painful class prejudice they experienced, which contrasted starkly with the reigning ideology of domesticity.

The Honky-Tonk, Al Dexter, and Ernest Tubb

Honky-tonk music initially flourished in the local roadhouses that emerged after the National Prohibition Act was repealed in 1933.[5] Within the newly built communities of former rural dwellers laboring in the oil fields of Texas, the honky-tonk became an emblem of displacement in its fraught relationship with modernity. For the working class, the honky-tonk and its nineteenth-century predecessor, the saloon, provided a means to counter the alienation of an increasingly mechanized society through musical entertainment, dancing, alcohol consumption, and casual sexual encounters.[6] Even though it could be a retreat from the pressures and rigidities of industrialism, the honky-tonk could also be a sordid entrapment for the downtrodden and abject and was often viewed as a site that needed to be policed by the dominant society. In fact, in 1943, Texas attempted to rein in and monitor debased and lewd behavior (indecent language, immoral activity, and violence) associated with working-class nightspots by passing the Moffett Bill, which banned the sale of alcohol in places that were deemed honky-tonks.[7]

The music that developed in such boisterous places of loud conversations possibly developing into altercations, clinking glasses, and feet shuffling on the dance floor adopted the instrumental and rhythmic components of 1930s swing: the use of amplification and melodic syncopation accompanied by a steady driving beat.[8] Western swing bands (for example, Milton Brown and His Musical Brownies and Bob Wills and His Texas Playboys) had incorporated the electric guitar and the electric steel guitar into their big-band sound of strings and, at times, horns and winds.[9] In smaller bars that could not accommodate or pay for a ten-member or larger band, tavern owners often relied on jukeboxes or smaller honky-tonk ensembles to entertain their patrons.[10] In turn, the musical conventions of honky-tonk came to feature the electric guitar and the electric steel guitar as lead instruments in addition to the fiddle and the piano. Coming from a swing music context, the lead instruments introduced and elaborated on the melody in solos and accompanied the vocal line with single-note rhythmic and melodic fragments over the insistent, driving beat of the rhythm section. Providing a boom-chuck rhythmic effect, the string bass stressed the strong beats, while the rhythm guitarist usually struck closed chords on the upbeats or backbeats, a technique known as "sock rhythm." Couples responded to this prominent steady pulse, dancing to music that ironically was lyrically focused on the fragility of romantic love.

The honky-tonk style's conceptual tie to the figurative working-class tavern, however, has prompted scholars to approach the music as an extension of an essentially masculinized domain. The "honky-tonk world," in the words of Joli Jensen, "is a man's world," a refuge from the rigidity of industrial labor.[11] Known for its raucous and homosocial atmosphere, the honky-tonk was not a "proper" or acceptable place for women, or rather for respectable women. Married women were supposedly home or at least not frequenting the neighborhood honky-tonk. Pamela Fox argues that the male honky-tonk became a "patriarchal locus delimiting women's participation . . . through nostalgia for an imaginary domesticity that signified a traditional, yet vanishing regional or home culture."[12] For men, the honky-tonk became a space for lamenting over the idealized past symbolically linked to the feminine.

Ethnomusicologist Aaron Fox also reinforces these arguments about the gendered codes of class in his study of how the representations of "a blue-blooded woman and a redneck man" play out in Texas honky-tonk. "Canonically, in thousands of songs, women wait at home with 'hungry eyes,' taking care of the children and the budget and dreaming of upward mobility, while their men carouse and drink in joyous anti-elitist solidarity." Sequestered in the domestic world, women are aligned with the lower middle class in their "embrace of respectability against the heroically disreputable male values of the labor process, shop-floor culture, military experience, and the utopian working-class space of the tavern."[13] From a male point of view, working-class wives often have been seen as middle-class agents who push their husbands and families for upper mobility and respectability.[14] Their work in the home or in the sex-segregated clerical sector or the service industries has also been aligned with consumerism and the values of the middle class.[15] In this respect, working-class women appear to defy the class-conscious roots of the working class, defined as white and male, according to Julie Bettie and Joan Acker.[16] Yet, as Nadine Hubbs reminds us, dominant society still regards working-class women as sexualized strumpets against which middle-class femininity is defined.[17] Within these double binds of class, working-class women are perceived as nagging shrews making demands on their husbands while they face the scrutinizing gaze of the middle class, which has cast them as the "bearer[s] of an exaggerated sexuality."[18] In both contexts, working-class women have suffered "the injury of invisibility" without a class-specific voice.[19]

Honky-tonk music has articulated the complexities and paradoxes of these gendered and class dynamics, in which the juke joint serves as a place of sexual and domestic negotiations. In honky-tonk, male protagonists appear to retreat from the expectations of heterosexual marriage and bemoan their failures in securing the promises of social mobility, while women are often cast as tantalizing temptresses of the honky-tonk or nagging wives of the domestic sphere. The Texas musician Al Dexter first presented these archetypical gendered and classed figures of the working-class tavern—the honky-tonk woman, the carousing husband, and the angry housewife—in narratives that pitted the domestic sphere against the sexual atmosphere of the juke joint. These particular tensions erupting from Dexter's music were fundamental not only in the honky-tonk music of other leading male artists but also in the songs of prominent female country performers.

In 1936, Dexter recorded "Honky-Tonk Blues," the first song to refer to the honky-tonk as a distinct architectural space.[20] Though some have dismissed his songs as inconsequential ditties of erotic suffering, Dexter expressed the sexual politics of the honky-tonk style with musical idioms that demonstrated the intricate relationship between country and popular music.[21] Chroniclers of country music usually focus on the ways in which Hank Williams, as a singer and songwriter, "brought the honky-tonk style to its apex."[22] Williams, combining the commercial practices of popular music with the "authentic" codes of southern vernacular traditions, spoke of the painful distinctions of southern white working-class masculinity, thereby serving as a performative model of male "hard" country in honky-tonk, the outlaw movement, and southern rock.[23] Well before the Tin Pan Alley–influenced songs and blues numbers of Hank Williams, however, Dexter drew on the instrumental and rhythmic components of swing and popular-music forms to portray his archetypical honky-tonk characters. In these narratives, Dexter demonstrated a theatrical flair for creating vignettes about the gendered dynamic of the working-class tavern. Perhaps following the traditions of the nineteenth-century saloon, in which musical performances of various kinds entertained working-class patrons, Dexter wrote self-referential songs that acted as comic-dramatic narratives of the actual space.

In "Honky-Tonk Blues," Dexter combines the heightened harmonic language typical of Tin Pan Alley with the rhythmic drive of 1930s dance music, shaping the figurative honky-tonk into a hedonistic site of sexual desire. Dexter's baritone melody opens to the chugging chords of the rhythm guitar and the syncopated melodic lines of the lead electric guitar as he explains in the opening phrases that he is afflicted with the "honky-tonk blues" in his yearning for his "honky-tonky baby girl." After declaring the object of his desire, the subject underlines his lustful pursuits through melodic shape and vocal delivery. The excitement of ogling his lover in her short skirt causes the vocal line to ascend to a new height, which Dexter can hardly sing given his normal baritone range. Abandoning any sense of vocal composure, Dexter's voice thins under the strain of reaching the melodic climax as he describes this "sneaky feeling in [his] spine." The harmony further underscores the tension of this moment with a secondary dominant seventh chord. In the concluding phrase, Dexter elaborates on the musical expressions of desire by singing, "When she sits on my knee, it's like a honeybee, oo-baby mine" with a bluesy melisma that accentuates the protagonist's libidinal cry on "oo." The vocal line is supported by a circle-of-fifth harmonic progression that finally resolves the prolonged tension as the protagonist depicts the sexual indulgence of the moment.

Following the release of "Honky-Tonk Blues," Dexter recorded "Answer to Honky-Tonk Blues" in 1938, which elaborates on the figure of the nagging wife in the unfolding drama of illicit pleasure. To the same music as the original, Dexter explains to his sexualized honky-tonk girl that he can no longer continue their liaison. With his wife now in tow, the male subject is forced to come home from his evenings of revelry at a decent hour. Situating the wife who monitors her husband's sexuality against the unchaste woman, Dexter's music creates a marked tension between domesticity and sexuality in which femininity and class play a fundamental role. The honky-tonk woman's sexuality, signaling her working-class status, contrasts with the wife's ambitions for marital fidelity.

Dexter next elaborated on these gendered roles in his narratives about the sexually fueled relationships in his 1942 jukebox hit, "Pistol Packin' Mama." Here, he hyperbolizes the anger of the betrayed wife, turning the domestic killjoy into a murderess, a dangerous woman. Failing to channel her mate's sexuality into a monogamous relationship, the outraged woman finally puts a stop to her partner's carousing. Bursting into the local cabaret, the woman shoots the male subject after she finds him dancing with another woman. Thus the male subject's virile ways in the honky-tonk result in death, and the wife emerges as a figure of fear. Dexter's song was a hit during World War II, at a significant time when women of various social classes were leaving their poorly paid service positions and homes for manufacturing jobs in wartime industries, which offered them newfound economic autonomy. The gendered depictions of the honky-tonk could serve as a warning to men about women's newly emerging material and cultural power. Instead of staying home and dreaming of upward mobility, the pistol packin' mama, a wench-like figure from the nineteenth-century popular stage, served as a parody of womanhood, a type of comic relief to lessen the anxieties spawned by the profound gender shifts of World War II.

Dexter's sexualized and gendered portraits of the honky-tonk further developed the character of the honky-tonk girl, who would become the well-known honky-tonk angel in many male and female honky-tonk songs. Besides this tragic fate of the male working-class patron who is unable to escape his wife's malice, Dexter also reveals what could happen to the honky-tonk woman who is unable to resist the entrapments of the dance hall. His "Poor Little Honky-Tonk Girl" (1940) tells a sordid tale of a young woman who is exploited by lecherous men. Far from the protection of her patriarchal home, the ingenue has promised her affections to a man who has left her heartbroken and bereft. The male narrator, however, offers to rescue the distressed damsel from a wanton life by promising her a respectable union, but she has to relinquish her dancing days in the honky-tonk. If "Pistol Packin' Mama" is a warning to men, then "Poor Little Honky-Tonk Girl" serves as a cautionary tale for young women who dare to venture into the masculinized honky-tonk. Only by chance would honky-tonk women find their happily-ever-after endings of domestic respectability in such a place. Thus in Dexter's music, women could be alluring sexual objects, fallen angels exploited by and also rescued by men, or angry wives who go to extreme lengths to insist on the fidelity of their husbands and sexual partners. Ernest Tubb and Hank Williams, considered the architects of the honky-tonk style, embellished themes in narratives that turned men, lured to the sexualized honky-tonk, into figures of masculine vulnerability and women into cold-hearted characters refusing to conform to gender norms.[24] In the 1950s, female country artists would take over these male-defined, often parodic representations of women (as Lulu Belle or Rose Maddox did with the wench character) and develop these models of womanhood in their narratives that articulated a class-specific voice defying the double binds of class and womanhood.

Tubb, also from Texas, popularized the honky-tonk style in Nashville right when the city was emerging as a major locale for the production of country music. As in Dexter's 1940s songs, Tubb's music underlines the conflicts of romantic love at a time when the ideals of domesticity were not readily available to the majority of Americans affected by the upheavals of World War II. The draft sent millions of men abroad to unfamiliar areas of the world, and the demands of wartime production pulled women into factory jobs and rural dwellers to urban centers. For example, those who had suffered through the Depression in the rural South and Southwest left their homes in droves to work in wage-earning factory jobs on the West Coast and in the Midwest and the North. Many displaced southerners turned to the emerging beer halls that dotted the landscape near the oil fields of Texas and the war plants of California or in the "hillbilly ghettos" of Chicago's Uptown or Detroit's Briggs neighborhoods.[25] In such places, honky-tonk songs, blasting from jukeboxes, underscored the contested terrain of the urban tavern through narratives that pointed to the sexual excesses linked to the working class. In Dexter's "Honky-Tonk Blues" or "Pistol Packin' Mama" or Tubb's "I Ain't Goin' Honky-Tonkin' Anymore," southern white masculinity appeared moored to the corporeal pleasures of the sordid honky-tonk.

Tubb further popularized not only the use of the electric guitar—a mainly commercial decision encouraged by jukebox operators—but also the theme of masculine vulnerability tied to the honky-tonk.[26] In his 1941 recording of "I Ain't Goin' Honky-Tonkin' Anymore" (one of his first recordings to feature the electric guitar), the male subject, suffering from a recent heartbreak, is weary of the tantalizing revelry of the juke joint. But the newly added electric guitar points in a different direction: the narrator's inability to resist the lively setting of the local roadhouse. In a call-and-response texture between Tubb's vocals and the electric guitar (accompanied by the acoustic rhythm guitar and the string bass), the lead instrument comments on the protagonist's repeated declaration—"I ain't goin' honky-tonkin' anymore"—with syncopated flat-thirds in its higher register. The electric guitar's string bending continues to punctuate the musical texture with rhythmically displaced blues notes, suggesting that the carnal enticements of the juke joint will indeed continue to attract the protagonist, despite his longing for the security of domestic love.

While Tubb portrays the honky-tonk as a sordid place of temptation, his 1941 hit "Walkin' the Floor over You" underscores the theme of romantic discord. Here the male subject pines for the return of his beloved to their shared domestic life. While the protagonist remains home, the woman is the one who appears out in the world in her refusal to adhere to normative definitions of gender. The music links the instabilities of romantic love to women's abandonment of the domestic sphere, a common theme in male honky-tonk songs, including Hank Thompson's "Wild Side of Life."[27] With such topics resonating with an audience affected by dislocation and the gender changes of World War II, Tubb became a rising star on jukeboxes and sought to expand on his commercial success by pursuing a radio and film career in Hollywood. But it was the Southeast that eventually diverted Tubb from his aspirations in California. During a live performance in Alabama in 1942, Tubb met Joseph Lee Frank, the first promoter and manager of country acts in Nashville. Frank convinced the Grand Ole Opry management to allow Tubb a guest performance on the radio program in 1943, just as he had persuaded the management to hire the Golden West Cowboys in 1937 and Roy Acuff in 1938.[28] The audience's welcome of Tubb's honky-tonk music ensured a regular spot for the Texas Troubadour on the *Opry* beginning in 1943.

Nashville and the Country Music Industry

Bringing honky-tonk from the Southwest to the Southeast, Tubb was instrumental in disseminating the style on the *Opry* at a significant moment when the country music industry rose to prominence in Nashville. Since its initial broadcasts in 1926, the *Opry* had played a pivotal role in circulating southern vernacular traditions: the banjo songs of Uncle Dave Macon, the string-band playing of the Fruit Jar Drinkers, and the virtuosic harmonica solos of DeFord Bailey.[29] By the mid-1930s, however, Harry Stone, the new station manager (replacing George D. Hay in 1930), encouraged the *Opry* to promote a broader range of musics. Just as Bill Monroe and His Bluegrass Boys revitalized the string-band tradition with breakneck tempos, Pee Wee King and His Golden West Cowboys performed Tin Pan Alley cowboy songs and love ballads, Roy Acuff sang gospel tunes, Eddy Arnold crooned tender sentiments in pop-infused pieces, and Tubb featured the electric guitar in honky-tonk songs about the conflicts of adult love. With such an arsenal of stars and styles, the *Opry* became a prominent barn-dance show (rivaling the success of WLS's *National Barn Dance*), especially when NBC started to broadcast a portion of the *Opry* to listeners throughout the country in 1939.[30]

In addition to promoting the *Opry*'s cast of performers through radio, Stone had established the WSM Artist Service, a booking department that organized package tours of *Opry* acts to perform in surrounding theaters and schoolhouses. Nashville, in turn, started to emerge as a viable center for country music that lured musicians who otherwise may have pursued their careers in California's film and music industries or in Chicago's recording and radio enterprises. With the musical talent that was congregating in Nashville, the recording industry also began to take root in the southern city. Paul Cohen, the country music A and R man for Decca, first recorded Red Foley in WSM's Studio B in 1945. Afterward, Cohen used the studios of the newly formed Castle Recording Company at the Tulane Hotel in Nashville for the majority of Decca's country recording sessions, including those with prominent performers of honky-tonk, such as Ernest Tubb and Kitty Wells.

On top of all of this, the establishment of Acuff-Rose Publications, a major country music publishing house, further contributed to country music's industrial foundation in Nashville.[31] Acuff approached Fred Rose (a prolific songwriter who understood the musical nuances of country music) to join forces in forming a publishing firm that developed copyrights and supported country songwriters, many of whom (for instance, Hank Williams and Floyd Tillman) contributed to the growing honky-tonk repertory of the 1940s and 1950s.[32] Thus by the late 1940s in Nashville, the components of the music industry—radio, touring, recording, song publishing, and songwriting— were firmly in place, enabling the country music industry to operate as a distinct, identifiable field within the larger commercial forces of the popular-music industry.[33]

Within this historical context of industrial growth and expansion, honky-tonk music emerged not only as a predominant style but also as part of the commercial foundation of the country music industry. "The commercial success first of honky-tonk styles and then rockabilly," as Diane Pecknold notes, "had paved the way for the development of a fully formed and relatively autonomous music production center in Nashville."[34] For example, when *Billboard* first charted the popularity of country music in 1944, the trade magazine based its country charts on jukebox play, in which Al Dexter's honky-tonk number "Pistol Packin' Mama" soared to the top.[35] Following the popularity of Dexter's songs (which continued to rise to the top of the charts throughout the 1940s), prominent honky-tonk artists such as Ernest Tubb, Floyd Tillman, Hank Williams, Kitty Wells, and Webb Pierce came to dominate *Billboard's* country music charts, once they were launched in 1944.

Nashville and Honky-Tonk

In the newly developed country music industry in Nashville, Hank Williams achieved national recognition in the late 1940s and early 1950s. His effective expressions adopted the musical conventions of the honky-tonk style:

the instrumentation (electric steel guitar, fiddle, acoustic rhythm guitar, and string bass) as well as the idioms of popular music and the blues. For example, Williams's "Honky-Tonk Blues" (a song that is similar only in title to Dexter's "Honky-Tonk Blues") is a twelve-bar blues tune about the figurative honky-tonk as a site of masculine defeat instead of licentious pleasures.[36] To the percussive beat of the rhythm section and the syncopated steel guitar part, Williams sings of leaving behind a rural culture for the city. But the conditions of displacement force the protagonist to turn to the honky-tonk, a place, according to Barbara Ching, where "the abject male literally and figuratively hits the bottom."[37] The honky-tonk appears not as a haven that protects the subject from the assaults of urban modernity but as an ensnaring trap from which the male subject cannot escape to forge his way in the modern world. Without any reprieve from the alienation of industrialism and dislocation, Williams's subject abandons all hope of economic mobility in his longing to return to the family farm.

For a listening audience affected by dislocation and the gender shifts of the post–World War II years, the possible failure of southern white working-class masculinity in an urban industrial setting must have weighed on the minds of many who listened to Williams's music. As George Lipsitz and Richard Leppert have noted, Williams's songs frequently underscore the ways in which the painful distinction of class contrasted with the ideological definitions of middle-class manhood.[38] In sitcoms such as *Father Knows Best* and *Leave It to Beaver*, the image of the caring father ensconced in the suburban home emerged as the primary configuration of masculinity. Historian Michael Kimmel declares, "It was often as fathers that men sought to anchor their identities and successes as men."[39] *Life* magazine even announced that 1954 was the year of "the domestication of the American man."[40] Domesticity appeared to be fundamental to establishing a social order that countered the concerns of the era. From the conformity that corporate America demanded of its gray suits (the middle-class) and its blue-collar workforce, men had few sources, apart from the home, in which to assert their masculinity. In fact, society stressed that men's domestic presence was instrumental in rescuing their sons from the feminization of the private sphere. Dedicated fathers could ensure that their sons would grow up to be patriotic, heterosexual men, capable of battling the evils of Communism in the Cold War period.

In contrast to the prevailing illustrations of manhood, Williams's musical expressions did not give the impression of stable heterosexual love within the domestic sphere. Instead, he longed for an intimate bond with the feminine in songs that voiced a "frustrated desire for traditional romantic/domestic happiness."[41] Known for his songwriting expertise, Williams was also an effective performer who realized the fraught complexities and contradictions of adult love through vocal nuance.[42] Williams could give the impression of impassioned angst as he belted the upper register of his melody in a strained, high nasal-twang voice, or he could promote a sense of ease in his lower range that gestured fleetingly to the promises of romance. In his 1951 hit "Cold, Cold, Heart," for example, Williams concludes the opening phrase in the lower register of his baritone range. With a warm vocal timbre, he swings the rhythm to lyrics that point to the warm security of love, "that you're my every dream," as if attempting to romance his love interest. At the end of the verse, however, he bemoans the emotional distance between him and his beloved ("a memory from your lonesome past keeps us so far apart"). The ascending melody reaches a climactic moment in which Williams struggles to hold on to the ending note (on the syllable "-part"). But this doesn't stop him from belting out this sound that falls somewhere between B-flat and B below middle C. Indeed, the longer he sings the note, the more pronounced his crescendo becomes until his voice sounds as if it is about to break under vocal strain, lending to a feeling of desperate yearning for the woman of his affections. The refrain concludes with the protagonist mourning the loss of domestic love: "Why can't I melt your cold, cold heart?"

In a musical context where men pined for romantic stability, female solo artists joined the musical dialogues that also signaled the burdens of class. As mentioned earlier, Kitty Wells's "It Wasn't God Who Made Honky-Tonk Angels" underscores the gendered conflicts of the working-class juke joint, bringing a woman's voice into the style. Yet the conceptual frame of the masculinized working-class tavern has placed women's music in a tangential position to the honky-tonk, thereby overlooking women's class-specific voice couched within the musical practices of the style. For Ching, "hard" country (defined lyrically rather than musically), a masculinized cultural form, is a mode of country expression that does not include the music of female artists. Women may engage with the lyrical tropes of masculine abjection but only through narratives of "revisionist scolding" that refuse to accept the onus of masculine failure.[43] In other words, women musicians can never enact the part of the downtrodden or the dispossessed to reveal the "hidden injuries of class."[44] Rather, they play the role of the demanding wife reprimanding her husband. Pamela Fox also finds that female artists of the 1950s could not fully embrace the male-defined "honky-tonk musical territory." Unlike the "authentic" expressions of class in male honky-tonk, women had to develop ways to promote an "outsider's status" not only to the music but also to the figurative working-class tavern.[45]

What has been overlooked in this conceptual division between the masculine honky-tonk and the feminine home are the ways women's narratives in honky-tonk evoked the uneasy relationship between class and womanhood. Wells and her female peers placed sonic models of womanhood directly within the sexualized terrain of the juke joint as a means to articulate subject positions that lay outside social norms. Here they complicated the constraints of working-class womanhood, of being viewed through the lens of an excessive sexuality that lacks the bodily control and refinement expected of the middle class or being dismissed for their dreams of upward mobility and respectability. Female country artists, for example, did not simply enact the sexualized role of the honky-tonk angel or the demanding shrew scolding her husband for not adhering to social norms of fidelity and domesticity in their narratives. Instead, their vocal performances infused their representations of sexuality, desire, and loss with a level of agency that revealed the complexities and contradictions of class and womanhood.

Kitty Wells's Early Musical Career

Wells certainly did not look the part of the honky-tonk angel or the rolling-pin-carrying wife refusing to accept her husband's philandering ways. In many ways, her visual presence in performance evoked the quintessential 1950s southern housewife, the woman who promised to stay home and not rejoin the paid labor market after World War II, despite the fact that so many other women balanced their domestic roles with working outside the home. In actuality, however, Wells emerged as a major recording star with honky-tonk hit after hit within a centralized country music industry located in Nashville.[46]

Well before her rise to her royal position as the first "Queen of Country Music," she was, like many other musicians, trying to eke out a career by performing regionally in local schoolhouses and theaters and on radio stations. Yet the usual historical accounts of Wells's ascendancy frame her musical pursuits as secondary to her primary domestic roles. Largely derived from country music journalism, this account, attempting to paint Wells's commercial success with the domestic tones of 1950s ideology, is one that has been continually repeated in country music scholarship. For example, Mary Bufwack and Robert Oermann in their historical survey of women in country music find that Wells was a "shy, soft-spoken dutiful housewife . . . the polite mother of three."[47] Others have echoed this vision of Wells by repeating the usual story of how the country singer was about to devote herself solely to her family before she realized she could sing chart-topping honky-tonk hits in Nashville.[48] "Over time the housewife label that originated as a promotional tool," as Georgia Christgau notes, "got hammered into history as fact that became code for Wells's supposed female traits such as compliance, obedience, passivity, even indifference."[49]

By taking a closer look at the historical details of her career, however, I find that Wells strove to be a professional musician before and during her marriage to her husband, musician Johnnie Wright, who was instrumental in guiding Wells to prominence in country music. Born Muriel Deason, she grew up in a musical family in the Nashville area. Her father played the guitar, and her mother sang hymns. As Wells recollected to biographer Walt Trott, "While I was growing up, we would go to church and to prayer meets, and she'd [Wells's mother] just sing her heart out."[50] Apart from participating in the rituals of prayer and singing at camp meetings, Wells and her family regularly sang gospel music in the congregation and choir of Nashville's Church of the Nazarene, a Protestant denomination that grew out of the Holiness movement in America.[51] Wells would later bring her southern vocality, cultivated in camp meetings and church, to her honky-tonk narratives.

In the mid-1930s, she formed her first ensemble with her sisters and cousin, the Deason Sisters, who performed regularly on Nashville's WSIX.[52] Soon she met and married Wright, with whom she performed, even after he teamed up with Jack Anglin to form the long-lasting duo Johnnie and Jack.[53] As the duo toured the Southeast and appeared on various radio stations in the region, Wells sang with the ensemble or performed as a soloist. Because of her growing success at Knoxville's WNOX in 1942, Lowell Blanchard, the station manager, encouraged Wells to adopt a stage name that was easy for her listeners to remember. Thus she became Kitty Wells, a name that her husband selected from a well-known song, "I Could Marry Kitty Wells," which *Opry* acts often performed.[54]

The male duo and Wells eventually landed a spot on what was then a relatively new but prominent radio program, the *Louisiana Hayride* in Shreveport.[55] Wells continued to establish her career by performing as a soloist on the *Hayride*, where she also had her own early-morning show playing records and selling quilting supplies.[56] Here she looked the part of the sentimental maiden dressed in a bonnet and old-fashioned rustic dress, and her radio success led to a recording contract. In the late 1940s, the Johnnie and Jack duo and Wells separately signed with RCA Records. Wells's contract lasted from 1949 to 1952, during which she recorded eight songs, none of which did well on the charts.[57] After RCA dropped her, Wright tried to secure another recording contract for Wells, even though his duo continued to record for RCA. He made a demo recording of Wells and gave it to Paul Cohen at Decca in Nashville. Cohen agreed to sign Wells with a song he had already picked for her, "It Wasn't God Who Made Honky-Tonk Angels." After twenty years of live performances and radio work, Wells emerged as a national star of country music. Like many women of her generation, she was not necessarily sequestered in the domestic sphere but rather balanced her roles as a wife and mother with her working life outside the home.

Women's Honky-Tonk

After her success in 1952, Wells's second hit song, "Paying for That Back Street Affair" (1953), responded to Webb Pierce's popular "Back Street Affair." The male subject in Pierce's song addresses his lover, a young woman, who at first is unaware that she is embroiled in a romantic union with a married man. He apologizes for deceiving her but justifies the affair by depicting the conditions of his unhappy marriage. Wells's song attempts to rescue femininity from the sexual excesses usually assigned to the working class by ending the illicit relationship. She orders her former lover to return to his forgiving wife, while she, the fallen woman, is left to suffer the moral and social consequences of their unchaste love. Because Wells had taken on the gendered tropes of class, her initial success involved reacting to the themes of male-centered narratives. Pamela Fox, for instance, finds that Wells's music was "hampered by its conventions" so that all her "songs, to some degree, would function as answer songs."[58] According to Fox, Wells's honky-tonk songs kept her in a sort of musical straightjacket where she could not entirely escape the gendered script of male honky-tonk.

If "popular music is nothing if not dialogic, the product of an ongoing historical conversation in which no one has the first or last word," as George Lipsitz asserts, then it could be argued that Wells effectively engaged with and transformed the honky-tonk style from a woman's perspective.[59] Her performances and song arrangements incorporated a shared vocabulary of musical and lyrical elements that disclosed the ways in which the social factors of class could also have a bearing on the imagined and real lives of women.[60] In musical and lyrical dialogue with her male and female peers, Wells drew on the well-established codes of musical practice to express sexual desire, longing, and heartache, promoting a sense of agency and disclosing the afflictions of working-class womanhood. In this sense, she exceeded the male-defined narratives of honky-tonk music by adopting and reshaping the models of gender with the particular sonic signifiers and conventions of the honky-tonk style.

In her 1953 song "You're Not Easy to Forget," for example, she reshapes the honky-tonk woman, an erotic object, into a subject that searches for sexual pleasure on her own terms.[61] In depicting the desires of the female subject, a southern white working-class woman, Wells's song explicitly incorporates the musical practices of the honky-tonk style, including the sonic gestures of southern rural music combined with popular music. The string bass and rhythm guitar provide the typical boom-chuck percussive effect, while the fiddle part embellishes the opening hook with strident-sounding double stops of a dominant to tonic drone, a vestige of southern fiddle playing, which underpins its introductory syncopated melody. In addition to the instrumental accompaniment, "You're Not Easy to Forget" was written by Henry Davis and Wilbur Jones, who deftly interwove a range of musical idioms to create a dramatic tale of a heartbroken woman searching for physical love in the working-class juke joint. The opening arch-shaped melody evokes a folklike gesture to depict the protagonist's quotidian inclination to turn to the honky-tonk as an escape from heartache. Adding to this effect, the bridge's heightened melody elaborates on the sonic narrative of abandonment and the protagonist's determination to once again enjoy the pleasures of physical and emotional love. Here, Wells's performance of the melodic line contributes to the dramatic nature of the sonic narrative as she reaches and sustains the bridge's higher melody in her strained, nasally inflected chest voice pushed above the vocal break. Just as Hank Williams produces a nasally strident vocal tone in his upper range, Wells also presents a constricted nasal-twang vocal quality to depict the angst and subject position of her protagonist. Her vocal delivery signals the vernacular singing traditions of the rural South, which she had largely learned from her mother and by singing gospel hymns in the local camp meetings and in the Church of the Nazarene.

Owen Bradley, Wells's producer at Decca, reportedly insisted that Wells record pieces in higher keys than those in which they were composed. Perhaps Bradley was aiming for this particular vocal sound of tension and traditionalism to heighten the dramatic narratives coming out of the honky-tonk as the symbolic meeting ground of displacement and southern white working-class culture.[62] Wells further elaborates on the vocal style of the southern vernacular by emphasizing and anticipating the downbeats with an accented, rhythmically strong grace note that ascends or descends a step to the main melodic note, a common vocal technique derived from the tradition of "lining out" psalms, known also as feathering.[63]

She also includes more-modern vocal approaches, such as a heightened use of vibrato, something one would not hear in traditional approaches to hymn singing or southern Appalachian singing styles. Moreover, in the closing refrain, where Wells reveals her true wishes of wanting the sexual intimacy of a former lover, she draws on the blues and sings a blues-inflected vocal line in which she sustains a flat third. With a constricted but labored singing voice that embellishes the melodic line with a range of vocal devices, Wells molds the sonic space of the honky-tonk into a figurative place where female subjects can disclose their sexual desires and heartache. The honky-tonk angel, in Wells's telling, is not just an object of desire or an unchaste figure of low moral character who refuses to conform to conventional norms. Instead, she is a central figure of the honky-tonk style in search of sexual pleasures and/or the stability of love in hope of securing the mythical security of the middle class. In this sense, Wells reshapes the honky-tonk angel into a transplanted southern white working-class woman grappling with the paradoxical tensions of the promised ideals of the American dream and the realities of not achieving those ambitions. By balancing musical convention with individual expression, Wells thus gives voice to the sexual agency of longing while exposing the unrealized hopes of working-class women.

The country music industry understood that Wells's voice carried emotional meaning that fit particularly well with honky-tonk music. In the 1960s, journalist Charles Newman described Wells's vocal mode as belonging to the "weeper style." This style, he explained, is "songs of the heart; simple love songs, broken romance, which Kitty puts over in such a way that one cannot help feeling moved by them, so sincere is her singing."[64] It was likely Wells's vocal tone of nasal-twang tension pronounced in her upper chest range combined with her use of vibrato that produced her "weeper style." With a sound that the country music industry understood as "authentic," Wells provided a nuanced voice (not only in the cultural but also the acoustical sense of "voice") for the honky-tonk woman. After the release of "You're Not Easy to Forget," *Billboard* commended the performer for her "potent reading" of the song, demonstrating that "Kitty Wells [was] still one of the hottest thrushes in the field."[65]

But Wells was not the only woman singer of the early 1950s who recorded honky-tonk music that effectively drew on the practices of popular music and the blues to address the hopes and desires of female subjects. Owen Bradley at Decca was intent on finding additional women performers who could sing effectively about the conflicts of romantic love. Bradley signed Goldie Hill, whose recording of "I Let the Stars Get in My Eyes" (1953) was a response song to "Don't Let the Stars Get in Your Eyes," recorded by Skeets McDonald. Hill's recording soared to the top of the country music charts, hot on the heels of Wells's hits. Marketed as the "Golden Hillbilly," Hill became the first solo woman to appear on the front cover of the prominent trade magazine *Country Song Roundup*, which heralded her as the most popular woman in country music in 1954.[66]

On a television broadcast of the 1950s program *The Country Show*, which featured Opry stars, Hill performs her bluesy honky-tonk numbers "Treat Me Kind," "Cry, Cry Darling," and "Say Big Boy." In her self-penned "Say Big Boy," a twelve-bar blues song, Hill does not mention the carnal setting of the honky-tonk.[67] Nevertheless, her performance gestures to the sexual frankness enabled by the style's relationship with the blues. In a fitted sequined western dress, the look that Patsy Cline would later adopt in the early part of her career, Hill looks knowingly into the camera as she addresses a former love interest. She slides to and from notes in her husky-sounding alto voice while swinging the beat with a swaggering confidence that is meant to entice the return of her lover. Here, she isn't a mere object or a figure overwrought with anguish but rather a subject who realizes her desires. Even *Billboard* noted the "provocative performance" of the chanteuse "as she [thought] about her man."[68]

While Wells and Hill took over the musical role of the honky-tonk angel, they also depicted female loss and dispossession in terms of heterosexual love in the honky-tonk style. Like the male protagonist whose frustrated desires for the domestic feminine underscored the sense of lack in songs by Williams or Tubb, Wells, and Hill elaborated on the shame and desolation of women subjects not necessarily living the American dream of domestic security and comfort. In "I'm the Loneliest Gal in Town," Hill, for example, sings from the position of the forlorn honky-tonk woman, a character introduced by Al Dexter's "Poor Little Honky-Tonk Girl" (1940).[69] In the strophic setting of the song, the refrain of each verse contrasts the image of the sexualized woman against her feelings of isolation and heartache: "Folks think I really get around, but I am the loneliest gal in town." Unlike Dexter's song, in her song Hill elaborates on the interiority and social position of the honky-tonk woman by explaining that the woman's convivial manner is only a facade to mask her loneliness and dejection. The steel guitar's blues-inflected embellishments of the melody, which introduce the song and reappear during the instrumental breaks, gesture to the lively atmosphere of the honky-tonk, whereas the fiddle's strident double stops point to the protagonist's rustic southern past. Such a sonic backdrop magnifies the displaced figure's alienation within an environment that seems unaware of her consuming despair.

Though Hill was nationally recognized for her honky-tonk recordings, it was Wells's mournful deliveries of the 1950s that best encapsulated the afflictions of class in narratives of emotional abandonment. Wells's songs, in particular, often portray the distress of failed love, in which the honky-tonk plays a central role. In the self-referential song "Honky Tonk Waltz" (written by Billy Wallace for Wells to record in 1953), Wells mourns the ending of a romantic relationship not in the privacy of her home, where one would expect a woman of the 1950s, but in the honky-tonk.[70] Listening to the languid tune "Honky Tonk Waltz," played on the jukebox, the song's subject recalls the physicality of dancing with her former lover, who has deserted her for the affections of another.

To depict the depth of the protagonist's anguish, Wells realizes the narrative with her usual singing style of a piercing nasal-twang timbre. The song's melodic design requires Wells to launch into her upper range of the chest voice at the beginning of each eight-bar phrase. The vocal effect is one of crying out in anguish before elaborating on the reasons for the protagonist's pain in the lower range. Yet even in her lower register, she produces a nasal-twang vocal quality on the downbeat attacks and elongation of vowels, also marked by tight vibratos. Unlike the warm, secure sound of Hank Williams's lower range or the resonance of Hill's chest voice, Wells maintains a timbral intensity throughout the song. Against the bodily constrictions of singing with what feels like a tight throat, raised larynx (even in the lower range), and clenched jaw, Wells's strident timbres emphasize the depth of emotional pain associated with betrayal in the licentious honky-tonk, the emblem of working-class displacement. With her characteristic weeper style, Wells's song of abjection voices the anxieties of class and gender—of failing to grasp the coveted possibilities of the 1950s. The song concludes with the image of the narrator alone in the honky-tonk, as a symbolic place of loss, while her beloved has moved on via the physical affections of another woman.

Alongside music that carved out a space for women's expressions of heartache in the honky-tonk, Wells also performed songs that centered on the negation of the family, the primary organizing unit of the 1950s. In one of her most daring examples, "Mommy for a Day" (which reached the top 40 on the country music charts in 1959), Wells enacts a divorced woman who has lost custody of her daughter.[71] Harlan Howard, a prominent Nashville songwriter, composed the song specifically for Wells's voice of constrained anguish. The song implies that the town's sexually tinged gossip about the protagonist led her former husband to believe she was unfit to be a wife and mother. Though there is no mention of the honky-tonk, in this era the divorcée was an incarnation of the fallen woman who had lost middle-class respectability.

With the usual markers that blend folk music with the idioms of popular music, "Mommy for a Day" catered to the sensibilities of a mass-mediated country audience. In an AABA song form, the first half of each A phrase suggests the use of pentatonicism, complementing the image of the mother visiting her daughter "each Sunday afternoon"—a traditional day of church and family for an audience of Protestant southerners. But as the song unfolds, the lyrical narrative completely undermines any sense of traditionalism evoked in the music. In the second phrase, the young daughter implores her mother to return to the family home, while the protagonist bravely attempts to face the bleak reality of seeing her "little girl" only once a week. Portraying the daughter's yearning for the constant reassuring love of the mother, the bridge's harmonic focus on the dominant—contrasting with the repetitive tonic-subdominant movement in the A phrases—infuses the music with a sense of longing for the domestic. The song concludes with the protagonist kissing her daughter goodbye in forlorn resignation to her degraded role as "mommy for a day." Removed from the domestic sphere of the family, the woman finds it impossible to define her class and gender status through normative models. She appears as an outcast not only from the family but also from the governing principles of 1950s womanhood.

In comparison to Wells's "Mommy for a Day," Hank Williams's "My Son Calls Another Man Daddy" (1949) also contributes to the lyrical tropes of domestic failure in honky-tonk music. Here Williams portrays a male protagonist, whose incarceration has alienated him from his son. His former wife has married a man who assumes the patriarchal role that he failed to realize. At a time when the criterion of domesticity upheld the middle-class values of men and women, Williams and Wells pointed to the realities of divorce while underlining the injuries of class—of failing to grasp the criterion integral to happiness and emotional fulfillment. Both the mother in Wells's song and the father in Williams's are therefore left to their desolate lives, divorced from the sanctity of the family.

If Williams's and Wells's songs spoke of class disenfranchisement against the backdrop of domesticity, Jean Shepard, who became a recording artist for Capitol Records in the early 1950s, performed music that clearly linked the abjection of divorce to the sordidness of the honky-tonk. In "My Wedding Ring" (1953), Shepard bluntly depicts a woman "drinkin' and livin' this honky-tonk life."[72] In the opening verses, she warns the women in her audience that her dismal existence as a divorced mother, an identity that is often coded as working class and abject, could easily be theirs. The chorus lyrically dramatizes the subject's cultural position of failure, "a girl . . . without a future." While her "baby boy . . . has his daddy's name, . . . another woman wears" her "wedding ring." With accompaniment that evokes the honky-tonk—syncopated piano melodies with a steel guitar lead—Shepard belts out the narrow melodic line. Even when the melody extends to the upper notes, Shepard projects her voice without providing a constricted sound like Wells's. Because the melodic line of "My Wedding Ring" is pitched lower than Wells's songs, including "Honky Tonk Waltz" and "Mommy for a Day," Shepard is not required to reach to the same melodic heights. However, she still projects a nasal-twang timbre in the upper range of her chest register and stresses nasal consonants throughout the song. But instead of completely tensing the throat muscles, Shepard is able to keep her throat more relaxed and inflect her tone with a bright-sounding belting voice by using nasal-twang techniques. She makes more use of the oral space and produces a sound from the back of the throat instead of projecting from the front of the mouth. In the lower range, where Shepard keeps the larynx in a lowered position, her voice resonates as she swings the beat and slides from note to note. As in Hill's "Say Big Boy," Shepard relies on the microphone to realize her phrasing, rhythmic play, and subtle shifts in dynamics, in effect providing her honky-tonk ballads with a more contemporary vocal sound that differed from Wells's strained, more-rigid singing voice, linked to the past.

Shepard's model of belting out the melody can be heard in the 1940s music of Rose Maddox, also a product of the California country scene (as discussed in chapter 5). This style of singing would later influence Loretta Lynn in her 1960s and 1970s songs in which Lynn asserted female agency in romantic unions. In fact, by the mid 1950s, Shepard was performing feminist songs in which she criticized the double standards of gender roles in "Two Whoops and a Holler" and played the role of the angry housewife in "Sad Singin' and Slow Ridin'," predating Loretta Lynn's forthright "Don't Come Home A-Drinkin'" by more than ten years.

In her recording of "Sad Singin' and Slow Ridin'" (written by Texas Ruby and Curly Fox), Shepard warns her husband that if he continues to stumble home in the wee hours of the night from an evening of drinking and philandering, he should expect some "sad singin' and slow ridin'" at his funeral procession. Here Shepard belts out the declamatory vocal line (based on a pentatonic scale) in a fast, clipped manner. Each A phrase of the song form begins with Shepard launching into a repetitive melodic line on the highest note of the song in her midrange to state emphatically her ominous threat. She follows her strident singing with bluesy melismas, giving the impression that she is not a naive housewife unaware of what an evening at the local honky-tonk may entail. In the bridge, she continues to inflect her melodic line with flatted thirds to accompany the sexualized image of her husband "struttin' out" for the evening. In the concluding phrase, she restates the dire consequences that could befall the carousing husband, recalling the murderous outrage enacted in Dexter's "Pistol Packin' Mama."

Yet for her televised 1955 performance of "Sad Singin' and Slow Ridin'" on *The Country Show: [With] Stars of the Grand Ole Opry*, Shepard, costumed in a gingham dress, sings in an humorous manner with her exaggerated vocal hiccups and use of nasality that evoke the singing style of the hillbilly.[73] She couches her critique of domestic gender roles in a comic performance that recalls the rustic buffoonery of Lulu Belle and Rose Maddox. Like her predecessors, Shepard could slip in and out of different vocal roles. In one instance, she could play the heartbroken protagonist singing a honky-tonk ballad, and the next she could be the comic angry wife threatening her husband with extreme consequences.

Women's songs carved out a distinct space within the symbolic honky-tonk to reveal their desires for romantic/sexual intimacy and domesticity or heartache from failing to secure the comfort of domestic unions. In other words, they articulated the emotional pain and desires of subjectivities that lay outside normative concepts of femininity through the archetypical characters of the musical style (the honky-tonk woman, the angry housewife, or the forsaken lover). Women artists also engaged directly with the style's male protagonists—heartbroken men, devoted mates, and cheating husbands—in solo songs and in duets that proved to be an integral part of honky-tonk. This sort of gendered dynamic played out in the performance territory of the duet, which realized the very act of two distinct subjects negotiating the conflicts and terms of heterosexual love and sexuality. Beginning in the late 1940s, pop singer Margaret Whiting and country artist Jimmy Wakely recorded Floyd Tillman's well-known "Slippin' Around," the first honky-tonk duet to hit the country charts and to establish the duet within honky-tonk. After this, prominent male and female stars recorded songs that imparted a shared unease about the mythos of the American dream.

Wells recorded a number of duets with Red Foley, Roy Acuff, and Webb Pierce; Shepard's first hit was a duet with Ferlin Husky, a rising star of honky-tonk; and Goldie Hill recorded several songs with Justin Tubb, the son of Ernest Tubb.

The duets of Pierce and Wells, in particular, matched two of the most popular voices in 1950s honky-tonk. Pierce, after beginning his performance career on the radio program *Louisiana Hayride*, moved to Nashville, where he secured a recording contract with Decca Records and became a star of the *Grand Ole Opry*, filling Hank Williams's former spot on the radio program.[74] Specializing in honky-tonk ballads, Pierce recorded his first hit, "Wondering," the same year that Wells recorded "It Wasn't God Who Made Honky-Tonk Angels." He continued to dominate the charts with his high, wailing tenor voice that linked the fragilities of masculinity to the fatalism of drinking, as in "There Stands the Glass" (1953), and to the painful expressions of heartache, as in "Crying over You" (1958).

When Pierce's resounding tenor voice joined Wells's strained alto, the singers illustrated the contested terrain of infidelity and monogamous love. In their 1956 song, "Can You Find It in Your Heart?," Pierce plays the role of the carousing husband begging to return to his domestic mate, enacted by Wells, who refuses to continue a relationship riddled with deception. Unlike the angry wife in Dexter's "Answer to Honky-Tonk Blues," who monitors her husband's sexuality, the female subject in "Can You Find It in Your Heart?" seeks to disentangle herself from the conflicts of infidelity. In essence the song positions the sexual man— who desires but fails to achieve domestic stability—against the monogamous woman, a model of femininity that points to domestic respectability.

The song's arrangement, however, does not clearly distinguish between the two vocal parts that represent the gendered subjects. The singers exchange melodic phrases of the same range in an antiphonal setting, achieving the effect of a shared sonic space in which the male subject longs for romantic love while the woman gestures to the failures of masculinity. The song opens with Pierce singing the opening A phrase, pleading for forgiveness of his sexual indiscretions. In response, Wells sings a similar melody in the following A' phrase, declaring her unwillingness to overlook his past extramarital affairs. As Pierce attempts to promise his loyalty in the bridge section, Wells interrupts and refuses to listen further to his professions of love. Instead, she carries the melody for the remainder of the bridge to explain her reasons for distrusting his continued pleas for reconciliation: "you'd just start foolin' around with someone new." Pierce asks once more for her heart in the first half of the reprise, which Wells concludes by rejecting his claims of affection. She emphasizes that there is no hope in continuing a romance that would be forever tainted with disloyalty. This dialogue of opposing views, however, blurs the gendered distinction of the performer's voices. Apart from the difference in their timbres—a wailing tenor voice and a piercing alto—there is little else to distinguish Wells's vocal part from Pierce's. Wells, for instance, does not sing a higher melody to separate her vocal line from that of Pierce. Through similar means of expression, the duet suggests that the anxieties of class—vying for the security of domestic love—can cross gender lines.

Conclusion

Kitty Wells and her female peers entered a dialogue initially shaped by 1930s honky-tonk, music that drew on the practices of popular music to realize dramas of the heart tied to class and displacement. The following chapter provides context for understanding Wells's domestic image in 1950s Nashville country music. For now, it is important to note that Wells, performing in her gingham dresses, appeared as a guardian of rural folk culture and domesticity, but her musical expressions provided an important layer of complexity. She performed music that blended the latest conventions of honky-tonk music with a singing style anchored in the southern vernacular. In her narratives of loss and desire, Wells's singing voice, full of acoustic tension, became the defining sound of 1950s women's honky-tonk in Nashville. Yet she was not alone in shaping the aural and cultural codes of class and gender. Wells along with Goldie Hill and Jean Shepard played the role of the honky-tonk angel by voicing the desires of the sexualized woman. No longer solely a bewitching sexualized object, the honky-tonk woman could be an identity in which some measure of sexual agency could be asserted. On the other hand, in songs of romantic abandonment, Wells and her peers instilled in the musical style a complex array of identities that pointed to the injuries of class intersecting with those of gender. They were the fallen women who lost middle-class respectability or the honky-tonk women alone and forsaken in a modern world. In a historical context where the ideals of domesticity reigned, Wells and her peers could move in and out of performative roles to disclose the paradoxes of class and contribute to removing the cloak of invisibility shrouding working-class women.

7 Domestic Respectability

The Marketing of Honky-Tonk Performers

While Kitty Wells, Goldie Hill, and Jean Shepard sang of the circumstances of divorce and broken relationships, the country music industry strove to market its female performers as examples of domestic respectability. Wells, for example, looked nothing like the honky-tonk angel. Dressed in a ruffled gingham dress, she presented a demure appearance, that of the ideal country wife far removed from the sexualized working-class world that her songs inhabited. Plenty of ink has been spilled in discussions of how Wells's domestic image aligned with normative concepts of gender. In particular, scholars have suggested that her domestic image and biographical narrative, which continually stressed her housewife status, made her a safe figure "to trespass into the honky-tonk musical territory," the masculinized realm of hard drinking, male heartache, and longing for the feminine.[1] As a woman who appeared devoted to her family, she personally could never be attacked for playing the role of the honky-tonk strumpet or the cold-hearted woman who refused to follow the gender script of the 1950s.[2]

I do not want to downplay Wells's domestic image and how it worked to mediate her poignant enactments of the honky-tonk angel, the divorcée, or the jilted lover hoping for domestic security. Rather I wish to broaden the conceptual understanding of the country music industry's marketing strategies. Wells's image wasn't simply about looking the part of a conventional woman so that she could distance herself from the narratives of her honky-tonk hit songs in a conservative country music industry dominated by male promoters, record producers, songwriters, and journalists. The framing of her gender performance also involved the country music industry's pursuit of respectability. Though the ideals of femininity have historically been intertwined with notions of domestic decorum, it is important to note that female artists were not the only performers pushed in the direction of middle-class propriety in the 1950s. Journalistic accounts of Hank Williams and Webb Pierce—known for their "hard" and "authentic" expressions of the honky-tonk loner—presented them as devoted husbands and fathers in their private lives, despite biographical details about both men that strongly suggested otherwise. This chapter explores why it was essential for the country music industry to push its artists closer to the ideals of bourgeois respectability when the music itself continually pointed in a different direction.

Country Music and the Popular-Music Industry

To better understand the marketing strategies for female honky-tonk artists, I place Wells, Hill, and Shepard in the historical and commercial context of the country music business striving for commercial acceptance. What was at stake for the country music industry was its growing presence within the popular-music industry, which had worked hard to exclude country music, rhythm and blues, and other forms of vernacular music associated with working-class audiences from the industrial fold of Tin Pan Alley. Yet by the 1940s, popular artists, drawing from country material, were offering their pop versions of country songs: for example, Bing Crosby and the Andrews Sisters covered Al Dexter's famous "Pistol Packin' Mama" in 1943, and Crosby recorded another country hit, "Sioux City Sue," in 1946. Given the commercial potential of country music, leaders of the industry continued to market the music to a more mainstream audience. In particular, Wesley Rose, the son of Fred Rose, introduced the songs written by Hank Williams to pop A and R men. Mitch Miller of Columbia Records was enthused about setting Williams's songs to the crooning voices of pop singers and orchestral strings and released a number of covers, including Tony Bennett's version of "Cold, Cold Heart" (1951), which became the first hit song for the pop singer. In addition to the success of pop covers of country songs, mainstream middle-class venues started to feature country music performances. In 1947, the stars of the *Grand Ole Opry* (including Ernest Tubb and Minnie Pearl) held a two-night concert in Carnegie Hall, an event that *Billboard* publicized as "the first hill country invasion of New York's musical literati."[3]

Even while country music was reaching a broader audience than previously, the popular-music industry in the 1940s and 1950s did not consistently embrace country music's expansion into the mainstream music market, as David Brackett and Diane Pecknold have demonstrated.[4] The popular media seemed surprised that simple rubes (the industrial leaders of country music) and the simplistic melodies of rural music had managed to achieve such commercial gains. For example, in a 1943 *Billboard* article, titled "Hillbillies Heat with Helium," the journalist Nat Green wrote, "Poking fun at the hillbillies is a favorite pastime of the intelligentsia and even some of the society's sub-stratas, but the rural rhythmites go blithely along with satisfied smiles on their kissers and coins that jingle, jangle, jingle in their kicks."[5]

Apart from portraying the country music industry as a bunch of hillbillies who had fortuitously stumbled on their success, *Billboard* warned its readers of the newfound shrewdness of these very country bumpkins: "Situation currently is so sharply reversed the diskers can't figure out what happened to the gullible zekes. . . . Explanations behind the big-biz atmosphere now pervading the folk-artist belt vary, but most diskers blame the war for part of their troubles. Claim that ridge-runners and stump-jumpers all got into the war and in course of their G.I. travels picked up enough metropolitan savvy to hoist their market value and asking price."[6] Other print sources joined *Billboard* in publicizing the growing concern that country music's ascendancy during and after World War II would change the commercial dynamics of the popular-music industry, whose economic foundation had depended on the marketing of Tin Pan Alley. In 1943, *Time* magazine reported: "The flood of camp-meetin' melody, which has been rising steadily in juke joints and on radio programs for a year, was swamping Tin Pan Alley. . . . All over the country were the Appalachian accents of the geetar and the country fiddle." Despite its popularity, however, country music was still seen as a simple, lowbrow music that paled in comparison to Tin Pan Alley's urban sophistication: "Almost any simple soul might write hillbilly words and the composition of hillbilly music has always been regarded by Tin Pan Alley as a variety of unskilled labor."[7] For the guardians of the popular-music industry, country music simultaneously appeared as a threat to the commercial enterprise of Tin Pan Alley as it remained a rustic outsider to popular music's middle-class aesthetics.

Two factors in particular contributed to country music's "lowbrow" status in the popular imagination: its association with long-held negative assumptions about the rural South, and the media's fixation (fueled by a sociological discourse) on the maladjusted, displaced hillbilly, one who sought refuge from city living in Chicago's or Detroit's infamous "hillbilly hangouts," where jukeboxes played honky-tonk.[8] After World War II, the South was a place of few employment opportunities due to the collapse of the timber and agriculture industries and the automation of the coal mining industry.[9] In reaction to the poor economic conditions of the South, 4.8 million white southerners had joined 2.5 million black southerners in the search for manufacturing and service jobs in the West and the North by 1950, and by 1970, 10 million southerners in total had left the region.[10] White southern migrants from the Upland South and southern Appalachia formed the largest group that poured into cities such as Chicago's Uptown neighborhood (where they represented 40 percent of all newcomers), Washington, D.C., Detroit, and Cincinnati.[11]

But the established communities of these urban areas did not necessarily embrace the newest arrivals. Chicago and Detroit were bursting at the seams without adequate resources to meet the demands of a rapidly growing population. With housing shortages and overcrowded schools, the Midwest often blamed southern migrants (black and white) for the escalating urban decay of its cities. For example, a 1958 article in *Harper's*, "The Hillbillies Invade Chicago," began by announcing, "The city's toughest integration problem has nothing to with Negroes. . . . It involves a small army of white, Protestant, Early American migrants from the South—who are usually proud, poor, primitive, and fast with a knife."[12] Shocked by such behavior, the author, Albert N. Votaw, declared: "These country cousins confound all notions of racial, religious, and cultural purity."[13] Southern migrants were, in the words of another writer, "the hillbillies from Arkansas and the Allegheny ridges, the rednecks and the crackers."[14] Especially in a historical context in which black southerners also sought the socioeconomic promises of the Midwest, dominant society conflated the markers of race with class and region. John Hartigan's study of post–World War II Detroit demonstrates that white southerners "disrupted the social conventions upon which the color line in Detroit had been implicitly established."[15] In reaction to the influx of not only black southerners but also white southerners to industrial cities, many city dwellers decided to flee the racial and class aspects of urban living for the manicured suburbs.

To allay concerns about class and displacement, white southerners who migrated to the Midwest and the North attempted to bring with them the comforts and the cultural symbols of home. They subscribed to southern newspapers, established Southern Baptist churches, and patronized hillbilly "hangouts" where jukeboxes played the latest country hits.[16] In 1943, *Billboard*, for example, reported on the relationship between white southerners and country music in Baltimore: "Music box operators here state that hillbillies are among the best patrons for spots which offer their kind of music. This is especially true of the spots in the immediate vicinity of war plants." The article also specifically cited the popularity of Dexter's "Pistol Packin' Mama" among the clientele.[17] With white southerners flocking to war plants and industrial centers, the Midwest and the North realized that southern migrants had money to spend on entertainment and music. In 1952, *Billboard* announced the opening of a country music club in Chicago's downtown area: "The greatest single effort ever attempted in the hillbilly field in a metropolitan area will break here about July 1 when Ben Orloff, local nitery operator, and Ray Singer open the Hayloft, an all Western and country night club in the heart of the [Chicago] Loop."[18] The dance halls, honky-tonks, and hillbilly nightspots, however, carried a certain degree of social stigma associated with the class status of newly arrived white southerners in urban areas. Though the honky-tonk style, in particular, and country music, in general, drew on a range of musical idioms, the music was linked to the white southern working class, whose honky-tonk songs had invaded not only the popular-music industry but also the very urban centers of the Midwest and the North.

Despite the migration out of the South, Nashville emerged at the center of the country music industry in the late 1940s as it promoted honky-tonk songs and recordings—music tied to working-class sensibilities and hillbilly nightspots—in an attempt to break into the larger popular-music market. Though the honky-tonk style was an integral part of the country music industry, its narratives of conflicted love, sexual longing, and heartache were not what shaped country music's selling image during the 1940s and 1950s. Instead, the country music enterprise worked to distance itself from the sordid juke joint and the concerns of industrialism by emphasizing the middle-class values of its artists. Yet it did so without alienating a fan base devoted to the aesthetics of white southern working-class music, notably the sonic elements of honky-tonk music.

The Marketing of Women in Country Music

The quest to elevate the status of country music, however, was nothing new. Beginning in the mid-1920s, the radio industry had developed particular strategies to introduce a sense of rustic propriety into the minstrel and vaudevillian traditions, which had been fundamental to its broadcasts of country music. After World War II, the country music industry continued to emphasize its rural southern roots while cloaking the commercial success of its performers in the attire of bourgeois respectability. Typically rising from humble rural origins, country artists appeared as reputable individuals, readily embracing the genteel principles of domesticity and untainted by the aspirations and pressures of their performance and recording careers. Kitty Wells, the most prominent woman country artist during this historic moment of growth and expansion in the country music industry, appeared to embrace her southern past and the predominant codes of domestic respectability. Attired in gingham dresses, she affected the look of the sentimental southern mother or the southern equivalent of June Cleaver in publicity photos and live performances. Models of propriety have long been particularly important to working-class women striving to dissociate themselves from the sexual excesses linked to the lower classes. As Beverley Skeggs has argued, "The Victorian feminine-domestic ideal could offer working-class women routes to respectability, status, self-worth and the ability to construct distinctions against other women."[19] Appearing as a rural wife, Wells gave her audience the impression that she had just stepped out of her southern kitchen to sing a song or two on the *Opry*. Yet the music that Wells usually performed articulated the subject positions of working-class women:

the longing and desires of the honky-tonk angel, the forsaken housewife, or the divorced single mother. Thus the complexity of Wells's musical image lies in the stark contrast between her domestic identity as a devoted, content wife and mother and her honky-tonk performances, which revealed the hidden pain and shame of the working class.

In general, the country music industry tried not only to sanitize women's honky-tonk narratives but also to downplay the ways their recording careers exceeded the parameters of the private sphere. For example, Wells's promotional material capitalized on her domestic identity, situating her success not in the honky-tonk or the recording studio but in the private sphere, a proper realm of music making for women.[20] In a series of photos from 1956, titled "At Home with the Stars: Kitty Wells," *Country Song Roundup* featured Wells sitting in her living room with her guitar, practicing her hit "You and Me" next to an image of her entire family gathered around the piano with her daughter, Ruby, playing the instrument. Other photographs in the series captured Wells in the kitchen, cooking breakfast and later baking a cake, as if she devoted most of her time to the preparation of meals for her family. The accompanying caption stated, "Kitty is a wonderful mother and housekeeper. Here she prepares breakfast," followed by "Nothing like a home-baked cake right out of the oven—the work of an expert!"[21] In another photo, Wells, as a dutiful wife, bids goodbye to her husband as he leaves their home for a music performance. Though Johnnie Wright was a prominent musician, by 1956, when *Country Song Roundup* released these photos, Wells's stardom often outshone her husband's. But according to the publicity machine, it was she who remained in the home while he pursued his career.

Though such marketing methods attempted to relegate Wells's identity to the home, her career as a prominent musician continually exceeded her domestic image. A 1952 article titled "Kitty Wells: A Star Is Born" stated, "Kitty Wells now holds the distinction of being one of the few women folk singers to ever rise to fame and fortune." The write-up further exclaims, "'It Wasn't God Who Made Honky-Tonk Angels' has caused the entire music industry to perk up and take notice. Her remarkably sincere and sad melodic voice is heard exclusively on the Decca label" (see figure 11).[22] A couple of years later, in 1954, the trade magazine *Country Song Roundup* bestowed on her the title "Queen of the Folk Singers" and exclaimed, "Never before had a girl made a serious dent in the circle occupied by the nation's top Country music artists." It went on to declare that Wells had "repeatedly been voted by every music trade magazine as the best female vocalist in the field."[23] *Billboard*, for example, recognized Wells as the most popular female country artist from 1954 to 1965.[24]

In other promotional material, Wells was billed not just as the leading "girl star" of country music but as a reigning artist who overshadowed many of her

Figure 11. "Kitty Wells: A Star Is Born," *Country Song Roundup*, December 1952.

contemporaries, including her husband, Johnnie Wright. A 1956 *Country & Western Jamboree* article, publicizing the accomplishments of the first country music show performed in a Broadway theater, stated that few country acts had been capable of drawing large crowds to their New York performances, adding, "That is until a *Grand Ole Opry* unit headed by Roy Acuff and Kitty Wells played the New York Palace." The piece suggested that the country music industry's campaign of expanding its commercial base depended on the talent and prominence of such figures as Acuff and Wells: "Roy Acuff did the emceeing with Kitty Wells doing a wonderful solo job. Kitty brought along daughter Ruby Wells as well as the comedy pair, Johnnie & Jack."[25] Acuff and Wells were clearly the stars of a show that included a number of musical acts, such as the Gillette Sisters, the Smokey Mountain Boys (Acuff's band with which he often performed), and Wells's performance entourage: her daughter and her husband's duo team along with their band, the Tennessee Mountain Boys. Thus it was Wells's central position in the country music industry that enabled the respective performances of her family members, including the duo Johnnie and Jack, in a prominent concert held in Broadway's Palace Theatre.

Following this country music show in New York, *Country & Western Jamboree* continued to promote the musical alliance between Acuff and Wells by marketing a songbook collection of country tunes, *Songs for Home Folks*, also recorded by Acuff, Wells, and Johnnie and Jack. The article again stressed Wells's hierarchal position to her husband. While Wells was the "Queen of Country Music," Acuff was the "King," and Johnnie and Jack were merely "Princes": "This is the royalty of country music: King Roy Acuff, the real old pro of the folk music set, and Miss Kitty Wells, who has led the ranks of the ladies for a long while. It is only natural that the King and Queen inevitably would get together, and they've done it in song. Completing the court are those princes of fellows, Johnnie and Jack."[26] Recognizing Wells as a leading entertainer in country music, the industry placed her in a higher position than her husband and linked her to the most illustrious of her male contemporaries.

With Wells looming large in the country music industry, her promotional material worked to navigate the conflicting tensions between her fame and dominant definitions of femininity. Often when Wells's publicity demonstrated her prominent standing in country music, it would follow with remarks that underscored her private life and devotion to her family. As one writer asserted, "Kitty is devoted to her career, but she is also most devoted to her family."[27] *Country Song Roundup* also tried to blend Wells's achievements as a performer with her domesticity: "During her many years at the top of the entertainment world, she has never let her career come ahead of her family. She is just as accomplished in the kitchen as she is on stage." When the article focused on her "plush suburban home near Nashville," it did so in a way that highlighted her public career by describing how the "paneled den [was] decorated with an unbroken string of accomplishments in the entertainment world."[28] The marketing of the "Queen of Country Music" thus involved the duel maneuver of pushing her into the public limelight and pulling her back into the sanctity of the home.

But how were female artists marketed if they were single within a country music industry that was intent on sticking to the codes of domestic propriety? Goldie Hill, who also had several honky-tonk hit songs and performed music that underlined female sexual desire and loss, did so as a recording soloist without a husband in sight. Her unwed status, however, did not stop Hills's publicity from suggesting that she had all the marketable attributes of a potential wife: "A true Texas beauty, Goldie stands a lovely 5' 4" and weighs a slim 129 pounds. The blue-eyed, browned-haired talent package is still single—but don't be fooled fellows. For we have it from good sources that Goldie is keeping an eye peeled for the right guy."[29] Hills's promotional material continued to emphasize that she was in search of a husband. A 1954 article titled "Goldie Hill: Beauty and Brains" stated, "Though still single, Goldie has an eye out for the right man.

Meanwhile, she keeps the neighbor's children happy with candy and cookies." A photo of Hill in her kitchen holding out a platter of cookies to a child gave the distinct impression that she was in the process of perfecting her domestic talents in preparation for marriage and children.[30]

In 1957, Hill married the country performer Carl Smith, with whom she had three children. Smith had previously been married to June Carter, though the promotional material would never have reported that Hill had married a divorced man, especially one who had been married to a member of the esteemed Carter family. The veneer of domestic happiness was a common ingredient in much of the 1950s promotional material for country artists. In fact, Hills's promotional material, once she was married, shared much in common with Wells's, especially the balance in coverage between female artists' professional achievements and their private domestic lives. The article "A Visit with Goldie Hill" (devoted to publicizing Hills's comeback to country music after a three-year hiatus) defined Hill as an "Epic Recording artist" as well as "talented, beautiful, charming and the perfect wife and mother." Though Hill described in detail the rigors of raising a family, she also gave the impression that she effortlessly combined her familial obligations with her public career: "I don't let my recording and my home life interfere with each other. I can find songs and practice songs without anybody around the house knowing it and it doesn't interfere with the things I have to do for the family." Announcing her recent releases, Hill exclaimed, "Since I started with Epic a year ago, I've had two albums and three singles within that year, which is doing pretty good."[31] Hill gave the distinct impression she could do it all—raise a family and maintain a recording career.

Domesticating Masculinity

Though women country artists may have appeared to be the most fitting symbols of domesticity, the country music industry's investment in normative gender coding extended to the publicity for its male stars, especially in an era when middle-class men defined themselves as fathers in their suburban homes. As mentioned in the previous chapter, society continually encouraged men to envision their domestic roles as essential to their identity, and *Life* magazine announced that 1954 was the year of "the domestication of the American man."[32] The country music industry followed suit and mediated the expressions of working-class masculinity in honky-tonk music with promotional material that placed male country artists in the bosom of their families. Even when promoting unmarried male musicians, the country music industry linked their sexual appeal to domesticity. In a 1952 article titled "Wondering Webb," the journalist found it surprising that Webb Pierce, an emerging recording star of country music, was still single: "Anyone would think by now he would be hitched for he's just as handsome, personable and versatile as a chap could be and you can well imagine all the girls that would find themselves available to the popular artist with black wavy hair and brown eyes."[33] In reality, though, Pierce had been divorced from his first wife since 1950, before he became a successful artist in Nashville's country music industry. Ignoring the fact that he was a man with a failed marriage in his past, his publicity preferred to market Pierce as an eligible and handsome bachelor.

After Pierce had married (for the second time) and started a family, *Country Song Roundup* in 1956 took full advantage of advertising him as a domesticated man: "Everyone knows Webb Pierce, the artist, but not many know Webb, the family man. On this page we proudly present exclusive photos of the Nation's Number One Country Singer at home with his charming family. We hope this will better acquaint you with Webb—and also serve to introduce his charming wife Audrey and baby daughter Debbie." The article continued by emphasizing the centrality of domesticity to Pierce's astounding career: "With a wonderful family to inspire his every effort, it's no wonder that Webb Pierce has been so successful."[34]

But unlike Wells, Pierce did not adopt a look that suggested domestic respectability. Rather he performed in brightly colored, elaborate western suits designed by Nudie Cohn, and in publicity photos he would stand next to his ostentatious 1962 Pontiac Bonneville, decorated with thirteen mounted guns, hand-tooled leather upholstery, "a thousand silver dollars mounted inside," and a floorboard "covered with unborn calf."[35] Pierce, the country music artist with the most number one hit songs in the 1950s, displayed his success by way of glitzy fashion, in this case, the conspicuous consumption of the working class. The industry's commitment to promoting middle-class values, however, distanced Pierce from any sense of flamboyancy or poor taste by situating him within heterosexual domesticity. In the late 1960s, *Country Song Roundup* once again insisted, "[Pierce is still] an easy going soft spoken gentleman whose wife, children, home, and business reflect exactly what he is. There is no show for showiness. There is no snootiness for the sake of looking down on others. There is none of the 'nouveau riche' attitude for appearance."[36] According to his publicity, Pierce remained a dignified figure of country music largely because of his role as a breadwinning father, despite his penchant for gaudy extravagance.[37]

Pierce was not the only male performer whom the industry shaped into a middle-class model of decorum. As Richard Peterson has demonstrated, even the publicity of Hank Williams (known for his alcoholism and marital conflicts) strove to place the artist in a middle-class context of domestic happiness during his ascendancy in country music. For example, *National Hillbilly News* stated in 1950 before Williams's death, "Got 'Lovesick Blues'?" No sir, not Hank Williams. . . . The real Hank Williams . . . is happily married to a beautiful girl and has two fine children."[38] Indeed, after his untimely death, Williams was still marketed as a family man who had flourished as a songwriter in the sanctity of his home, despite the fact that he was divorced from his first wife, Audrey Sheppard, and married to his second, Billy Jean Jones, by the time he died in 1953. A journalist asserted, "The Williams home . . . became the talk of the nation . . . for here Hank Williams penned the songs that all America took to their hearts. Songs of love, hope and faith and songs of the common man. Hank's pretty wife, Audrey, was the inspiration for some of his greatest compositions."[39] According to the publicity, Audrey's warm domestic presence had inspired Williams to write love songs, even though many believed that it was their fraught relationship that had fueled the themes of heartache and marital strife in his music, notably "Cold, Cold Heart" and "Your Cheatin' Heart."[40] Not until after his death would Williams's performance persona emerge as an authentic model of country music masculinity to which other artists would continually aspire. In fact, during his career, Williams often competed with a host of young male honky-tonk artists, including Lefty Frizzell, Webb Pierce, Carl Smith, Ray Price, and Faron Young, in the popularity polls of prominent country music trade magazines. And he often did not occupy first place.[41]

Jean Shepard and Country Friendliness

Yet not all country performers from the 1950s could be packaged as domestic icons. Like Goldie Hill, Jean Shepard was a single woman recording honky-tonk songs throughout the 1950s. But her publicity did not point to the possibilities of marriage or market her as a viable domestic partner, as had the early promotional material of Hill and Pierce. Instead, the industry seemed to grapple with the effects of the full sound of Shepard's voice in performance, especially combined with her songs that explicitly critiqued gender roles, such as "Two Whoops and a Holler" and "Sad Singin' and Slow Ridin'." A 1957 article, "The Girl with the 'Big Heart,'" asked, "What's behind the big voice of Jean Shepard, Capitol recording star? . . . First you'll find a cute blonde girl who stands only about 5'1" tall and weighs a small 100 pounds."[42] By pointing to her diminutive but attractive stature, the country music industry seemed to counter the powerful impression of her voice, linking the performer to normative definitions of beauty and femininity—cute and petite. Her publicity continued to contrast her small stature with the power of her voice. A 1963 account of Shepard's career in the trade magazine *Music City News*, for example, stated: "Jean is a little thing. She stands five feet and one inch tall and weighs one hundred and ten pounds, but from the way she belts out a song, you would think she was twice that size."[43]

Apart from the comments on her physicality, the trade magazines shaped her image into one of country friendliness—a similar strategy that the country music industry would employ in the early years of George Jones's career, despite his growing reputation as a hard-drinking country performer, following in the footsteps of Williams.[44] The marketing strategy of painting country artists as personable and approachable was even used to plug the young Johnny Cash early in his career in the 1950s. Before he became the "Man in Black," he was a country performer with a personality of "warmth" and "sincerity" as well as a "beloved family man" and "the friend of all those who admire him."[45]

In building a community of artists with whom fans could form personal connections, the country music industry underlined that fact that Shepard was no different, even as a single woman who sang about infidelity and divorce. *Country Song Roundup* stated, "The first thing you will notice is the big friendly smile and the warm personality that makes you feel as though you have known her all your life. . . . She is one of the nicest, most sincere, and lovable persons in the business and she is a girl who has a big heart—a heart for singin' Country music and a heart to help those who need help."[46] Since the industry couldn't depict Shepard as a wife and mother, it molded her into a thoughtful, caring, and modest woman—all the qualities associated with the feminine ideal—even as she emerged as a commercial success. "In spite of her standing in entertaining circles," for instance, "Jean remains modest and down-to-earth." "To her fans and friends, she'll always be 'Just Plain Jean.'"[47] Instead of being viewed as a threat to normative culture because of her honky-tonk repertory, Shepard, at all times, appeared to be the essence of affability: "On-stage the capable young blonde reaches out magnificently over an entire audience with a surprisingly resonant voice, at the same time, appears to be carrying a message of friendship for each individual listener."[48]

But in 1960 Shepard did indeed marry, and her wedding to the country star Hawkshaw Hawkins received much press. Shepard finally could be marketed as a married woman (though Hawkins would die tragically in the same 1963 plane accident that took the lives of Patsy Cline and Cowboy Copas). The ceremony itself took place in the Forum Auditorium of Wichita, Kansas, and was broadcast as part of the *Grand Ole Opry*—mixing entertainment with the actual ceremony. The show began with "a great line up of stars, featuring Jean Shepard and Hawkshaw Hawkins, Tex Ritter with his side kick Hank Morton, Carl Perkins, The Plainsmen Quartet, The LeGarde Twins from Australia, Moon Mullican, Gary Van and his Western Starlighters from Dallas, and Billy Thompson." Four thousand people attended this grand event. After the country music portion of the show, "the curtain closed," and organ music could be heard. "The Plainsmen Quartet sang a moving rendition of "True Love" and "Her Hand in Mine" to set the stage for the main act: Shepard's wedding ceremony. "Nick Sanders, the owner of the Country Music station KSIR in Wichita, Kansas, was at the microphone, explaining the procedure as the wedding progressed" for radio listeners. *Country Song Roundup* described in detail the country show and the ceremony for those who had missed the radio broadcast.[49] Shepard and Hawkins made their own wedding into entertainment for their fan base, blurring the divide between private and public.

Rustic Traditions and Domestic Propriety

While the industry promoted the personable and reputable principles of its performers, it continued to foster the loyalty of its fan base, including white southern migrants, by emphasizing the regional and rural roots of country music. Along with her domestic identity, Wells, for instance, was also a country musician rooted in the practices of southern vernacular culture. *Country Song Roundup* revealed that Wells received her first music lessons in folk balladry from her father: "She learned her art as a child from her guitar playing railroader father, big Charlie Carey Deason. As big Charlie used to pick and sing 'Casey Jones' in the evenings, little Kitty began to learn the true American art of the folk ballad."[50] *Country & Western Jamboree* echoed similar claims: "Kitty was born the daughter of a railroader and learned the sad folk songs of America at her father's knee. Her voice has the sincerity and wistful melody that is the true mark of a ballad singer."[51] By connecting Wells's to her father's musical ability and his working-class vocation, the country music industry suggested that she herself embodied the musical heritage associated with plebeian life.

Indeed, it was her musical background and commitment to southern working-class culture that made Wells a star who fully deserved her commercial success as the "Queen of Country Music." Her background story certainly helped authenticate Wells's links to honky-tonk music. Yet her publicity carefully managed the class elements of her childhood largely by aligning her with the southern rendition of the feminine ideal. Introducing the performer onto the stage in the 1960s, Grant Turner, a master of ceremonies for the *Opry*, trumpeted Wells's particular devotion to the esteemed traditions of the South—country music, family, and the church: "Well, our next singer is right at home. She should feel that way, for Nashville is her hometown. She has three loves in her life, her singing, her family, and her church. We call her the Queen of Country Music. And she certainly earned that title and carries it well."[52]

Wells's publicity, which strove to balance her commercial prominence with 1950s gender ideals, was a common phenomenon of this era. Joanne Meyerowitz, for instance, argues that postwar mass culture embraced the contradictions "between domestic ideals and individual achievement."[53] Popular culture discourse, found in magazines aimed at a middle-class readership, supported women's participation in both the public sphere and the domestic realm.

In addition, the industry's emphasis on traditional southern values, domesticity, and rusticity did not necessarily frame it exclusively as a "feminine enterprise."[54] The country music trade magazines frequently conflated the rural traditions of country music with those of domesticity in marketing male musicians. Contributing to the industry's memorializing of Hank Williams, *Country Song Roundup* included a series of articles in addition to letters, written by country music's most prominent figures, attesting to Williams's character and musical contributions.[55] The opening article gave the impression that Williams's illustrious career sprang from the cherished musical traditions of southern rurality, church, and family: "When he was only a little shaver, Hank began singing in the choir of the church where his mother played the organ. Like many typically American farm boys, Hank grew up to the strains of the strong yet tender hymns that the deeply religious simple folk of this country love. From these hymns, Hank Williams learned early in life that a singer must put his heart into a song in order to get across the true meaning of the lyrics." Surrounding this account of Williams's musical expressions were photos of his domestic life: his singing and playing the guitar to his infant son and another photo in which he and his former wife, Sheppard, are smiling into the camera.[56]

Country fans of the 1950s applauded the industry's strategies for infusing country music with a sense of middle-class propriety and listeners finding refuge in the industry's investment in respectability, assuaging their concerns about class and dislocation. As Pecknold states, fans viewed the "growing acceptance of country music as an indicator of their own respectability."[57] The country music industry worked hard to illustrate that its performers and by extension its fans were not maladjusted hillbillies trapped in the sordid honky-tonks of the Midwest and the North or working in factories and living in overcrowded cities. Instead, Wells and her peers remained safely ensconced in the South, linked to the Nashville country music industry and untouched by the upheavals of post–World War II America. The domestic lives of country artists, who were often pictured with their families, were meant to constitute stable sites for their listening audience grappling with the disorienting effects of industrial modernity. Even in the face of mass-mediated commercialism, Wells and her male and female peers remained anchored in the rural past and the sanctity of the home. They were seen as devoted fathers and mothers or reputable individuals, dedicated to preserving the musical heritage of country music.

Conclusion

While the country music industry worked to shed its lowbrow status in the mass-mediated popular-music market, it attempted to shape its musicians—including male honky-tonk artists—into individuals who adhered to middle-class values in their private lives despite the narratives of their music. Country music trade magazines offered especially tantalizing glimpses into the ways leading stars—Hank Williams, Kitty Wells, Webb Pierce, Jean Shepard, and Goldie Hill—appeared as examples of respectability to a fan base of displaced southerners grappling with the pressures and uncertainties arising from geographic and social mobility. Yet their musical voices underscored the subject positions of men and women who fell short of the domestic ideals of the 1950s. Specifically, the complex relationship between female country artists' domestic/rural images and their musical enactments of honky-tonk culture assuaged and articulated the anxieties of class and dislocation intersecting with those of gender. As Wells, in particular, seemed to protect rural folk culture and domesticity from the dramatic changes of postwar America, she voiced the desires and fears of her audience. And she wasn't alone. Shepard and Hill, in performance, provided poignant expressions that spoke of the class-driven realities of desire and the possibilities of female agency. With the immediacy of their singing voices pushing against the ideals of 1950s America, women in country music remind us that the process of adopting or performing the look and physicality of middle-class decorum is never a straightforward process. Instead, the musical images of female honky-tonk artists illuminated the paradoxical tensions of white, rural, and working-class women's relationships to dominant expectations of gender.

Conclusion

Country Vocalities and Gendered Theatrics

Bringing the key figures of my study together, I have demonstrated the many ways in which women were fundamental to the musical developments of country music within specific geographical locales. Not only did female performers help shape the styles of early country music in the Midwest, California, and Nashville, but they also addressed the economic, social, and geographical concerns of their audiences with a range of musical enactments of gender. From Chicago's WLS, Lulu Belle introduced unruly versions of southern womanhood, and Patsy Montana presented independent cowgirls to a Depression-era audience grappling with the effects of migration and the gender strife of the era. To a distinct Okie audience in California, Carolina Cotton brought the vocal virtuosity and glamour of the singing cowgirl to the dance idioms of western swing, and Rose Maddox extended the comedic rebellion of the hillbilly to her rockabilly performances. In Nashville, women in honky-tonk—Kitty Wells, Jean Shepard, and Goldie Hill—unveiled the desires of working-class female subjects through sexual and domestic metaphors against a backdrop of geographic and social mobility.

Within these musical representations, the singing voice combined with the theatrical conventions of the popular stage have been instrumental in shaping specific visions of womanhood. Lulu Belle's and Maddox's vocal parodies of southern culture offered transgressive forms of humor that pointedly challenged social and gender norms. Montana's and Cotton's "sweet" singing style and yodeling virtuosity painted glamorous and, at times, comic pictures of female autonomy. And Wells's strident, nasal-twang singing voice of constraint and tradition underscored the cultural nuances of the honky-tonk angel. As we have seen, no single mode of expression gave voice to the complexities and paradoxes of class, region, and gender. Yet important recurrent themes have emerged in this study and remain integral to the musical idioms and aural reception of female country artists.

Early country music's performative legacy grew out of the conventions of minstrelsy and vaudeville, in which female performers (such as Sophie Tucker and Fanny Brice) transformed male-defined thespian roles of the wench or the old maid into humorously defiant models of womanhood. Emerging from the practices of the nineteenth-century popular stage, Lulu Belle vocally played the rube comedienne in narratives that critiqued gender roles, helping carve out a discursive space that enabled female performers to contest the regional and class premises of domestic respectability. Patsy Montana, in her cowgirl role, incorporated the gender-bending tropes of the West in staged shows, dime novels, and early film to write and perform songs that resisted the confines of domesticity and even critiqued the cultural standing of masculinity. On the stages of California's nightspots, Carolina Cotton and Rose Maddox drew on the singing roles of the cowgirl and the hillbilly comedienne, with Cotton playing a variety of rustic roles in film. Kitty Wells, Jean Shepard, and Goldie Hill also transformed the female objects of male honky-tonk into subjects that articulated desires and longings that could not be neatly contained. Wells's vocal enactments of heartbroken women's longing for sexual love and material comfort were very much an act, but one that she fully embodied in each performance.

From Lulu Belle's songs about marital discord to Kitty Wells's honky-tonk ballads about heartache and yearning, women in country have employed domestic and sexual metaphors to signify subject positions that do not fall within the middle-class tropes of blissful love and happy unions. Early country music is especially significant because the theatrics of the rustic comedienne, the singing cowgirl, and the honky-tonk angel have lingered in the narratives and musical images of more recent country music. Musically, we can hear the aural acts of defiance in the past and in contemporary narratives of gun-toting women confronting their ex-lovers; angry, forsaken housewives contesting the terms of marriage; honky-tonk angels disclosing the shame and desires of working-class women; and "redneck" women flaunting their class status.

By taking a look at some key figures in women's country music beginning with Loretta Lynn and Dolly Parton, we get a glimpse of how individual artists used a range of vocal practices that combined past conventions with personal style in performances of gender and country identity. As a songwriter and performer, Loretta Lynn, for example, drew on the themes of her predecessors with a vocal style indicative of southern vernacular idioms. Lynn broke into the Nashville country music scene with her first hit, "I'm a Honky-Tonk Girl" (1960), in which the female subject turns to the honky-tonk to listen to the jukebox and drown her sorrow over her beloved's abandonment of her. In the opening phrase, Lynn immediately depicts the protagonist's heartache and emotional depravity: "Ever since you left me I've done nothing but wrong." Similar to Wells's vocal production, Lynn's singing style forefronts the acoustic tension of the voice to depict the painful social realities of class. In each A phrase of the song, she pushes her chest voice well above the vocal break to the higher midrange (B-flat$_4$) to realize the upper melody. She thus infuses her drama of the heart with a strident nasal-twang voice and further embellishes the melody with a pronounced vibrato at the end of phrases to heighten the pathos of the narrative. Out of complete desperation, the narrator declares that she is now a "honky-tonk girl" with a blues-inflected melodic line to connect the downtrodden to the licentious atmosphere of the juke joint. The subject's feelings of shame have everything to do with her emotional and material vulnerability that leads to the honky-tonk, where the "low Other" resides. Like her predecessors, Lynn elaborates on the identity of the honky-tonk angel. Instead of being a woman who chooses the pleasures of the night over a so-called respectable lifestyle, the honky-tonk girl suffers from the pain of the working class—the shame of living a life that refuses to deliver the promises of economic stability and domestic happiness.

Lynn, however, did not persist in elaborating on these gendered themes of abjection in her honky-tonk tunes. In her well-known songs of the 1960s and 1970s, "Don't Come Home A-Drinkin' (with Lovin' on Your Mind)," "Fist City," and "The Pill," Lynn refuses to play the part of the downtrodden. In "Don't Come Home A-Drinkin'," for example, Lynn enacts the position of a no-nonsense woman giving a stern warning to her husband, who spends his evenings in the local bar, similar in narrative tone to that of Shepard's 1956 recording of "Sad Singin' and Slow Ridin'." If the husband in "Don't Come Home A-Drinkin'" continues to pursue alcohol and extramarital dalliances at the local juke joint, Lynn's protagonist will refuse to participate in a marital sexual relationship.[1]

The female protagonist's assertive character lies not only in the lyrical narrative but also in Lynn's vocal delivery. Unlike the marked use of nasal-twang tension in "I'm a Honky-Tonk Girl," Lynn sings in a more resonant chest voice at the beginning of her vocal phrases with a vocal styling that resembles Maddox's and Shepard's open-throat vocalities. Though "Don't Come Home A-Drinkin'" is in the same key as "I'm a Honky-Tonk Girl," the tessitura of the song accentuates Lynn's lower chest range. With a chest-dominant vocal technique, Lynn sings a declamatory vocal line of repeated pitches and ascending triadic movement to her midrange.[2] The song's melodic design combined with Lynn's delivery gives the distinct impression of clipped speech developing into louder admonishments produced by a belting tone inflected with some degree of nasal twang when she sings the upper melody of the tune. In live performance, when Lynn would increase in volume by belting her ascending melodic lines in her chest voice, she would often have to move the microphone away from her mouth, to avoid overloading the sound equipment.

With her dynamic, sonorous voice, marked by her eastern Kentucky accent, Lynn performed songs that negotiated the terms of heterosexual relationships. In "Fist City" (1968), she could sing about confronting the other woman, warning her to "lay off my man" with the same singing voice that proclaimed her rural Appalachian roots in nostalgic narratives (such as "Blue Kentucky Home" and "Coal Miner's Daughter") for an audience of former rural dwellers. Just as Lulu Belle and Rose Maddox could critique gender conventions while singing nostalgically about the South, Lynn also publicized her geographical ties by evoking the regional tropes of country with an anti-bourgeois attitude in songs like "When You're Looking at Me, You're Looking at Country" (1971). She replaced country's early hillbilly imagery with representations encapsulating a rural working-class way of life. In short, Lynn drew on the defiant woman archetype, wielding it in a manner that could contest the marginalized social positions of women while asserting a country identity that lay outside normative society. Lynn continually makes it clear that the female subjects of her songs are not from the middle class. Even when she takes up contemporary topics, such as women's rights, sexuality, and birth control, as in "The Pill" (1972), she sings from the position of a rural white working-class woman negotiating the terms of her sexual and romantic life within a heterosexual context.

Like Lynn, Dolly Parton initially built her musical career on these sonic and thematic conventions by performing songs that highlighted the unjust double standards of male and female sexuality and depicted the authority and competence of female subjects in negotiating the fraught terrain of heterosexual adult love. Similar in theme to Wells's "It Wasn't God Who Made Honky-Tonk Angels" or "I'm No Angel," the protagonist in Parton's "Just Because I'm a Woman" (1968) freely admits to a sexualized past and demands not to be judged by the man in her new relationship. Though she declares that she is "no angel," she explains that her former dalliances do not make her an immoral woman. She elaborates that she "was just the victim of a man that let" her down, and her "mistakes" are no worse that any man's sexual past. In another example, the up-tempo tune "You're Gonna Be Sorry" (1968), Parton explains what to do when a man takes for granted the love and affection of a woman. While the man of the tale was "busy makin' out" with another woman, Parton's protagonist was "making plans for checkin' out." In shaping vocally her assertive stance of leaving emotionally and sexually unrewarding relationships, Parton sings with a chest-dominated vocality. She embellishes her vocal lines with the use of vibrato and a range of vocal dynamics from quietly singing to belting the melodic high points. Thus early in Parton's career, she extended predominant practices to her country narratives of confrontational and determined women.

Yet as Parton climbed the commercial ladder to star status, she cultivated a distinct singing style that highlighted her light, tremulous, head voice and her use of vocal embellishments.[3] While Parton still maintains her Tennessee accent, her singing voice, known for its distinct use of register and timbre, also encapsulates the different facets of her commercial success and the well-crafted persona that balanced authenticity with commercialism. Drawing on the theatrics of barn-dance radio's dueling dynamics of rustic sentimentality and hillbilly parody, Parton performs what the lyrics to her 2008 song "Backwoods Barbie" describe as "country girl's ideal of glam." Parton's stylized image evokes the sexualized, man-hungry rube paradigm (perfected by Al Capp's cartoon illustrations of Daisy Mae), or as Leigh Edwards puts it, Parton has combined the "pure mountain-girl" identity with the "subversive image of a 'poor white trash hillbilly hooker'" in a composite version of working-class womanhood used to critique middle-class norms.[4] In all of this, Parton's signature vocal style has helped dramatize her feminized rustic masks. That is, her soft, head voice comes across as the persona of a country girl putting on a musical costume of feminine charm and glitz, which is similar in effect to Lulu Belle's early vocal performances of the naive country rube. However, Parton's vocal manner can also switch from a quieter, lighter, and higher vocality toward a more pushed-sounding chest voice accompanied by a piercing nasal-twang tone that evokes Appalachian mountain culture. All these techniques underline how Parton's use of contrasting vocal approaches has shaped her fluid play of gender.[5]

Stylized displays of rusticity and working-class womanhood, confrontational narratives challenging the confines of patriarchy, and vocalities redolent of past traditions have all had a lasting influence on some of the most compelling performances of recent female artists. The Dixie Chicks, a female trio that *Rolling Stone* referred to as the "badass queenpins of country," burst on the country scene in 1990s Nashville by bringing the long-standing musical traditions and imagery of early country music to the present.[6] Playing an assortment of string instruments—fiddle, banjo, dobro, and mandolin—band members Martie Erwin Maguire and Emily Erwin Robison highlight string-band or bluegrass instrumental idioms in a contemporary setting of electric guitars and drums. The vocals of the trio also mediate past and present expressions in their imaginative sonic narratives of the southern pastoral or the exotic eeriness of the gothic South, the loneliness or revelry of the honky-tonk, and the mythos of the American West.

The Dixie Chicks' "Cowboy Take Me Away" (1999), for example, is about escaping to the promises of the West through the cowgirl's romantic relationship with the cowboy. Similar in theme to Montana's "I Want to Be a Cowboy's Sweetheart" (recorded by an earlier version of the Dixie Chicks with band mates Robin Lynn Macy and Laura Lynch before Natalie Maines had joined), this song reflects the Dixie Chicks' understanding of the musical and romanticized visions of female autonomy. Just as the cowgirl in "I Want to Be a Cowboy's

Sweetheart" wishes to "pillow" her "head near the sleeping herd while the moon shines down from above," the protagonist in "Cowboy Take Me Away" yearns to sleep on the "hard ground" under a "blanket made of stars." Depicting this mythical landscape, Maines departs from her usual nasal-twang style of singing. To the quiet playing of the acoustic guitar and fiddle, Maines begins the tune by singing close to the microphone in a whispery, soft manner, engendering a level of intimacy in the trio's portrait of romance and freedom. When the backup vocals enter, the higher harmony singing of Maguire brings a clear soprano voice to the vocal production, and Maines in her chest register works to match the rounded tones of her band mates, in a singing manner recalling that of the 1930s and 1940s cowgirl.

But when the trio conjures the sonic image of the honky-tonk, as in "Tonight the Heartache's on Me" (1999) or depicts the hurried circumstances of a "White Trash Wedding" (2002), Maines accentuates her nasal-twang chest vocality, locating her vocal styling within southern vernacular traditions. Indeed, in the raucous number "White Trash Wedding," all three singers underline a strident nasal-twang singing style in their three-part harmony, accompanied by their bluegrass playing, to convey the aural tropes of class and region in their satirical description of a "shotgun" wedding ceremony.

These sorts of conflations of sexuality, rusticity, and rejection of middle-class social values formed the basis of Gretchen Wilson's 2004 "Redneck Woman" (as demonstrated by the recent work of Nadine Hubbs) and have continued to inflect the music of women in country.[7] Miranda Lambert, one of the most successful women in Nashville, has built her persona and career on these past examples of rebellion. The *New York Times* has declared that she is "a certain kind of hell-raiser: volatile, irrepressible, out for blood."[8] What initially cemented her reputation are her early hits, "Kerosene" (2005) and "Crazy Ex-Girlfriend" (2007), which dramatically underscore the irrepressible wrath of a scorned woman. In "Crazy Ex-Girlfriend," Lambert sings of tracking down her former boyfriend and his new girlfriend in the local bar, where her anger and jealousy explode in violence. Her tune gestures to a lineage of songs that depict the unbridled anger of women erupting into threatening and vindictive acts such as Shepard's "Sad Singin' and Slow Ridin'" (1956), Lynn's "Fist City" (1968), or the Dixie Chicks' "Goodbye Earl" (2000). In her songs of revenge and protest, Lambert sings with a characteristic resonant chest voice, yielding a confrontational, punctuated sound to her vocals.

Lambert is also known for her strident nasal-twang vocality, accentuated in her higher chest range, in her plaintive ballads, such as "Bathroom Sink" (2014). Gazing at herself in the bathroom mirror, Lambert sings of learning the lessons her "mama" taught her, "how to pray and drink, and how to clean the bathroom sink." With a rising melodic line, Lambert realizes the lyricism of the slow ballad with a strident chest voice, giving symbolic weight to those maternal ties that bind the protagonist to her past. Like the musical voices of Loretta Lynn, Dolly Parton, and Natalie Maines, Lambert carries the recurrent themes of the past to the dynamic present, shaping and reimagining the paradoxes and complexities of female subjectivities that go against the vocal and social grains of society.

In our current postindustrial environment, the working class has become a social category far removed from its former masculinized identity, the virile proletariat, as once imagined by theorists. Instead, the feminization of the service industry (the driving force of the current economy in the United States) has extended to the working class, transforming our understandings of the gendered processes of social class. No longer can working-class women be overlooked in a socioeconomic environment that depends on their labor and has made it increasingly difficult for working-class men to hold on to their breadwinning status in the industrial sector. With their musical depictions of redneck women and crazy ex-girlfriends, contemporary female country artists underscore the complex transformations of contemporary social relations, especially in respect to the feminization of the working class and the shrinking of the middle class, a category of identity whose members have worked hard to keep a safe distance from the sexualized bodies of the lower class. Invoking the vocalities and theatrics of hillbilly maidens, singing cowgirls, and honky-tonk angels, the acoustic and cultural voices of women in country continue to underline the contestations of class and gender for contemporary audiences struggling to understand the shifting demographics of the twentieth-first century.

Notes

Introduction

1. For more information about *The Country Show*, see Lange, *Smile*, 222–223.

2. *Memories: Grand Ole Opry Stars of the Fifties.*

3. Female country artists did not host the *Grand Ole Opry* until Bob Whittaker took over as manager of the program in 1993. For more information about women as emcees of the *Opry*, see Escott, *Grand Ole Opry*, 186–187.

4. Scholars have echoed contemporary claims that women in country music were used as a form of window dressing in country music before the mass appeal of Patsy Cline opened new avenues for female country soloists. For example, see Bufwak and Oermann, *Finding Her Voice*, 209, quote of Dottie West; and Hofstra, *Sweet Dreams*, 107, which includes George Hamilton IV's account of Cline's success.

5. Haslam, *Workin' Man Blues*, 14.

6. Berish, *Lonesome Roads*, 19 and 3.

7. Felski, *Gender of Modernity*, 37.

8. For more details about the formation of the middle class in the United States during the nineteenth century, see Archer and Blau, "Class Formation in Nineteenth-Century America," 17–41; and Blumin, *Emergence of the Middle Class.*

9. Bourdieu, *Distinction*, 169–225.

10. Blumin, *Emergence of the Middle Class*, 183–184, points to the perceived moral superiority of women over men in the nineteenth-century middle-class home.

11. McRobbie, "Notes on 'What Not to Wear,'" 101.

12. Skeggs, *Formations of Class and Gender*, 99.

13. Skeggs, *Formations of Class and Gender*, 99, states that working-class women were "involved in forms of labour that prevented femininity from ever being a possibility."

14. Hubbs, *Rednecks, Queers, and Country Music*, 122.

15. Skeggs, *Formations of Class and Gender*, 99.

16. Skeggs, *Formations of Class and Gender*, 118. Sherry Ortner has posited that the working class has been repeatedly "cast as the bearer of an exaggerated sexuality against which middle-class respectability is defined" (*Anthropology and Social Theory*, 33).

17. McNay, "Agency and Experience," 186.

18. Skeggs, "Exchange, Value, and Affect," 88.

19. McCusker, "Gendered Stages," 358.

20. McCusker, *Lonesome Cowgirls and Honky-Tonk Angels*, 3.

21. P. Fox, *Natural Acts*, 11.

22. P. Fox, *Natural Acts*, 7.

23. I am influenced by the methodological approaches of musicologist Robert Walser. He argues that an "analysis of the music . . . that is grounded in the history and significance of actual musical details and structures" can reveal a "dialectic environment in which meanings are multiple, fluid, and negotiated" (*Running with the Devil*, 21).

24. Morris, *Persistence of Sentiment*, 183.

25. Edwards, *Dolly Parton*, 6.

26. Hamessley, *Unlikely Angel*.

27. Hubbs, *Rednecks, Queers, and Country Music*, 127.

28. For more about the gendered strife within working-class families, see Ortner, *Anthropology and Social Theory*, 29–31.

29. Hubbs, *Rednecks, Queers, and Country Music*, 19.

30. See P. Fox, *Natural Acts*, 9, for a discussion of the process of identification and disavowal in relation to the rustic masks of minstrelsy and barn-dance radio.

31. Brackett, *Categorizing Sound*, 57.

32. Brackett, *Categorizing Sound*, 115–136.

33. McClary, *Conventional Wisdom*, 5 and 6.

34. McClary, *Conventional Wisdom*, 44.

35. Leppert and Lipsitz, "'Everybody's Lonesome for Somebody,'" 270–271 and 260.

36. Leppert and Lipsitz, "'Everybody's Lonesome for Somebody,'" 266.

37. Leppert, "Gender Sonics," 196.

38. Neal, "'Nothing but a Little Ole Pop Song,'" 146.

39. Stilwell, "Vocal Decorum," 57, offers a useful critique of Robert Oermann's narrative in the documentary *The Women of Rockabilly: Welcome to the Club*.

40. Stimeling, "Narrative, Vocal Staging, and Masculinity," 348.

41. Stimeling, "Taylor Swift's 'Pitch Problems,'" 86.

42. I also write about country singing styles in "The Singing Voice in Country Music," in Stimeling, *Oxford Handbook of Country Music*, 157–176.

43. S. Cusick, "Feminist Theory, Music Theory." For other scholarly works that consider the relationship between the body and music, see Cizmic, *Performing Pain*; Eidsheim, *Race of Sound*; and Le Guin, *Boccherini's Body*.

44. S. Cusick, "On Musical Performance," 29, italics original.

45. Since the eighteenth century, vocal pedagogues have found that the singing voice can be divided into three distinct registers: the low chest, the extensive midrange, and the higher head range.

46. See Neal, "Twang Factor in Country Music," 51–53, for a discussion of the aesthetics and perceptions of twang as a style of vocal delivery that signifies regional, class-, and race-based identities.

47. Vocal pedagogues distinguish between oral twang (used in opera and musical theater) and nasal twang (the vocal style heard in country music) and offer "corrective" measures to open up the vocal sound in the oral cavity, keeping with a bel canto aesthetic of rounded

tones. See Chapman, *Singing and Teaching Singing*, 99; Kayes, *Singing and the Actor*, 70; and McKinney, *Diagnosis and Correction of Vocal Faults*, 137.

48. Kayes, *Singing and the Actor*, 112; and Sundberg and Thalén, "What Is Twang?"

49. McKinney, *Diagnosis and Correction of Vocal Faults*, 137. Kayes, *Singing and the Actor*, 112, warns that the singer's tightening of the larynx can fall into constriction when producing vocal tones inflected by nasal twang.

50. Wicks, "Belated Salute," 59.

51. For a history of how singing schools inculcated a level of musical literacy to discourage lined-out psalm singing, see Bealle, *Public Worship, Private Faith*, 10–11; Kiri Miller, *Traveling Home*, 7; and Steel and Hulan, *Makers of the Sacred Harp*, 40.

52. White and King, *Sacred Harp*, 24.

53. White and King, *Sacred Harp*, 23.

54. Quoted in Wicks, "Belated Salute," 61.

55. *White Spirituals from the Sacred Harp*.

56. Stilwell, "Vocal Decorum," 72.

57. Boyer, *How Sweet the Sound*, 11.

58. Eidsheim, *Race of Sound*, 25 and 27.

59. P. J. Smith, "Brit Girls," 159. See also Catherine Clément, "Through Voices, History," 21–24, for how voice types in opera represent distinct versions of womanhood.

60. Wolf, *Problem like Maria*, 102.

61. Maureen Mahon refers to Big Mama Thornton's "powerful chest voice" ("Listening," 11). For examples of popular media referring to Natalie Maine's strong and powerful voice, see Bacon, "Culture"; and Rayburn, "No Sign of Controversy."

62. Stras, "Voice of the Beehive."

63. Warwick, *Girl Groups, Girl Culture*, 49.

Chapter 1. Early Country Music: The Crossing of Musical Hierarchies on Chicago's WLS

1. See McCusker, *Lonesome Cowgirls and Honky-Tonk Angels*, 7–27; and Pecknold, *Selling Sound*, 13–52, for radio's role in the commercial developments of country music before Nashville emerged as the center of the country music industry in the late 1940s.

2. See Brackett, *Categorizing Sound*, 113–121, for a detailed history of recording labels and early country music.

3. Brackett, *Categorizing Sound*, 113–141, discusses at length the ways the recording industry could not agree on a conceptual term to market early country music, as it did with the designation of "race" records.

4. Kibler, *Rank Ladies*, 8, opines that vaudeville houses brought high and low culture together, linking divergent cultures divided by gender, class, and ethnicity.

5. See Berry, *Hayloft Gang*, for a collection of essays that explain how WLS provided its listeners with musical escapes from the conditions of the Great Depression.

6. B. Anderson, *Imagined Communities*, 25. Anderson explains that beginning during the Enlightenment, the technology of print contributed to the circulation of new forms of literature (such as the newspaper and the novel) that "provided the technical means of 'representing' the kind of imagined community that is a nation," replacing previous social orders, the monarch, and religious authorities, which had largely structured society. With millions partaking in the ritual of reading a daily newspaper, this new medium organized

time and presented information about a given area, contributing to strangers forming some sort of connection, an identity as a specific group.

7. Berry, *Hayloft Gang.*

8. *WLS Family Album*, 1930, 5.

9. *WLS Family Album*, 1930, 18.

10. *WLS Family Album*, 1936, 17.

11. Chad Berry, introduction to Berry, *Hayloft Gang*, 15.

12. See Berry, *Southern Migrants, Northern Exiles*; and Gregory, *Southern Diaspora*, for historical accounts of white southern migration to the Midwest.

13. Gregory, *Southern Diaspora*, 13–14, makes the point that the out-migration of white southerners was larger than previous historians have depicted. In comparison to the 3 million whites who were living outside the South, in the 1930s around 1.5 million black southerners had left for the North, the Midwest, and the West.

14. Palmer, *Social Backgrounds*, 34.

15. Bertrand, "Race and Rural Identity," 130, argues that the *National Barn Dance* attracted an audience of midwestern "farm folks." Pecknold states that Edgar Bill, the station manager of WLS, "consciously targeted a middle-class audience," specifically, "the prosperous and pious farmers of the Midwest" (*Selling Sound*, 19–20). On the other hand, Tyler points to the "surprising breadth of the audience" for the *National Barn Dance* ("Rise of Rural Rhythm," 23).

16. See Salamon, *Prairie Patrimony*, 15–23, for a discussion of the various ways a shared ethnic Germany identity, distinct from native-born Americans, materialized in the Midwest.

17. Cohen, *Making a New Deal*, provides a detailed historical account of the different ethnic working-class communities in Chicago before the Depression (11–52) and their relationship to the emerging radio industry in Chicago (133–37).

18. Levine, *Highbrow/Lowbrow*, 85–168.

19. Kibler, *Rank Ladies*, 7.

20. Harrison-Kahan, *White Negress*, 20.

21. The "angel in the house" was a Victorian idealization of womanhood based on the principles of middle-class domesticity. The term comes from Coventry Patmore's poem titled "Angel in the House," published between 1854 and 1862.

22. Kibler, *Rank Ladies*, 7, 9–10. Additional scholars have demonstrated the ways vaudeville navigated the boundaries of middle-class sensibilities with explicit displays of female sexuality and bawdy humor. See Erdman, *Blue Vaudeville*, 5–14.

23. Goodman, *Radio Civic Ambition*, 144.

24. See Radway, "Book-of-the-Month Club," for a discussion of the emergence of middlebrow culture and the middle class.

25. Rubin, *Making of Middlebrow Culture*, xii.

26. *WLS Family Album*, 1934, 8.

27. *WLS Family Album*, 1937, 40. Christine was heard on daily programs and the Saturday evening broadcasts of the *National Barn Dance.*

28. *WLS Family Album*, 1930, 12.

29. *WLS Family Album*, 1934, 31.

30. Montana, interview, June 9, 1984, 63.

31. *Stand By!*, March 2, 1935, 11.

32. *Standby!,* July 4, 1936, 3 and 15.

33. *WLS Family Album,* 1930, 18.

34. *WLS Family Album,* 1932, 15.

35. *WLS Family Album,* 1937, 45; and *WLS Family Album,* 1933, 19.

36. *WLS Family Album,* 1933, 19.

37. Edgar Bill quoted in Biggar, "WLS National Barn Dance Story," 106.

38. Each week *Stand By!* listed the performers for the different segments of the *National Barn Dance.* See, for example, *Stand By!,* March 23, 1935, 8; July 29, 1935, 14; March 14, 1936, 14; and May 2, 1936, 14.

39. McCusker, *Lonesome Cowgirls and Honky-Tonk Angels,* 62, explains that by 1937, the NBC broadcast of WLS's *National Barn Dance* attracted middle-class and lower-middle-class listeners nationwide. Brackett, *Categorizing Sound,* 115–127, and Karl H. Miller, *Segregating Sound,* 210–211, demonstrate that the recording industry's 1920s country music appealed significantly to audiences outside the South.

40. *Souvenir WLS Program,* 1939, 3.

41. *WLS Family Album,* 1931, 39.

42. *WLS Family Album,* 1930, foreword.

43. McCusker, *Lonesome Cowgirls and Honky-Tonk Angels,* 3.

44. Haytock, *Middle Class,* 11.

45. Nelson, *Farm and Factory,* 118.

46. Nelson, *Farm and Factory,* 116.

47. Pecknold, *Selling Sound,* 20.

48. Jellison, *Entitled to Power,* 78; Kennedy, *Freedom from Fear,* 195–197.

49. Jellison, *Entitled to Power,* 72.

50. Jellison, *Entitled to Power,* 67–68.

51. Jellison, *Entitled to Power,* 105

52. Cohen, *Making a New Deal,* 243.

53. Denning describes the Depression years as "a time of gender strife and change" resulting in part from "the crisis in masculinity that accompanied the massive unemployment" of the era (*Cultural Front,* 30).

54. Kimmel, *Manhood in America,* 192.

55. For a history of women's employment during the Great Depression, see Milkman, *On Gender, Labor, and Inequality,* 16–31; Parrish, *Anxious Decades,* 401; and Scharf, *To Work and to Wed,* 107–8.

56. May, *Homeward Bound,* 49–51.

57. Gregory, *Southern Diaspora,* 60–61.

58. Adamic, "Hill-Billies Come to Detroit," 177.

59. Berry, *Southern Migrants, Northern Exiles,* 60–62.

60. Berry, *Southern Migrants, Northern Exiles,* 62, 7–8, also explains that southern white migrants often alternately sojourned in the South and in the Midwest, trying to reconcile a "divided heart" torn between the economic promise of the industrial Midwest and the familiarity and comfort of home.

61. Berry, *Southern Migrants, Northern Exiles,* 41; and Nies, "Defending Jeeter," 122.

62. See Pecknold, *Selling Sound,* 28–30, for more about hillbilly music's relationship to the folk preservationist movement.

63. *WLS Family Album,* 1931, 44.

64. Malone, *Country Music USA*, 56.

65. See McGinley, *Staging the Blues*, for more about the relationship between constructions of folk authenticity and the theatrics of the urban popular stage.

66. Kincaid, *Favorite Old-Time Songs*, 6.

67. McCusker, "Patriarchy and the Great Depression," 153–159.

68. As musicologist Susan McClary and others have observed, musical expression has historically been linked to notions of the feminine. To distance themselves from the charge of effeminacy, male musicians have laid claims to music's masculine virtues, such as valor or power. See McClary, *Feminine Endings*, 17.

69. See Greenberg, "Singing Up Close," 97–137, and McCracken, *Real Men Don't Sing*, about the gendered implications of the tenor crooning voice.

70. Greenberg, "Singing Up Close," 104.

71. I have written previously about Gene Autry in "Lavender Cowboy."

72. *WLS Family Album*, 1933, 20.

73. *WLS Family Album*, 1937, 24.

74. *Stand By!*, February 8, 1936, 9.

75. *WLS Family Album*, 1933, 21.

76. Harkins, *Hillbilly*, 81–84, points to Lair's use of derisive mountain imagery in shaping comic representations of the hillbilly. See also Gopinath and Schultz, "Sentimental Remembrance," 486, for more about the ways in which Lair shaped the Cumberland Ridge Runners into hillbilly stereotypes.

77. *WLS Family Album*, 1934, 11.

78. McCusker, *Lonesome Cowgirls and Honky-Tonk Angels*, 30–40, addresses the ways in which Lair shaped Parker into a representation of what she terms a "Southern sentimental mother."

79. *WLS Family Album*, 1933, 22.

80. For a discussion of "the restrained lady versus the unruly woman" in vaudeville, see Kibler, *Rank Ladies*, 13–14.

81. Cockrell, *Demons of Disorder*, 80.

82. Austin, "*Susanna*," 246–252.

83. See Cantwell, *Bluegrass Breakdown*, 241, for the ways in which country music continued blackface minstrelsy's themes of sentimentality and ridicule. Karl H. Miller, *Segregating Sound*, 34–50, explores how the sentimentality and parody in minstrelsy informed the popular music market at the turn of the twentieth century.

84. P. Fox, *Natural Acts*, 17.

85. *WLS Family Album*, 1932, 41; 1934, 18; and *Stand By!*, March 2, 1935, 15.

86. *Stand By!*, March 23, 1935, 9.

87. *WLS Family Album*, 1936, 16; and 1937, 47.

88. *WLS Family Album*, 1943, 40.

89. *WLS Family Album*, 1934, 20.

90. *WLS Family Album*, 1932, 12.

91. "Listener's Mike," *Stand By!*, July 17, 1937, 2.

92. Gopinath and Shultz, "Sentimental Remembrance," 485–488, explores the tensions between sentimental expressions and comic hillbilly imagery in the duo act Karl and Harty, who were also part of the larger ensemble the Cumberland Ridge Runners. Karl H. Miller, *Segregating Sound*, 212, underlines the recording industry's promotion of old-time music in terms of the "dual legacy" of nostalgia and hillbilly parody.

93. Tyler, "Rise of the Rural Rhythm," 29.

94. Douglas, *Listening In*, 102.

95. Goodman, *Radio's Civic Ambition*, 227.

96. For more about Burridge D. Butler's attempts to promote a respectable image for the *National Barn Dance*, see Pecknold, *Selling Sound*, 21–22.

97. "Listener's Mike," *Stand By!*, January 25, 1936, 2.

98. "Listener's Mike," *Stand By!*, July 24, 1937, 2.

99. "Listener's Mike," *Stand By!*, February 20, 1937, 2.

100. "Listener's Mike," *Stand By!*, May 22, 1937, 2.

101. "Listener's Mike," *Stand By!*, October 2, 1937, 2.

102. "Listener's Mike," *Stand By!*, February 20, 1937, 2.

103. "Listener's Mike," *Stand By!*, December 26, 1936, 2; *WLS Family Album*, 1937, 25.

104. "Listener's Mike," *Stand By!*, February 20, 1937, 2.

105. "Listener's Mike," *Stand By!*, July 17, 1936, 2.

106. "Listener's Mike," *Stand By!*, December 28, 1935, 2.

107. "Listener's Mike," *Stand By!*, December 4, 1935, 2.

108. "Listener's Mike," *Stand By!*, January 4, 1936, 2.

109. "Listener's Mike," *Stand By!*, January 23, 1937, 2.

110. "Listener's Mike," *Stand By!*, November 19, 1935, 2.

111. "Listener's Mike," *Stand By!*, October 16, 1937, 2.

112. "Listener's Mike," *Stand By!*, February 5, 1938, 2. See Douglas, *Listening In*, 92–93, for the history and racialized reception of radio broadcasts of jazz and African American musicians during the 1920s and 1930s.

113. "Listener's Mike," *Stand By!*, December 5, 1936, 2.

114. "Listener's Mike," *Stand By!*, December 5, 1936, 2.

115. "Listener's Mike," *Stand By!*, January 2, 1937, 2.

116. "Listener's Mike," *Stand By!*, October 5, 1935, 2.

117. "Listener's Mike," *Stand By!*, September 19, 1936, 2.

118. P. Fox, *Natural Acts*, 9, discusses the process of identification and disavowal in relation to barn-dance radio, drawing on the love and theft concept of blackface minstrelsy developed by Lott, *Love and Theft*.

Chapter 2. *The Rural Masquerades of Gender: Lulu Belle and Her Radio Audience*

1. Daniel, "Lulu Belle and Scotty," 72.

2. *Lulu Belle's and Skyland Scotty's Homefolk Songs*, 2–3.

3. McCusker, *Lonesome Cowgirls and Honky-Tonk Angels*, 51; and P. Fox, *National Acts*, 61.

4. I am applying the theatrical approach to understanding the blues in McGinley's, *Staging the Blues*, 34, to early country music.

5. See Goodman, *Radio Civic Ambition*, for a history of how radio continued the notions of musical hierarchy in broadcasts.

6. Wiseman, interview, June 7, 1982, 9–10.

7. Cockrell, *Demons of Disorder*, 55; Kibler, *Rank Ladies*, 114. Lott, *Love and Theft*, 165–169, also suggests that the misogynistic tropes of blackface transvestism could be a mask to conceal the homoerotic dynamic of two men singing to each other about desire.

8. Kibler, *Rank Ladies*, 114.

9. Wiseman, "Belle of the Barn Dance," 8.

10. McDonald, *Jeepers Creepers*.

11. McDonald, *Grand Ole Opry*.

12. Wiseman, interview, June 7, 1982, 10.

13. M. A. Williams, "Home to Renfro Valley John Lair," 91; and Wiseman, "Belle of the Barn Dance," 12.

14. Wiseman, interview, June 7, 1982, 15.

15. In Lulu Belle's interview, she made it clear that her use of the hope chest and her chewing-gum skits were her own ideas and not scripted by WLS writers. Wiseman, interview, June 7, 1982, 15. Moreover, Patsy Montana has stated in interviews that the *National Barn Dance* was "more or less an ad-lib show" without skits when she first arrived in 1933. Montana, interview, June 9, 1984, 37–38.

16. Wiseman, interview, June 7, 1982, 15.

17. Wiseman, interview, June 7, 1982, 15, italics original.

18. Lulu Belle, "Chewing Chawing Gum," in *Lulu Belle and Skyland Scotty: Mountain Songs*, 3; and *Lulu Belle's and Skyland Scotty's Homefolk Songs*, 15.

19. Harkins, *Hillbilly*, 53, points to Marion Hughes's *Three Years in Arkansaw* (1904), in which the figure of the female hillbilly was characterized as mannish and uncouth.

20. Wiseman, interview, June 7, 1982, 15.

21. Red Foley and Lulu Belle, "Hi Rinktum Inktum Doodle," on *Old Shep 79*. In the *Alka-Seltzer Song Book*, the title is listed as "Hi Rinktum Inktum."

22. Sharp, *English Folk Songs*, 200.

23. Linn, *That Half-Barbaric Twang*, 116–118, explains that the five-stringed banjo was an instrument that popular culture associated with rural southern black culture of the nineteenth century. In the twentieth century, the instrument transitioned from its association with black slave culture to white mountain culture. Conway, "Black Banjo Songsters in Appalachia," traces the influences of African American banjoists on the developments of old-time music.

24. Cockrell, *Demons of Disorder*, 146–149, argues that the banjo's association with noise and social rebellion faded when the blackface minstrel show, beginning in 1843, incorporated mainstream aesthetics of melody over rhythm in order to cater to the musical tastes of middle-class audiences.

25. The singing styles of Roba Stanley, Sara and Maybelle Carter, Cousin Emmy, and the Coon Creek Girls use various degrees of nasal twang in their chest-dominant vocal tones.

26. Wiseman, interview, June 7, 1982, 9.

27. Wiseman, interview, June 7, 1982, 9.

28. See Stras, "Voice of the Beehive," 33–56, for more about the vocal development and tone of young female singers.

29. See Greenberg, "Singing Up Close," 43–50, for how operatic singers' vocal practices signified moral and aesthetic standards for radio singing.

30. Greenberg, "Singing Up Close," 2.

31. A fan declared that Lulu Belle was at her best when she sang "Little Black Moustache" and "Chewing Chewing Gum." See "Listener's Mike," *Stand By!*, January 9, 1937, 2.

32. Kibler, *Rank Ladies*, 68–69, points to the history of the old-maid stock character in vaudeville.

33. Red Foley and Lulu Belle, "Little Black Moustache," on *Old Shep*.

34. Wiseman, interview, June 7, 1982, 12. Red Foley had married Eva Overstake of the Three Little Maids, and Eva had asked to work with Foley, leaving Lulu Belle without a duet partner.

35. Wiseman, interview, June 7, 1982, 16.

36. "Madam, I've Come to Marry You" was also included in *100 WLS Barn Dance Favorites*, 67.

37. *Lulu Belle's and Skyland Scotty's Homefolk Songs*, 19; and *Lulu Belle and Skyland Scotty: Mountain Songs*, 1. The main source of income for radio performers was not necessarily from their radio appearances or royalties on recording sales but from the money they earned selling their songbooks on live tours throughout the region.

38. *100 WLS Barn Dance Favorites*, 2.

39. Though "Single Girl, Married Girl" and "Wish I Was a Single Girl" are similar in title, I have found no evidence that "Single Girl, Married Girl" was part of Lulu Belle's repertory. Lulu Belle never recorded the song, nor did she include it in any of her songbooks. In "Listener's Mike," *Stand By!*, March 4, 1937, 2, a fan did mention that Lulu Belle performed "Single Girl," which could have been either "Single Girl, Married Girl" or "Wish I Was A Single Girl" since both tunes also circulated under the title "The Single Girl." See Sharp's collection *English Folk Songs*, 32–34, and *100 WLS Barn Dance Favorites*, 2.

40. Cockrell, *Ingalls Wilder Family Songbook*, 92.

41. Lulu Belle and Scotty included repertory from blackface minstrelsy (such as "Aunt Jemima's Plaster" and "Uncle Eph's Got the Coon") in their songbooks and their recordings.

42. Lulu Belle and Scotty, "Wish I Was a Single Girl Again," on *Flowers in the Wildwood: Women in Early Country Music*. Russell and Pinson, *[Country Music Records]*, 516, lists a fiddle, guitar, banjo, and bass for Lulu Belle's and Scotty's recording of "Wish I Was a Single Girl Again," even though there is not a bass playing on this recording.

43. See Goertzen, *Southern Fiddlers and Fiddle Contests*, 96–100, for a description of southern fiddling.

44. Cousin Emmy, "I Wish I Was a Single Girl Again," on *Cousin Emmy and Her Kinfolks*.

45. *Stand By!*, July 18, 1936, 12.

46. Kibler, *Rank Ladies*, 55–78.

47. Kibler, *Rank Ladies*, 62.

48. Lavitt, "Red Hot Mamas," 261, draws on the work of Kibler in *Rank Ladies* by situating Tucker and Brice in a history of unruly comediennes.

49. A manager of a Harlem theater suggested that Tucker blacken up to mask the ways she did not conform to conventional beauty and the ideals of white femininity. Harrison-Kahan, *White Negress*, 28; Kibler, *Rank Ladies*, 129–130; and Lavitt, "Red Hot Mamas," 253–254.

50. Antler, "One Clove," 128.

51. Antler, "One Clove," 129; and Harrison-Kahan, *White Negress*, 16–17.

52. S. Green, *Great Clowns on Broadway*, 3.

53. Fanny Brice, "Becky Is Back in the Ballet," "Second Hand Rose," "Mrs. Cohen at the Beach" on *Fanny Brice*. For a summary of these pieces and their performance context, see Goldman, *Fanny Brice*, and Grossman, *Funny Woman*.

54. Hoberman and Shandler, *Entertaining America*, 154.

55. As quoted in Grossman, *Funny Woman*, 102.

56. P. Fox, *Natural Acts*, 9, addresses fans' identification and disavowal of the theatrical tropes of white rusticity; Kibler, *Rank Ladies*, 63, also underlines the ways vaudeville audiences could identify with and distance themselves from female clowns.

57. Jenkins, *What Made Pistachio Nuts?*, 225.

58. "Listener's Mike," *Stand By!*, January 2, 1937, 2.

59. "Listener's Mike," *Stand By!*, February 13, 1937, 2.

60. "Listener's Mike," *Stand By!*, January 2, 1937, 2.

61. "Listener's Mike," *Stand By!*, October 16, 1937, 2.

62. "Listener's Mike," *Stand By!*, September 18, 1937, 2.

63. "Listener's Mike," *Stand By!*, January 2, 1937, 2.

64. "Listener's Mike," *Stand By!*, April 16, 1938, 2.

65. "Listener's Mike," *Stand By!*, April 23, 1938, 2.

66. "Listener's Mike," *Stand By!*, December 12, 1936, 2.

67. "Listener's Mike," *Stand By!*, January 2, 1937, 2

68. "Listener's Mike," *Stand By!*, February 26, 1938, 2.

69. "Listener's Mike," *Stand By!*, May 29, 1937, 2.

70. "Homecoming Time in Happy Valley" was also included in the published songbooks *Lulu Belle's and Skyland Scotty's Home Folk Songs*, 2 and 3; and *Lulu Belle and Skyland Scotty: Mountain Songs*, 32 and 33.

71. Lulu Belle and Scotty included "Homecoming Time in Happy Valley" in a series of radio transcriptions for *Breakfast in the Blue Ridge* in the early 1950s. The radio transcriptions have been released on Lulu Belle and Scotty, *Tender Memories Recalled*.

72. Lulu Belle and Scotty also recorded "Homecoming Time in Happy Valley" in the early 1960s. In this rendition they raised the key of the song from E-flat major (1950s recording) to G major, which encouraged Lulu Belle to elaborate on the lyricism of the head voice. Lulu and Scotty, *Sweethearts of Country Music*.

73. "Have I Told You Lately That I Love You?" is included in *Lulu Belle and Scotty: Hayloft Jamboree Song Book*, 2–3.

74. Wiseman, "Belle of the Barn Dance," 10.

75. "Listener's Mike," *Stand By!*, March 13, 1937, 2.

76. "Listener's Mike," *Stand By!*, January 15, 1938, 2.

77. "Listener's Mike," *Stand By!*, November 27, 1937, 2.

78. Kane, *Shine on Harvest Moon*. After their film debut, Lulu Belle and Scotty appeared in a number of Republic films, including *Village Barn Dance* (1940), *Hi, Neighbor* (1942), *Swing Your Partner* (1943), *Sing, Neighbor, Sing* (1944), and *National Barn Dance* (1944).

79. McCusker, *Lonesome Cowgirls and Honky-Tonk Angels*, 44–45.

80. *WLS Family Album*, 1934, 21.

81. *WLS Family Album*, 1935, 14.

82. *WLS Family Album*, 1935, 10.

83. P. Fox, *Natural Acts*, 60 and 62.

84. Hurst, "Barn Dance Days," 62.

85. *Stand By!*, September 18, 1937, 4.

86. Lulu Belle, "The Royal Family: Lulu Belle, Winner of Queen Contest, Thanks Her Fans," *Stand By!*, October 31, 1936, 3.

87. *WLS Family Album*, 1936, 25.

88. *WLS Family Album*, 1951, 12

89. *WLS Family Album*, 1946, 38.

90. *WLS Family Album*, 1945, n.p.

Chapter 3. Gendering the Musical West: Patsy Montana's Cowgirl Songs of Tomboy Glamour

1. Malone states that the singing cowboy could become "a reassuring symbol of independence and mastery, a collection of traits that the nation had once possessed and might once again assert" (*Singing Cowboys and Musical Mountaineers*, 91). Stanfield argues that the singing cowboy may have been the "most important cultural figure to emerge from the tumultuous years of the Great Depression—a character that represented the fantasies, desires, and ambitions of those who felt keenly the economic hardship and threat (and fact) of dispossession and dislocation" (*Horse Opera*, 3).

2. Montana, interview, June 9, 1984, 6.

3. In interviews, Montana would always clarify that she was a violinist not a fiddler of southern music. Montana, interview, October 16, 1974 30.

4. Montana, interview, June 9, 1984, 6.

5. Montana, interview, June 9, 1984, 7–8; "Girl on the Cover" (Patsy Montana), *Stand By!*, November 30, 1935, 11.

6. Montana, interview, June 9, 1984, 7–14.

7. Montana, interview, June 9, 1984, 11.

8. See Montana, *Patsy Montana*, 19, for her praise of Elton Britt's yodeling.

9. In an interview and a published article, Montana recalled that she made many film shorts, including *Lightning Express*, though I have not found a copy of this film in my research. Montana, interview, June 6, 1984, 8, 17–18; "Girl on the Cover" (Patsy Montana), *[Stand By!]*, 11.

10. Montana, interview, August 30, 1985, 37–38.

11. See McCusker, *Lonesome Cowgirls and Honky-Tonk Angels*, 68–81, for more information about the radio career of the Girls of the Golden West.

12. In an interview (Good, "Two Cowgirls on the Lone Prairie," 9), Millie Good also stated that Montana had written to the Girls of the Golden West about her western-themed repertory and performance persona. Dolly and Millie gave the letter to their manager, William Alford, who contacted Montana about auditioning for WLS.

13. Montana, interview, October 16, 1974, 31.

14. See Tyler, "Rise of Rural Rhythm," 35, for more about how WLS's broadcasts framed a stylistic range of music within the concept of home and hearth.

15. Girls of the Golden West on *Back in the Saddle Again*.

16. *Louise Massey and the Westerners' Song Folio*.

17. D. Cusick, *Cowboy in Country Music*, 41–43.

18. "Man on the Cover" (Dott Massey), *Stand By!*, May 18, 1935, 9.

19. In an interview (September 2, 1985, 12), Montana recalled that the radio executives were impressed with the music of the Westerners and included "Louise Massey and the Westerners quite a bit on the network show because they were such a polished act."

20. *Stand By!*, March 2, 1935, 10.

21. "Listening In with WLS Daily Programs," *Stand By!*, June 1, 1935, 15.

22. "Girl on the Cover" (Louise Massey), *Stand By!*, February 23, 1935, 7.

23. "Man on the Cover" (Dott Massey), *Stand By!*, May 18, 1935, 9.

24. "Man on the Cover" (Dott Massey), *Stand By!*, May 18, 1935, 9.

25. Daniel, "Ranch Romance."

26. Young and Young, *Music*, 153.

27. In an interview (September 2, 1985, 11), Montana maintained that she was never a star of the NBC broadcast of the *National Barn Dance*, even though in her autobiography (*Patsy Montana*, 75), she states that by 1936, she had finally made it on the NBC broadcast. In my own research of *Stand By!*'s weekly advertisements of Saturday-evening programming, Patsy Montana was never mentioned as part of the cast of performers for the Alka-Seltzer-sponsored NBC broadcast in the 1930s.

28. In an interview (June 9, 1984, 34), Montana stated, "I was part of their [the Prairie Rambler's] act, but yet, I was a soloist."

29. By September 28, 1935, *Stand By!* (p. 14) was listing Montana with her own daily 9:00 a.m. show with the Prairie Ramblers (sponsored by Peruna and Kolor-Bak) and as one of the main performers in the 8:30–12:00 p.m. regional broadcast of the *National Barn Dance*, and by October 5, 1935, *Stand By!* (p. 14) was also listing Montana and the Prairie Ramblers as the main act of the daily morning program *Smile-A-While*. *WLS Family Album*, 1938, 14, also mentioned that Montana was a regular feature of *Smile-A-While*.

30. Montana, interview, June 9, 1984, 57.

31. Montana, interview, October 16, 1974, 13; and interview, June 9, 1984, 63.

32. Montana, interview, September 2, 1985, 60.

33. Montana, interview, August 30, 1985, 33.

34. Montana, *Best of Patsy Montana*.

35. Montana, interview, June 9, 1984, 77.

36. In an interview (June 9, 1984, 52), Montana recalled that though she was "sick of singing 'Texas Plains,'" it had become her style of song and influenced her writing of "I Want to Be a Cowboy's Sweetheart."

37. In an interview (August 30, 1985, 10–11), Montana explained that during her guest performance on NBC's broadcast of the *National Barn Dance* Lulu Belle was seated in the audience throwing peanuts. Also during that broadcast the barn dance featured songs about states. Montana felt compelled to represent the state of Montana by changing the title and lyrics of Stuart Hamblen's song to "Montana Plains." Afterward, he accused Montana of trying to steal his song.

38. For more detailed accounts about the physiological demands of yodeling, see Plantenga, *Yodel-Ay-Ee-Oooo*, 12–15, and Wise, "Yodel Species."

39. R. Miller, *Structure of Singing*, 132.

40. Wise, "Yodel Species," claims that the vocal break for female yodelers occurs between the head register and the higher whistle register, even though the vocal break for women is between the chest register and the head register.

41. Wise, *Yodeling and Meaning*, 73.

42. Wise, *Yodeling and Meaning*, 77–78, includes reviews of Henriette Sontag's 1852 performance in New York.

43. Graeme Smith, "Australian Country Music," 303, notes that the yodeling of Swiss family singing ensembles served as a model for burlesques in minstrel shows. During the 1850s, the minstrel troupe Rainer's Original Ethiopian Serenaders toured Australia as well as the rest of the world.

44. See Wise, *Yodeling and Meaning*, 101–188, for more about the career of J. K. Emmet and his influence on the German ethnic character and the yodel.

45. Abbott and Seroff, "America's Blue Yodel."

46. See Koegel, *Music in German Immigrant Theater*, 233–238, for a history of cross-dressing in German ethnic theatrical productions.

47. Abbott and Seroff state, "Anderson and other black Southern vaudeville yodelers—particularly Monroe Tabor and Beulah Henderson—bring out the previously unexplored commercial side of 'black yodeling' and show precisely how, during the decade 1910 to 1920, black professional yodelers brought blues and yodeling into intimate juxtaposition" ("America's Blue Yodel," 6). The connection between blues and yodeling is evident further with the vaudevillian blues performer Sara Martin in "Yodeling Blues" (1923), where she sings, "I'm going to yodel my blues away," followed by Eva Taylor and Bessie Smith each recording the same song in 1923.

48. Neal, *Songs of Jimmie Rodgers*, 22–23, points out that the yodeling passages of Anderson, Puckett, and Rodgers in their respective recordings of "Sleep, Baby, Sleep" resemble one another melodically and rhythmically.

49. Mazor, *Meeting Jimmie Rodgers*, 66, suggests that Jimmie Rodgers did not find the virtuosic Alpine yodel fitting for his lyrical narratives and referred to an Alpine-influence yodeler as a "friek [sic] yodeler."

50. See Neal, *Songs of Jimmie Rodgers*, 19–25, and Wise, *Yodeling and Meaning*, 128–160, for further details about Rodgers's yodel melodies.

51. Wise, *Yodeling and Meaning*, 181, makes the point that "Chime Bells" is a modernized version of "Mountain High."

52. Britt, "Chime Bells," on *RCA Years*.

53. Abbate, *Unsung Voices*, 6 and 10.

54. *WLS Family Album*, 1938, 32, marketed the DeZurik Sisters as "trick yodelers."

55. *WLS Family Album*, 1939, 19; and *WLS Family Album*, 1937, 40.

56. "Swiss Miss," *Stand By!*, May 9, 1936, 9.

57. See Berish, *Lonesome Roads*, 41–43, for a discussion of "sweet" as an aesthetic category that implied white middle-class and mainstream popular music in the 1930s.

58. Montana, interview, October 16, 1974, 28.

59. "Listener's Mike," *Stand By!*, June 12, 1937, 2.

60. "Listener's Mike," *Stand By!*, November 27, 1937, 2.

61. For example, fans never described Lulu Belle's singing voice in terms of sweetness of tone, even though many appreciators commented on her sweetness of character.

62. "Listener's Mike," *Stand By!*, April 2, 1938, 2.

63. Montana, interview, June 9, 1984, 46.

64. "Listener's Mike," *Stand By!*, March 19, 1938, 2.

65. "Listener's Mike," *Stand By!*, May 7, 1938, 2.

66. "Listener's Mike," *Stand By!*, January 11, 1936, 2, italics mine.

67. "Listener's Mike," *Stand By!*, January 25, 1936, 2.

68. "Listener's Mike," *Stand By!*, January 4, 1936, 2.

69. Skeggs, *Formations of Class and Gender*, 110.

70. Skeggs, *Formations of Class and Gender*, 111.

71. Jellison, *Entitled to Power*, 76–77.

72. Montana, *Patsy Montana, America's No. 1 Cowgirl*, 9, 14, 16, and 27. The title "I Want to Be a Cowboy's Dream Cowgirl" has some variation, appearing in the songbook's table of contents as the title given here, in the song's sheet music included in the songbook as "I Want to Be a Cow Boy's Dream Cow Girl," and in the lyrics as "I want to be a cowboy's dream girl." See also Montana, interview, June 9, 1984, 52.

73. In "Listener's Mike," *Stand By!*, October 23, 1937, 2, a fan "wished Patsy Montana would sing her new song more often, 'The Answer to I Want to Be a Cowboy's Sweetheart.'"

74. Montana, *Patsy Montana, America's No. 1 Cowgirl*, 78 and 94.

75. Etulain, "Origins of the Western," 56–60, discusses the political and cultural impulses that contributed to the popularity of the western novel. Bill Brown in the introduction to *Reading the West*, 1–40, explains the material and cultural conditions that fostered the mass production of dime novels. Denning, *Mechanic Accents*, provides a broader historical perspective of the different types of narratives constituting the genre of dime novels. Though his study focuses on the archetypical characters of western plots, Denning also concentrates on detective and mystery tales situated in urban settings and consumed by the working class.

76. For detailed analyses of western heroines in dime novels, see McLaird, *Calamity Jane*, 85–100; and Henry Nash Smith's "Dime Novel Heroine," in H. N. Smith, *Virgin Land*, 112–122. Edward Wheeler, a well-known author of dime novels in the 1870s and 1880s, penned *Hurricane Nell, the Girl Dead Shot*. He also wrote the Deadwood Dick series, in which Calamity Jane appeared in half the narratives. It was common for authors to use actual western figures, such as Buffalo Bill (William Cody) and Davy Crockett, in dime novels.

77. Jones and Wills demonstrate that Mrs. George Spencer's *Calamity Jane: A Story of the Black Hills* (1887) was the "first full length novel to take the Calamity Jane myth" and focus it on Calamity Jane and Meg's relationship of "empathy, sisterhood and an inference of romantic attachment" (*American West*, 155–156). See also Hubbs, *Rednecks, Queers, and Country Music*, 122.

78. Bell-Metereau, *Hollywood Androgyny*, 80.

79. Bell-Metereau, *Hollywood Androgyny*, 82.

80. Montana, *Best of Patsy Montana*.

81. See White, *Git Along, Little Dogies*, 137–147, for a historical account of the publication and performances of "The Strawberry Roan."

82. See Fife, "Strawberry Roan and His Progeny," for the different parodies of the original song.

83. Fletcher includes the twenty-measure chorus of the Tin Pan Alley rendition of "The Strawberry Roan" as a possible way to retaliate against the songwriters Howard and Vincent for plagiarizing his ballad in their Tin Pan Alley version. Guy William Logsdon, "*Whorehouse Bells Were Ringing*," 86–107, provides a historical account of Fletcher's bawdy parody of his own song.

84. Kibler, *Rank Ladies*, 13.

85. Wise, *Yodeling and Meaning*, 177–178, interprets Montana's yodel in "The She Buckaroo" as an example of drawing on past traditions of nostalgia and gender conventions without recognizing that her song is modeled after "The Strawberry Roan."

86. Austin, "*Susanna*," "*Jeanie*," 159.

87. Montana, interview, June 9, 1984, 20.

88. *WLS Family Album*, 1936, 22.

89. McCusker, *Lonesome Cowgirls and Honky-Tonk Angels*, 77, points out in the marketing of the cowgirl duo the Girls of the Golden West, WLS's trade magazines continually underlined Dolly's and Millie's domestic lives.

90. "Girl on the Cover" (Patsy Montana), *Stand By!*, November 30, 1935, 11.

91. *WLS Family Album*, 1937, 52.

92. *WLS Family Album*, 1938, 15.

93. Patsy Montana, "On the Santa Fe Trail," *Stand By!*, June 12, 1937, 3 and 15, italics original.

94. Montana, "On the Santa Fe Trail," 15.

95. *WLS Family Album*, 1940, 18.

96. After 1937, *WLS Family Album* and *Stand By!* stopped featuring photos of Montana with the Prairie Ramblers, though her separate shots were often juxtaposed on the opposite page to those showing the Prairie Ramblers. Montana at times performed live without the string-band ensemble in the late 1930s. However, she continued to record with the Prairie Ramblers throughout the 1940s.

97. Sherman, *Colorado Sunset*.

Chapter 4. Carolina Cotton: Yodeling Virtuosity and Theatricality in California Country Music

1. Tucker, *Swing Shift*, demonstrates that there were hundreds of all-women swing bands in the 1940s. There were also all-women western swing bands in the 1940s and 1950s, including the Oklahoma Sweethearts, the Rangerettes, and Jean Shepard's Melody Ranch Girls, to name a few.

2. Haslam, *Workin' Man Blues*, 112–148, connects the rhythmic vitality of western swing to the later developments of honky-tonk cultivated in Bakersfield.

3. La Chapelle, *Proud to Be an Okie*, 77 and 99.

4. Brackett notes that the popular-music press still understood the hybridized style of western swing numbers, such as Bob Wills's "New San Antonio Rose," to be an example of hillbilly music and conflated it "with the easily digestible corn" imagery associated with early country music (*Categorizing Sound*, 202).

5. Malone, *Country Music USA*, 2nd. ed., 148.

6. Diege, *Singing Cowgirl*; *Water Rustlers*; and *Ride 'Em Cowgirl*.

7. Knapp, *American Musical*, 10.

8. For data about the migration from the Southwest to California, see Gregory, *American Exodus*, 6. For a historical account of the two migrant streams, one to the urban cities and the other to the agricultural valleys of California, see Gregory, *American Exodus*, 39–62.

9. Sharon Marie (Carolina Cotton's daughter), email communication with author, November 11, 2014. During their journey from the South to the West Coast, the Hagstrom family lived briefly in different parts of the country, including Klamath Falls and Portland, Oregon; Casper, Wyoming; Sacramento; Phoenix; and Los Angeles, before settling in San Francisco in late 1936 or early 1937.

10. Gregory, *American Exodus*, 81.

11. Gregory, *American Exodus*, 65–69.

12. Gregory, *American Exodus*, 106–108.

13. La Chapelle, *Proud to Be an Okie*, 34–36.

14. La Chapelle, *Proud to Be an Okie*, 40–41.

15. Goggans, *California on the Breadlines*, 200–202.

16. Gregory, *American Exodus*, 6.

17. La Chapelle, *Proud to Be an Okie*, 101–103.

18. La Chapelle explains that "1940s-era women had long before created a young women's fan culture in which it was permissible to assert themselves in sexually aggressive ways" (*Proud to Be an Okie*, 108). In this context, female fans tore at the clothing of male western swing performers and likely hollered and screamed to the music.

19. See Boyd, *Dance All Night*, 5–14; Malone, *Country Music USA*, 2nd ed., 158–174; and Stimeling, *Cosmic Cowboys and New Hicks*, 95–97, for historical accounts of the musical developments of western swing.

20. Malone, *Country Music USA*, 1968 ed., 179.

21. Giordano, *Country and Western Dance*, 9. This was a "Season's Greetings from Milton Brown and the Musical Brownies."

22. Stimeling, *Cosmic Cowboys and New Hicks*, 96.

23. Berish, *Lonesome Roads*, 3.

24. Haslam, *Workin' Man Blues*, 90.

25. Henderson, "San Francisco Area."

26. See also Tucker, *Swing Shift*, for a history of all-women swing bands.

27. Haslam, *Workin' Man Blues*, 92.

28. Marie, email.

29. Malone, *Country Music USA*, 2nd ed., 201. See also Haslam, *Workin' Man Blues*, 121–128, for more details about Cooley's career and personal life.

30. La Chapelle, *Proud to Be an Okie*, 81–95.

31. "Folk Artists Profiles," *The Billboard 1944 Musical Year Book*, 364.

32. La Chapelle, *Proud to Be An Okie*, 90.

33. Jack Scholl's film short *Spade Cooley: King of Western Swing* evokes western swing's multicultural roots with numbers like "Topeka Polka," a song that points to a specific place where the polka was popular among Polish and German immigrants and their descendants as well as to the city Topeka, named after Siouan Native Americans. The film also features a rodeo setting of Native Americans in stereotypical dress dancing to Cooley's "Indian Scout," alluding to Cooley's Cherokee ethnicity.

34. Wise, *Yodeling and Meaning*, 180.

35. Cotton's yodels compare with the best of Britt's and outshine many of her contemporaries, including the yodels of McBride and the McKinney Sisters, singing cowgirls in Bob Wills's ensemble. In McBride's 1950 recording of "I Betcha My Heart I Love You" with Bob Wills and His Texas Playboys, she yodels after each of her verses, which acts as an instrumental break that precedes the piano's solo and later the electric steel's solo. Though she tries to keep up with the swing band with her vocalizations, her yodeling passages do not compare to Carolina Cotton's impressive level of rhythmic and melodic virtuosity.

36. Plantenga, *Yodel in Hi-Fi*, 75–95, gives a history of how European romantic composers included yodel melodies in their compositions and how European operatic vocalists included the yodel in their performances. See also Wise, *Yodeling and Meaning*, 73–78.

37. Wise points out that Jimmie Rodgers's yodel break often "functions as a vocalized version of an instrumental break" (*Yodeling and Meaning*, 138).

38. Goodwins, *Singing Sheriff*.

39. Davis, *Il Trittico*, 25.

40. "Folk Artists Profile," 364.

41. Swan, "People and Things."

42. Marie, email. Bobbie Bennett also oversaw the careers of the Deuce Spriggens, Merle Travis, and Jimmy Wakely.

43. Swan, "People and Things."

44. La Chapelle demonstrates that Spade Cooley's publicity included Carolina Cotton to create "fictional communal spaces in which neighborly cattlemen and ranch women worked together as coequals" (*Proud to Be an Okie*, 167).

45. Marie, email.

46. May, *Homeward Bound*, 68.

47. Hegarty, *Victory Girls, Khaki-Wackies, and Patriotutes*, 87.

48. Hegarty, *Victory Girls, Khaki-Wackies, and Patriotutes*, 109.

49. McBee, *Dance Hall Days*, 6–10.

50. Gotfrit, "Women Dancing Back," 179.

51. Skeggs, *Formations of Class and Gender*, 110–111.

52. "Pic for Carolina Cotton," *Billboard*, May 6, 1944, 22.

53. Carolina Cotton, "I Love to Yodel," on *Yodeling Blonde Bombshell*.

54. See Wise, *Yodeling and Meaning*, 100–112. Wise's research on J. K. Emmet, who played the Dutch character Fritz van Vonderblinkinstoffen and wrote his 1878 "Lullaby" for his character, does not address how the song could be using the yodel in theatrical skits and productions that explicitly parodied gender roles. See Koegel, *Music in German Immigrant Theater*, 233–238, for examples of the cross-dressed Dutch character offering masculine parodies of ethnicity.

55. Lander, *I'm from Arkansas*.

56. Nat Green, "American Folk Tunes: Cowboy and Hillbilly Tunes and Tunesters," *Billboard*, October 28, 1944, 64.

57. Archainbaud, *Apache Country*.

58. Bell-Metereau, *Hollywood Androgyny*, 88.

59. Bell-Metereau, *Hollywood Androgyny*, 82.

60. See Warren, *Buffalo Bill's America*, 190–206, for the history of Native Americans in Buffalo Bill's Wild West shows. Like Cody, many of the Native Americans came from the frontier and were involved in the Indian wars. Johnson, *Hunger for the Wild*, 188–189, points to the growing anxiety arising from the transformation of the mythical West into a region of industry and commerce.

61. Though the film still largely panders to Native American stereotypes by reinscribing the exoticism of the noble savage, Gene Autry did hire Tony White Cloud, acknowledged in the film credits and publicity, to choreograph the musical and dance scenes of his performance troupe of Jemez Indians. The film largely continues many of the themes of Wild West shows, namely, that corrupt white people are the ones who are responsible for conflicts with Native Americans.

62. Parler, "Musical Radicalism," 232. See also pp. 221–224 for details about Gene Autry's professional relationship with Tony White Cloud and his performance troupe of Jemez Indians that extended beyond their roles in *Apache Country*.

63. Nazarro, *Hoedown*.

64. The song is a comic number about turning one's lost dog into bologna. It was recorded by singing actors who played the Dutch character. Wise, *Yodeling and Meaning*, 95, for a discussion of Septimus Winner's "Der Deitcher's Dog." See also Plantenga, *Yodel in Hi-Fi*, 61.

65. Cotton, "Singing on the Trail," on *Yodeling Blonde Bombshell*.

66. "Record Reviews," *Billboard*, January 18, 1947, 101.

67. "American Folk Tunes: Cowboy and Hillbilly Tunes and Tunesters," *Billboard*, March 20, 1948, 106.

68. "Country and Western (Folk) Record Reviews," *Billboard*, August 2, 1952, 102.

69. Archainbaud, *Blue Canadian Rockies*.

70. Marie, email.

71. D. Cusick, *Cowboy in Country Music*, 72, points out that Rosalie Allen was also a woman disc jockey on WOV's *Prairie Stars* from 1944 to 1946 and had a regular column promoting country music in the leading trade magazines such as *National Jamboree, Country Song Roundup*, and *Hoedown*.

72. *Rustic Rhythm*, July 1956, 4. La Chapelle, "'Spade Doesn't Look Exactly Starved,'" 25, notes that women played an important role in fan journalism of country music in 1940s Southern California.

73. Marie, email.

Chapter 5. Rose Maddox: Roadhouse Singing and Hillbilly Theatrics

1. The collapse of the agricultural industry pushed more farmers off their land. With fewer landowners, the number of sharecroppers increased in the South. By 1930, 60 percent of southern farmers did not own their own land, and by 1937 two-thirds of the nation's tenant farmers and sharecroppers lived in the South. See Nies, "Defending Jeeter," 122.

2. Maddox, interview, 1.

3. Maddox, interview, 3. Rose Maddox recalled camping alongside the road, staying in migrant and hobo camps, and receiving food and shelter from the Salvation Army during the Maddox family's travels to California.

4. Maddox, interview, 5; and Whiteside, *Ramblin' Rose*, 20.

5. In her interview with John Rumble (p. 5), Maddox gave an account of the hard work of trying to make a living by following the crops and being called a fruit tramp.

6. Gregory, *American Exodus*, 67.

7. P. Taylor, "Again the Covered Wagon," 351.

8. La Chapelle, *Proud to Be an Okie*, 29–33, makes the interesting point that a significant portion of the white middle-class were transplants who had recently left the Midwest prior to the Okie migration. Their push for political and social containment may have had more to do with their attempts to distance themselves from migrants who reminded them of home and their own economic vulnerability in Depression-era California.

9. Maddox, interview, 12 and 15–16. According to Rose Maddox, the early morning broadcasts from Modesto's KTRB could carry as far away as Alaska. The Maddox family performed on radio for free to become better known in the region so that they could play in the local honky-tonks and bars for tips. Before World War II, the ensemble, including Cal on rhythm guitar, Fred on bass, Don on fiddle, and Rose as lead singer, started to play in the local dance halls as well.

10. McCusker, *Lonesome Cowgirls and Honky-Tonk Angels*, 3–5, demonstrates that female country artists were integral in pushing the image of country music closer to that of middle-class respectability to attract the financial support of radio sponsors.

11. Maddox Brothers and Rose, *On the Air*. The Maddox Brothers and Rose had won a state competition for the best hillbilly band at the 1939 Sacramento State Fair celebrating the state centennial. The prize was a yearlong network radio program sponsored by Anacin Pain Reliever on Sacramento's KFBK, whose broadcast reached a number of states beyond California (including Arizona, Nevada, Oregon, and Washington) and therefore expanded their listening audience. Maddox, interview, 13, and Whiteside, *Ramblin' Rose*, 42.

12. Lott, *Love and Theft*, 215.

13. See R. Rubin, "Sing Me Back Home," for a discussion of the ways in which country music acts on the West Coast, beginning with the Maddox Brothers and Rose, modeled their personae after the parodies of rural southern culture prevalent in minstrelsy.

14. Rose Maddox emphatically stated that the Sons of the Pioneers "were [her] idols," and admitted, "I wanted to sing just like them. Wanted to sing just exactly like them." Maddox, interview, 19.

15. Stras, "Voice of the Beehive," 41–42, discusses the vocal development of young women.

16. Maddox, interview, 18. Maddox stated that she did some performance work with Arkie and His Hillbillies during World War II without her brothers.

17. Maddox, interview, 19. This story is also featured in Whiteside, *Ramblin' Rose*, 54, and in Haslam, *Workin' Man Blues*, 171.

18. Maddox, interview, 13.

19. Arhoolie Records has reissued the Four Star recordings of the Maddox Brothers and Rose: *America's Most Colorful Hillbilly Band*, vol. 1, *1946–1951*; and *America's Most Colorful Hillbilly Band*, vol. 2, *1947–1951*.

20. Maddox, interview, 39.

21. Maddox, interview, 40.

22. Maddox, interview, 16–18.

23. An important example of country music's relationship to the blues is Hank Williams's 1947 "Move It On Over," the musical precursor to Bill Haley's 1955 "Rock around the Clock."

24. See Malone, *Don't Get above Your Raisin'*, 79–80 and 135–136, for a historical and cultural account of rockabilly music.

25. Whiteside, *Ramblin' Rose*, 81.

26. Johnny Sippel, "Folk Talent and Tunes," *Billboard*, December 4, 1948, 32. The blurb also announced that the Maddox Brothers and Rose were regulars on a number of radio stations, including Modesto's KTRB, San Diego's XERB, Clint, Texas's XELO, and XEG, the Mexican radio station across the border, demonstrating their growing national appeal.

27. *Billboard*, November 12, 1949, 111.

28. Maddox Brothers and Rose, *America's Most Colorful Hillbilly Band*, vol. 1.

29. Maddox interview, 20, Maddox recalled that instead of including drums, she also learned how to play the bass. When she sang, however, she would put the bass on its stand and come up to the microphone.

30. T. D. Taylor points out that "vaudeville and other popular singers cultivated a piercing, nasal singing style" so that they could be heard in the back of the theater ("Music and the Rise of Radio," 260).

31. Rose Maddox, interview, 13 and 20; Whiteside, *Ramblin' Rose*, 58.

32. McNamara, *New York Concert Saloon*, 1–10 and 117–122.

33. Rodger, *Champagne Charlie and Pretty Jemima*, 17.

34. Maddox, interview, 20.

35. Woody Guthrie had a successful radio career in California during the Great Depression and wrote, performed, and broadcast many of his songs that spoke of the economic and social exploitations of Okies. See La Chapelle's "Refugees: Woody Guthrie, 'Los Angeles,'" and the Radicalization of Migrant Identity," in his *Proud to Be an Okie*, 45–75.

36. Guthrie, *Woody Guthrie*.

37. Maddox, interview, 14; Whiteside, *Ramblin' Rose*, 27. According to Rose Maddox, she learned "Philadelphia Lawyer" from listening to Woody Guthrie perform the song live in a California bar. Both the Maddox Brothers and Rose and Guthrie followed the rodeos and initially played for tips in bars close to the rodeos.

38. Maddox Brothers and Rose, *America's Most Colorful Hillbilly Band*, vol. 1.

39. For more about the production of nasal twang, see McKinney, *Diagnosis and Correction*, 137; and Kayes, *Singing and the Actor*, 110–117. Note that most vocal pedagogues instruct their students in how to include twang in vocal production without an explicit nasal sound.

40. Whiteside, *Ramblin' Rose*, 90–91.

41. Glenn, *Female Spectacle*, 77.

42. La Chapelle, *Proud to Be an Okie*, 10, argues that it was not until the 1960s that southern plains migrants lost their distinct Okie identity by adopting the social values of middle-class Californians.

43. Maddox Brothers and Rose, *America's Most Colorful Hillbilly Band*, vol. 1.

44. Ching, "The Hard Act to Follow: Hank Williams and the Legacy of Hard Country Stardom," in her *Wrong's What I Do Best*, 54.

45. Lefty Frizzell recorded a similarly themed honky-tonk tune, "If You Got the Money, I've Got the Time" (1950), about a man who promises the object of his affection an evening of "honky-tonkin'" as long as she can foot the bill.

46. Ortner, *Anthropology and Social Theory*, 33; and Skeggs, *Formations of Class and Gender*, 99.

47. Kibler, *Rank Ladies*, 67.

48. Maddox Brothers and Rose, *America's Most Colorful Hillbilly Band*, vol. 1.

49. Liner notes by Ken Davidson, in Cox, *Bill Cox: The Dixie Songbird*.

50. Eric Lott, *Love and Theft*, 163–173, for the history of wench songs in blackface acts.

51. May, *Homeward Bound*, 74.

52. Milkman, *Gender at Work*, 100.

53. May, *Homeward Bound*, 87.

54. La Chapelle, *Proud to Be an Okie*, 107–108, discusses the ways female defense workers asserted their sexuality

55. For more about the *Hayride*, see Laird, *Louisiana Hayride*.

56. Maddox, interview, 25–26. Maddox recalled that the performances of the Maddox Brothers and Rose were just as popular in the South as in the western part of the United States.

57. *Hillbilly & Western Hoedown*, March 1954, 18 and 19.

58. Maddox Brothers and Rose, *On the Air*.

59. For critical understandings of the ways the country music industry pursued respectability and acceptance within the popular music market, see Brackett, *Interpreting Popular Music*, 101–107.

60. "From Southern Rags to Western Riches," *Country Song Roundup*, December 1950, 22.

61. "Women in the News," *Cowboy Songs*, June 1954, 8.

62. *Country & Western Jamboree*, December 1956, 8 and 9.

63. *Country & Western Jamboree*, June 1957, 24.

64. Maddox Brothers and Rose, *Most Colorful Hillbilly Band in America*, includes Rose Maddox's solo recordings for Columbia Records.

65. "That Girl from Oklahoma," *Country & Western Jamboree*, November 1956, 15.

66. *Country Music People*, September 1971, 10.

67. *Billboard*, September 12, 1953, 23, lists the recording under "Top Sellers—Country and Hillbilly." Shepard, *Beautiful Lies*.

68. "That Girl from Oklahoma," 15. The country music trade press continually contrasted Shepard's small stature with her loud and resonant voice.

69. *Country Song Roundup Yearbook*, Spring 1967, 78.

70. *Folk and Country Songs*, January 1957, 19.

71. Maphis and Maphis, *Ridin' the Frets*.

72. See Bufwack and Oermann, *Finding Her Voice*, 196–200, for further details about female rockabilly artists in California.

73. Homer Escamilla wrote "Hey Little Dreamboat" and shared songwriting credits with Rose Maddox for her Columbia recordings of "Looky There (Over There)" and "Old Man Blues." Maddox Brothers and Rose, *Most Colorful Hillbilly Band in America*, CD booklet, 26–27.

74. Maddox Brothers and Rose, *Most Colorful Hillbilly Band in America*.

75. See Sanjek, "Can a Fujiyama Mama?," 137–167, for a history of women rockabilly artists. Sanjek briefly notes the significance of Rose Maddox in the history of rockabilly.

76. As quoted in Bufwack and Oermann, *Finding Her Voice*, 201.

77. Harrington, *Women of Rockabilly*.

78. Sanjek, "Can a Fujiyama Mama?," 156.

79. See Neal, *Country Music*, 178–179, for a discussion of how Wanda Jackson combined the stylistic elements of honky-tonk with rockabilly in the song "I Gotta Know."

80. *Country & Western Jamboree*, December 1956, 8–9.

81. Kimmel, *Manhood in America*, 236.

82. W. Jackson, *Wanda Rocks*.

83. For more about Brenda Lee's singing style, see Stilwell, "Vocal Decorum," 83.

84. Maddox, interview, 36.

85. Carson, Lewis, and Shaw, *Girls Rock!*, 117.

Chapter 6. Voices of Angels: Kitty Wells and the Emergence of Women's Honky-Tonk

1. See A. Fox, "Jukebox of History."

2. See Skeggs, *Formations of Class and Gender*, 47, for a discussion of the fallen woman's relationship to respectability and conventional gender codes.

3. Lawler argues that class is often "displaced on to individual and familial lack" ("Rules of Engagement," 124).

4. Lipsitz, *Class and Culture*, 2; and Coontz, *The Way We Never Were*, 36–38.

5. Malone, *Country Music USA*, 2nd ed., 153.

6. Shank, *Dissonant Identities*, 34–35.

7. "Texas Bill Defines 'Honky Tonk' for Officers' Guidance," *Billboard*, July 3, 1943, 62.

8. See Malone, *Country Music USA*, 2nd ed., 162–164; and Haslam, *Workin' Man Blues*, 74, for a broader history of amplification used in country music.

9. In the mid-1930s, the guitarist Bob Dunn of the Musical Brownies became the first country musician to amplify his guitar. He also modified his electric instrument into a steel guitar to imitate the Hawaiian playing style (popular in the United States) by magnetizing and raising the strings.

10. The Wurlitzer Company introduced the first jukebox in 1928. Malone, *Country Music USA*, 2nd ed., 154.

11. Jensen, *Nashville Sound*, 27.

12. P. Fox, *National Acts*, 64–65.

13. A. Fox, *Real Country*, 250–251.

14. See Ortner, *Anthropology and Social Theory*, 27–41, for more details about working-class women as "agents of middle-class value."

15. See Felski for more about the gendered biases of class analysis. She makes the point that the working class has been "represented through images of a virile proletariat in left rhetoric," whereas "the lower middle class is often gendered female, associated with the triumph of suburban values and the symbolic castration of men" (*Doing Time*, 48).

16. Bettie argues "that 'class' as a signifier has problematically become a historically outdated code for white male industrial labor" (*Women without Class*, xvi). Likewise, Acker notes that the concept of class emerged from "the economic experiences of white men," and not from women or people of color (*Class Questions, Feminist Answers*, 1).

17. Hubbs, *Rednecks, Queers, and Country Music*, 126.

18. See Ortner, *Anthropology and Social*, 32–33, for a discussion of the relationship between the working class and exaggerated sexuality.

19. Bettie, *Women without Class*, 199.

20. "Honky-Tonk Blues," on Dexter, *Honky Tonk Blues 1936–40*.

21. Ching, *Wrong's What I Do Best*, 54.

22. Brackett, *Interpreting Popular Music*, 107.

23. Ching explains how the portrayals of Williams after his death made him into "the model of the hard country star" (*Wrong's What I Do Best*, 62).

24. Pamela Fox argues that male honky-tonk songs of heartache and aching desire "registered a deep sense of betrayal aimed not at romance narrative itself but at women who have failed to comply with the script" (*Natural Acts*, 87).

25. Pecknold, *Selling Sound*, 49, discusses the role of the honky-tonk in depicting displaced southerners in negative stereotypes.

26. Pugh, *Ernest Tubb*, 66. Responding to the requests of a Forth Worth jukebox operator who complained to Tubb that the acoustic sounds of his recordings could not be heard above the evening noise, Tubb included the electric guitar in his next recording session.

27. See P. Fox, *Natural Acts*, 64–65, for a discussion of the themes in male honky-tonk.

28. Pugh, *Ernest Tubb*, 82–85. J. L. Frank also managed the career of Roy Acuff and booked traveling tours of country musicians Minnie Pearl, Eddy Arnold, and Pee Wee King.

29. See Wolfe, *Good-Natured Riot*, for a history of WSM's radio program *Grand Ole Opry*.

30. See Rumble, "'I'll Reap My Harvest,'" 356–357, for a historical account of how the *Grand Ole Opry* gained prominence in the country music industry.

31. See Rumble, "'I'll Reap My Harvest,'" 350–377, for a history of Fred Rose's career in the music industry and how he formed a partnership with Roy Acuff in Nashville.

32. What largely made this alliance possible was the 1940 formation of BMI (Broadcast Music, Inc.), the first songwriters' collection agency to monitor the licensing of country music and other popular-music genres—blues, jazz, and Latin music—that had been excluded by ASCAP. See Pecknold, *Selling Sound*, 53–58, for more details about the significance of Acuff-Rose Publications and the formation of BMI to the developments of the country music industry in Nashville.

33. Peterson, *Creating Country Music*, 14–25, and Pecknold, *Selling Sound*, 53–54, provide a historical overview of the constituent elements of the country music industry.

34. Pecknold, *Selling Sound*, 121–122.

35. Pecknold, *Selling Sound*, 59.

36. Beginning in 1947, Hank Williams recorded several different versions of "Honky-Tonk Blues." In 1952, MGM Records released a successful rendition of the song that reached number 2 on the country charts.

37. Ching, *Wrong's What I Do Best*, 35.

38. For discussion of the ways in which Hank Williams's musical expressions resisted normative society, see Leppert and Lipsitz, "'Everybody's Lonesome for Somebody,'" 266–267.

39. Kimmel, *Manhood in America*, 226.

40. Kimmel, *Manhood in America*, 245.

41. Leppert and Lipsitz, "'Everybody's Lonesome for Somebody,'" 268. P. Fox, *Natural Acts*, 88.

42. Leppert and Lipsitz, "'Everybody's Lonesome for Somebody,'" 264–265, and Brackett, *Interpreting Popular Music*, 91–92, each discuss the ways in which Williams emphasized the timbral differences of his upper and lower registers.

43. Ching, *Wrong's What I Do Best*, 32.

44. See Sennett and Cobb's landmark study of class, *Hidden Injuries of Class*.

45. P. Fox, *Natural Acts*, 94.

46. Though Wells's accomplishments are significant, it is worth noting the success of female country artists prior to *Billboard*'s inclusion of country music charts in 1944. As previous chapters have demonstrated, Lulu Belle was the most popular woman on radio in 1936, Patsy Montana was the first female country artist to sell a million copies of a record, and Rose Maddox contributed to establishing country music on the West Coast.

47. Bufwack and Oermann, *Finding Her Voice*, 152.

48. For examples of this narrative, see Wolfe, *Classic Country*, 56; and P. Fox, *Natural Acts*, 94.

49. Christgau, "Kitty Wells, Queen of Denial," 218.

50. Trott, *Honky Tonk Angels*, 2.

51. For more about the Church of the Nazarene and gospel music, see Malone, *Southern Music, American Music*, 67.

52. Murray Nash, "Miss Country Music and Her Family," *Country & Western Jamboree*, December, 1955, 7, and Dunkleburger, *Queen of Country Music*, 12, reiterated the details of Wells's personal life and career.

53. Nash, "Miss Country Music," 7; and Dunkleburger, *Queen of Country Music*, 34. Jack Anglin married Louise Wright, Johnnie's sister.

54. Nash, "Miss Country Music," 7; Dunkleburger, *Queen of Country Music*, 38; and Wolfe, *Classic Country*, 58.

55. Dunkleburger, *Queen of Country Music*, 35–38.

56. Wolfe, liner notes to Wells, *Queen of Country Music*, 4.

57. Wells recorded two songs written by Johnnie and Jack, "Death at the Bar" and "Love or Hate," and the popular gospel numbers "Gathering Flowers for the Master's Bouquet" (previously recorded by the Maddox Brothers and Rose) and "Don't Wait the Last Minute to Pray." The following year, Wells recorded four more pieces, including a tune made popular by Linda Parker on Chicago's WLS, "I'll Be All Smiles Tonight." Wolfe, liner notes to Wells, *Queen of Country Music*, 36.

58. P. Fox, *Natural Acts*, 99.

59. Lipsitz, *Time Passages*, 99.

60. I am drawing from Susan McClary's arguments about the ways "conventions always operate as part of the signifying apparatus" (*Conventional Wisdom*, 6) to make a case for Wells's balance of convention and individual expression.

61. Wells, *Queen of Country Music*.

62. Wolfe, liner notes to Wells, *Queen of Country Music*, 7.

63. See Wicks, "Belated Salute," 77–85, for examples of how country singers have continued the tradition of lining-out in their vocal renditions.

64. Charles Newman, "The Kitty Wells Story," *Country News and Views* 2 (April 1964): 9–10.

65. *Billboard*, June 5, 1954, 53.

66. *Country Song Roundup*, September 1954.

67. *Memories of the Fifties*, vol. 1.

68. *Billboard*, May 16, 1953, 26.

69. Hill, *Don't Send Me No More Roses*.

70. Wells, *Queen of Country Music*.

71. Wells, *Queen of Country Music*.

72. Shepard, *Beautiful Lies*.

73. *Memories of the Fifties*, vol. 1.

74. For more about Webb Pierce's career and musical voice in honky-tonk, see my "Weeping and Flamboyant Men."

Chapter 7. Domestic Respectability: The Marketing of Honky-Tonk Performers

1. P. Fox, *Natural Acts*, 94.

2. Pamela Fox explains how male honky-tonk voiced a deep level of betrayal aimed at women who "failed to comply with the script" (*Natural Acts*, 87).

3. *Billboard*, September 13, 1947, 20.

4. Brackett, *Interpreting Popular Music*, 101–107; Pecknold, *Selling Sound*, 58–66.

5. Nat Green, "Hillbillies Heat with Helium," *The Billboard 1943 Music Year Book*, 99.

6. "Today's Platter Pilgrimages Show Folk Fellahs Plenty Hep," *Billboard*, February 16, 1946, 20 and 31.

7. *Time*, "Music: Bull Market in Corn."

8. Gregory, *Southern Diaspora*, 66; Pecknold, *Selling Sound*, 49.

9. Berry, *Southern Migrants, Northern Exiles*, 99–100.

10. Gregory, *Southern Diaspora*, 14 and 65.

11. Guy, "Common Ground," 49–50.

12. Votaw, "Hillbillies Invade Chicago," 64.

13. Votaw, "Hillbillies Invade Chicago," 64.

14. E. Brown, "Truth about the Detroit Riot," 489.

15. Hartigan, "'Disgrace to the Race,'" 145.

16. Berry, *Southern Migrants, Northern Exiles*, 144–166.

17. "Big Favorite with Baltimore Patrons," *Billboard*, July 3, 1943, 62.

18. *Billboard*, April 26, 1952, 17.

19. Skeggs, *Formations of Class and Gender*, 48.

20. As with the fanzines that promoted the career of Lulu Belle in the 1930s on WLS (see chapter 2), the country music trade magazines positioned Wells's music making in the home.

21. "At Home with the Stars: Kitty Wells," *Country Song Roundup*, June 1956, 6.

22. "Kitty Wells: A Star Is Born," *Country Song Roundup*, December 1952, 9.

23. *Country Song Roundup*, September 1954, 9.

24. Mike Hyland, "Wells Still Riding Charts; Pushes Her Ruboca Label," *Billboard*, September 15, 1979, 53.

25. "*Opry* Group Smashes Records at the Palace," *Country & Western Jamboree*, February 1956, 10.

26. "Country Music's King and Queen," *Country & Western Jamboree*, October 1956, 30.

27. *Country & Western Jamboree*, January 1957, 53.

28. "The Queen of Country Music: Kitty Wells," *Country Song Roundup*, January 1969, 15.

29. *Country Song Roundup*, August 1953, 15.

30. "Goldie Hill: Beauty and Brains," *Country & Western Jamboree*, October 1954, 8.

31. "A Visit with Goldie Hill," *Country Song Roundup*, August 1969, 8.

32. Kimmel, *Manhood in America*, 245.

33. *Country Song Roundup*, June 1952, 8.

34. *Country Song Roundup*, February 1956, 7.

35. "Country Music's Pride and Joy," *Country Song Roundup*, August 1962, 19.

36. *Country Song Roundup*, 1969 annual, 28.

37. For more about Webb Pierce's career, see my "Weeping and Flamboyant Men."

38. Quoted in Peterson, *Creating Country Music*, 182.

39. Charlie Lamb, "A Girl Named Audrey," *Country & Western Jamboree*, September 1956, 10.

40. See R. M. Williams, *Sing a Sad Song*, 166–170.

41. Peterson, *Creating Country Music*, 182.

42. "The Girl with the 'Big Heart,'" *Country Song Roundup*, June 1957, 10.

43. "Opry Star: Jean Shepard," *Music City News*, December 1963, 2.

44. "The George Jones Story," *Country Song Roundup*, May 1962, 9, describes Jones as "one of the friendliest people in the business and one of the best-loved by ardent country fans."

45. Frieda Barter, "No Bumps for Johnny Cash," *Country & Western Jamboree*, October 1956, 12 and 25.

46. "The Girl with the 'Big Heart,'" *Country Song Roundup*, June 1957, 10.

47. *Folk and Country Songs*, January 1957, 19.

48. "That Girl from Oklahoma," *Country & Western Jamboree*, November 1956, 15.

49. Ginger Willis, "A Shepard Catches A Hawk," *Country Song Round Up*, May 1961, 6 and 7.

50. *Country Song Roundup*, "A Star Is Born: Kitty Wells," December 1952, 9.

51. *Country & Western Jamboree*, January 1957, 53.

52. *Saturday Night at the Grand Ole Opry*.

53. Joanne Meyerowitz, "Beyond the Feminine Mystique: A Reassessment of Postwar Mass Culture," in *Not June Cleaver*, 232.

54. Pamela Fox argues that country music trade presses, such as *Rustic Rhythm*, framed "traditional rural culture as a feminine enterprise" (*Natural Acts*, 110).

55. Not until after Hank Williams's death did the country music industry memorialize him as an iconic creator of honky-tonk music. See Peterson's analysis of Williams's career and how the country music industry worked to create his legendary status (*Creating Country Music*, 182–183).

56. *Country Song Roundup*, June 1953, 6.

57. Pecknold, *Selling Sound*, 124.

Conclusion: Country Vocalities and Gendered Theatrics

1. I also write about country singing styles and Loretta Lynn's vocality in "Singing Voice in Country Music."

2. Heidemann, "Remarkable Women and Ordinary Gals," 172–173, also discusses and makes similar observations about Lynn's vocal style in the song "Fist City."

3. See Hamessley, *Unlikely Angel*, for more details about Parton's singing voice.

4. Morris, *Persistence of Sentiment*, 183–184; Edwards, *Dolly Parton*, 4.

5. Morris, *Persistence of Sentiment*, 179, mentions that Porter Wagoner and Dolly Parton could suddenly transform their glitzy stage sets "into the audible recollection of a camp meeting, thrilling their down-home audience." Lydia Hamessley's forthcoming book on Dolly Parton's songwriting, *Unlikely Angel*, also points to the ways that Parton vocally drew on vocal traditions of southern vernacular practices in her narratives about mountain culture.

6. *Rolling Stone*, special double issue, December 24, 1998–January 7, 1999, 161.

7. Hubbs, *Rednecks, Queers, and Country Music*.

8. Chinen, review of Miranda Lambert's *Revolution*.

Bibliography

Primary Sources

100 WLS Barn Dance Favorites. Compiled by John Lair. Chicago: M. M. Cole, 1935.

Alka-Seltzer Song Book. Elkhart, IN: Miles Laboratories, 1937.

American Folk Music. Edited by Harry Smith. Washington, DC: Smithsonian Folkways Records and Sony Records, 1997. CD.

Anderson, G. M., dir. *The Girl from Montana.* Selig Polyscope, 1911.

Archainbaud, George, dir. *Apache Country.* Written by Norman S. Hall. Gene Autry Productions, 1952.

———. *Blue Canadian Rockies.* Gene Autry Productions, 1952.

Back in the Saddle Again: American Cowboy Songs. New York: New World Records, 1983. CD.

Bennett, Hugh, dir. *National Barn Dance.* Written by Lee Loeb and Hal Fimberg. Paramount, 1944.

Billboard. 1943–.

Brice, Fanny. *The Rose of Washington Square.* London: Jasmine Records, 2012. CD.

Britt, Elton. *The RCA Years.* BMG Music and Collectors Choice Music, 1997. CD.

Cotton, Carolina. *Yodeling Blonde Bombshell.* Kit Fox Records, 2005. CD.

Country & Western Jamboree. 1955–1957.

Country News and Views. April 1964–.

Country Song Roundup. 1952–1969.

Cousin Emmy. *Cousin Emmy and Her Kinfolks, 1939–1947.* Hambergen, Germany: Bear Family Records, 2007. CD.

Cox, Bill. *Bill Cox: The Dixie Songbird.* CDTR705. Dayton, OH: Tri-agle-far Records, 2005. CD.

Cowboy Songs. June 1954.

Dexter, Al. *Honky Tonk Blues 1936–40: The Early Recordings.* London: Jasmine Music, 2004. CD.

Diege, Samuel, dir. *Ride 'Em Cowgirl.* Grand National Pictures, 1939.

———. *The Singing Cowgirl.* Grand National Pictures, 1938.

———. *Water Rustlers.* Grand National Pictures, 1939.

Flowers in the Wildwood: Women in Early Country Music. Munich: Trikont, 2003. CD.

Foley, Red. *Old Shep: The Red Foley Recordings, 1933–1959.* Hambergen, Germany: Bear Family Records, 2006. CD.

Folk and Country Songs. January 1957.

Good, Millie. "Two Cowgirls on the Lone Prairie." Interview by Tony Russell and Charles Wolfe in *Old Time Music* 43 (Winter 1986/87): 6–13.

Good, Millie, and Bill McCluskey. Interview by John Rumble, November 4, 1988. Interview OHC3680LC transcript, Country Music Foundation Oral History Project, Country Music Hall of Fame Library, Nashville, TN.

Goodwins, Lesley, dir. *The Singing Sheriff.* Universal Pictures, 1944.

Guthrie, Woody. *The Asch Recordings.* Washington, DC: Smithsonian Folkways, 1999. CD.

Hill, Goldie. *Don't Send Me No More Roses.* London: Righteous, 2009. CD.

Jackson, Wanda. *Wanda Rocks.* Hambergen, Germany: Bear Family Records, 2002. CD.

Kane, Joseph, dir. *Shine On Harvest Moon.* Republic Pictures, 1938.

Kincaid, Bradley. *Favorite Old-Time Songs and Mountain Ballads.* Chicago: WLS, the Sears, Roebuck Radio Station, 1928.

Lamont, Charles, dir. *Hi, Neighbor.* Republic Pictures, 1942.

Landers, Lew, dir. *I'm from Arkansas.* PRC Pictures, 1944.

Louise Massey and the Westerners' Song Folio. New York: Peer International, 1941.

Lulu Belle and Scotty. *Lulu Belle and Scotty: Hayloft Jamboree Song Book.* Chicago: Hilliard-Currie, 1944.

———. *Lulu Belle and Skyland Scotty: Mountain Songs, Western Songs, and Cowboy Songs.* 1937. Reprint, Chicago: M. M. Cole, 1941.

———. *Lulu Belle's and Skyland Scotty's Homefolk Songs.* N.p.: S. Wiseman, 1937.

———. *The Sweethearts of Country Music.* Dearborn, MI: Highland Music, 1991. CD.

———. *Tender Memories Recalled.* Vol. 2. United States: Mar-Lu, 1989. LP.

Maddox, Rose. Interview by John Rumble, January 15, 1995. Interview OHC178-LC, transcript, Country Music Foundation Oral History Project, Country Music Hall of Fame Library, Nashville, TN.

The Maddox Brothers and Rose. *America's Most Colorful Hillbilly Band.* Vol. 1, *1946–1951.* El Cerrito, CA, Arhoolie, 1993. CD.

———. *America's Most Colorful Hillbilly Band.* Vol. 2, *1947–1951.* El Cerrito, CA, Arhoolie, 1995. CD.

———. *The Most Colorful Hillbilly Band in America.* Includes CD booklet with biographical essay by Robert K. Oermann, notes on the music by Deke Dicerson, and discography by Richard Weize and Kevin Coffey. Hambergen, Germany: Bear Family Records, 1998. CD.

———. *On the Air: The 1940s.* El Cerrito, CA: Arhoolie, 1996. CD.

Maphis, Joe, and Rose Lee Maphis. *Ridin' the Frets.* London: Jasmine Records, 2010. CD.

Marie, Sharon (Carolina Cotton's daughter). Email communication with author. November 11, 2014.

McDonald, Frank, dir. *Grand Ole Opry.* Republic Pictures, 1940.

———. *Jeepers Creepers.* Republic Pictures, 1939.

———. *Sing, Neighbor, Sing.* Republic Pictures, 1944.

———. *Swing Your Partner.* Republic Pictures, 1943.

———. *Village Barn Dance*. Republic Pictures, 1940.

Memories: Grand Ole Opry Stars of the Fifties. 12 DVD set. Gannaway, 1996. DVD.

Montana, Patsy. *The Best of Patsy Montana: Deluxe Edition of Famous Original Cowboy Songs and Mountain Ballads*. Itasca, IL: Collector's Choice Music; New York: Sony Music Special Products, 2001. CD.

———. Interview by Dorothy Gable, October 22, 1967. Interview OH348-LC, transcript, Country Music Foundation Oral History Project, Country Music Hall of Fame Library, Nashville, TN.

———. Interview by Douglas B. Green, October 16, 1974. Interview OH122-LC, transcript, Country Music Foundation Oral History Project, Country Music Hall of Fame Library, Nashville, TN.

———. Interview by John Rumble, June 9, 1984. Interview OHC195-LC, transcript, Country Music Foundation Oral History Project, Country Music Hall of Fame Library, Nashville, TN.

———. Interview by John Rumble, August 30, 1985. Interview OHC196 transcript, Country Music Foundation Oral History Project, Country Music Hall of Fame Library, Nashville, TN.

———. Interview by John Rumble, September 2, 1985. Interview OHC197-LC transcript, Country Music Foundation Oral History Project, Country Music Hall of Fame Library, Nashville, TN.

———. *Patsy Montana, America's No. 1 Cowgirl: Deluxe Edition of Famous Original Cowboy Songs and Mountain Ballads*. Chicago: M. M. Cole, 1941.

———. *Patsy Montana: The Cowboy's Sweetheart*. With Jane Frost. Jefferson, NC: McFarland, 2002.

———. "Portraits from the Most Popular Country Show on the Air, 1924–1939." *Journal of Country Music* 10 (1985): 33–48.

Music City News. December 1963.

Nazarro, Ray, dir. *Hoedown*. Columbia Pictures, 1950.

———. *The Rough, Tough West*. Columbia Pictures, 1952.

The Prairie Ramblers and Patsy Montana's Collection of Songs. New York: Bob Miller, 1937.

Saturday Night at the Grand Ole Opry. Vol. 2. New York: Decca DL 4539, 1964. LP.

Scholl, Jack, dir. *Spade Cooley: King of Western Swing*. Warner Brothers Pictures, 1945.

Shepard, Jean. *Beautiful Lies . . . the Early Years*. London: Jasmine Records, 2009. CD.

Sherman, George, dir. *Colorado Sunset*. Republic Pictures, 1939.

Stand By! (WLS fan magazine). 1935–1938.

Wells, Kitty. *The Queen of Country Music*. Liner notes by Charles Wolfe. Hambergen, Germany: Bear Family Records, 1993. CD.

White Spirituals from the Sacred Harp: The Alabama Sacred Harp Convention. Recorded by Alan Lomax at the Sacred Harp Singing Convention in Fyffe, Alabama, 1959. New York: New World Records, 1977. CD.

Wiseman, Lulu Belle. "Belle of the Barn Dance: Reminiscing with Lulu Belle Wiseman Stamey." Interview by William E. Lightfoot. *Journal of Country Music* 12 (1987): 2–18.

———. Interview by Bill Lightfoot, June 7, 1982. Interview OH443, transcript, Country Music Foundation Oral History Project, Country Music Hall of Fame Library, Nashville, TN.

WLS Family Album (WLS fan magazine). 1930–1957.

Secondary Sources

Abbate, Carolyn. *Unsung Voices: Opera and Musical Narrative in the Nineteenth Century.* Princeton, NJ: Princeton University Press, 1991.

Abbott, Lynn, and Doug Seroff. "America's Blue Yodel." *Musical Traditions* 11 (1993): 2–11.

Acker, Joan. *Class Questions, Feminist Answers.* Lanham, MD: Rowman and Littlefield, 2006.

Adamic, Louis. "The Hill-Billies Come to Detroit." *The Nation,* February 13, 1935, 177–178.

Adkins, Lisa, and Beverley Skeggs, eds. *Feminism after Bourdieu.* Malden, MA: Blackwell, 2004.

Anderson, Benedict. *Imagined Communities: Reflections on the Origins and Spread of Nationalism.* London: Verso, 1991.

Antler, Joyce. "One Clove Away from a Pomander Ball: The Subversive Tradition of Jewish Female Comedians." *Studies in American Jewish Literature* 29 (2010): 123–138.

Archer, Melanie, and Judith R. Blau. "Class Formation in Nineteenth-Century America: The Case of the Middle Class." *Annual Review of Sociology* 19 (1993): 17–41.

Austin, William W. *"Susanna," "Jeanie," and "The Old Folks at Home": The Songs of Stephen C. Foster from His Time to Ours.* New York: Macmillan, 1975.

Bacon, Peter. "Culture: Nothing Fluffy about These Chicks." *Birmingham Post,* September 11, 2003, 15.

Banfield, Stephen. "Stage Screen Entertainers in the Twentieth Century." In *The Cambridge Companion to Singing,* edited by John Potter, 63–82. Cambridge: Cambridge University Press, 2000.

Bealle, John. *Public Worship, Private Faith: Sacred Harp and American Folksong.* Athens: University of Georgia Press, 1997.

Bell-Metereau, Rebecca. *Hollywood Androgyny.* New York: Columbia University Press, 1985.

Berish, Andrew. *Lonesome Roads and Streets of Dreams: Place, Mobility, and Race in Jazz of the 1930s and 40s.* Chicago: Chicago University Press, 2012.

Berry, Chad, ed. *The Hayloft Gang: The Story of the National Barn Dance.* Urbana: University of Illinois Press, 2008.

———. *Southern Migrants, Northern Exiles.* Urbana: University of Illinois Press, 2000.

Bertrand, Michael T. "Race and Rural Identity." In Berry, *Hayloft Gang,* 130–152.

Bettie, Julie. *Women without Class: Girls, Race, and Identity.* Berkeley: University of California Press, 2003.

Biggar, George C. "The WLS National Barn Dance Story: The Early Years." *JEMF Quarterly* 7 (Autumn 1971): 105–112.

Blumin, Stuart M. *The Emergence of the Middle Class: Social Experience in the American City, 1790–1900.* Cambridge: Cambridge University Press, 1989.

Bourdieu, Pierre. *Distinction: A Social Critique of the Judgement of Taste.* Translated by Richard Nice. Cambridge, MA: Harvard University Press, 1984.

Boyd, Jean A. *Dance All Night: Those Other Southwestern Swing Bands, Past and Present.* Lubbock: Texas Tech University Press, 2012.

———. *The Jazz of the Southwest: An Oral History of Western Swing.* Austin: University of Texas Press, 1998.

Boyer, Horace Clarence. *How Sweet the Sound: The Golden Age of Gospel.* Washington, DC: Elliott and Clark, 1995.

Brackett, David. *Categorizing Sound: Genre and Twentieth-Century Popular Music.* Berkeley: University of California Press, 2016.

———. *Interpreting Popular Music.* Cambridge: University Press, 1995; reprint, Berkeley: University of California Press, 2000.

Brown, Bill, ed. *Reading the West: An Anthology of Dime Westerns.* Boston: Bedford Books, 1997.

Brown, Earl. "The Truth about the Detroit Riot." *Harper's,* November 1943, 488–500.

Bufwack, Mary A., and Robert K. Oermann. *Finding Her Voice: Women in Country Music, 1800–2000.* Nashville: Country Music Foundation Press and Vanderbilt University Press, 2003.

Cantwell, Robert. *Bluegrass Breakdown: The Making of the Old Southern Sound.* Urbana: University of Illinois Press, 1984.

Carson, Mina, Tisa Lewis, and Susan M. Shaw. *Girls Rock! Fifty Years of Women Making Music.* Lexington: University Press of Kentucky, 2004.

Chapman, Janice L. *Singing and Teaching Singing: A Holistic Approach to Classical Voice.* San Diego, CA: Plural Publishing, 2017.

Chinen, Nate. Review of Miranda Lambert's *Revolution.* Critic's Choice, *New York Times,* September 28, 2009, C3.

Ching, Barbara. *Wrong's What I Do Best: Hard Country Music and Contemporary Culture.* New York: Oxford University Press, 2001.

Christgau, Georgia. "Kitty Wells, Queen of Denial." In Pecknold and McCusker, *Country Boys and Redneck Women,* 229–248.

Cizmic, Maria. *Performing Pain: Music and Trauma in Eastern Europe.* Oxford: Oxford University Press, 2012.

Clément, Catherine. "Through Voices, History." In Smart, *Siren Songs,* 17–28.

Cobb, B. E., and B. F. White. *The Sacred Harp: A Tradition and Its Music.* Athens: University of Georgia Press, 1978.

Cockrell, Dale. *Demons of Disorder: Early Blackface Minstrels and Their World.* Cambridge: Cambridge University Press, 1997.

———, ed. *The Ingalls Wilder Family Songbook.* Middleton, WI: Published for the American Musicological Society by A-R Editions, 2011.

Cohen, Lizabeth. *Making a New Deal: Industrial Workers in Chicago, 1919–1939.* New York: Cambridge University Press, 1990.

Conway, Cecelia. "Black Banjo Songsters in Appalachia." *Black Music Research Journal* 23, no. 1/2 (Spring, Autumn 2003): 149–166.

Coontz, Stephanie. *The Way We Never Were: American Families and the Nostalgia Trap.* New York: Basic Books, 1992.

Cusick, Don. *The Cowboy in Country Music: An Historical Survey with Artist Profiles.* Jefferson, NC: McFarland, 2011.

Cusick, Suzanne. "Feminist Theory, Music Theory and the Mind/Body Problem." *Perspectives of New Music* 32 (Winter 1994): 8–27.

———. "On Musical Performance of Gender and Sex." In *Audible Traces: Gender, Identity, and Music,* edited by Elaine Barkin and Lydia Hamessley, 25–48. Zürich: Carciofoli Verlagshaus, 1999.

Daniel, Wayne W. "Lulu Belle and Scotty: 'Have I Told You Lately That I Love You?'" *Bluegrass Unlimited* (March 1986): 70–76.

———. "The Ranch Romance of Louise Massey and the Westerners." *Journal of Country Music* 2, no. 3 (January 1999): 3–7.

Davis, Andrew. *Il Trittico, Turandot, and Puccini's Late Style*. Bloomington: Indiana University Press, 2010.

Denning, Michael. *The Cultural Front: The Laboring of American Culture in the Twentieth Century*. London: Verso, 1996.

———. *Mechanic Accents: Dime Novels and Working-Class Culture in America*. London: Verso, 1987.

Douglas, Susan J. *Listening In: Radio and the American Imagination*. New York: Times Books, 1999.

Dunkleburger, A. C. *Queen of Country Music: The Life Story of Kitty Wells*. Nashville: Ambrose, 1977.

Edwards, Leigh H. *Dolly Parton, Gender, and Country Music*. Bloomington: Indiana University Press, 2018.

Eidsheim, Nina Sun. *The Race of Sound: Listening, Timbre, and Vocality in African American Music*. Durham, NC: Duke University Press, 2019.

Erdman, Andrew L. *Blue Vaudeville: Sex, Morals, and the Marketing of Amusement, 1895–1915*. Jefferson, NC: McFarland, 2004.

Escott, Colin. *Grand Ole Opry: The Making of an American Icon*. New York: Center Street, 2006.

Etulain, Richard W. "Origins of the Western." In *Critical Essays on the Western American Historical Novel*, edited by William T. Pilkington, 56–60. Boston: G. K. Hall, 1980.

Felski, Rita. *Doing Time: Feminist Theory and Postmodern Culture*. New York: New York University Press, 2000.

———. *The Gender of Modernity*. Cambridge, MA: Harvard University Press, 1995.

Fife, Austin E. "The Strawberry Roan and His Progeny." *JEMF Quarterly* 8 (1972): 149–65.

Fox, Aaron. "The Jukebox of History: Narratives of Loss and Desire in the Discourse of Country Music." *Popular Music* 11, no. 1 (January 1992): 53–72.

———. *Real Country: Music and Language in Working-Class Culture*. Durham, NC: Duke University Press, 2004.

Fox, Pamela. *Natural Acts: Gender, Race, and Rusticity in Country Music*. Ann Arbor: University of Michigan Press, 2009.

Giordano, Ralph G. *Country and Western Dance*. Santa Barbara, CA: Greenwood, 2010.

Giroux, Henry A., ed. *Postmodernism, Feminism, and Cultural Politics: Redrawing Educational Boundaries*. Albany: State University of New York Press, 1991.

Glenn, Susan A. *Female Spectacle: The Theatrical Roots of Modern Feminism*. Cambridge, MA: Harvard University Press, 2000.

Goertzen, Chris. *Southern Fiddlers and Fiddle Contests*. Jackson: University Press of Mississippi, 2008.

Goggans, Jan. *California on the Breadlines: Dorothea Lange, Paul Taylor, and the Making of a New Deal Narrative*. Berkeley: University of California Press, 2010.

Goldman, Herbert G. *Fanny Brice: The Original Funny Girl*. Oxford: Oxford University Press, 1992.

Goodman, David. *Radio Civic Ambition: American Broadcasting and Democracy in the 1930s*. New York: Oxford University Press, 2011.

Gopinath, Sumanth, and Anna Schultz. "Sentimental Remembrance and the Amusements of Forgetting in Karl and Harty's 'Kentucky.'" *Journal of the American Musicological Society* 69, no. 2 (2016): 477–524.

Gotfrit, Leslie. "Women Dancing Back: Disruption and the Politics of Pleasure." In Giroux, *Postmodernism, Feminism, and Cultural Politics,* 174–195.

Green, Stanley. *The Great Clowns on Broadway.* New York: Oxford University Press, 1984.

Greenberg, Jonathan. "Singing Up Close: Voice, Language and Race in American Popular Music, 1925–1935." PhD diss., University of California, Los Angeles, 2008.

Greene, Paul D., and Thomas Porcella, eds. *Wired for Sound: Engineering and Technologies in Sonic Cultures.* Middletown, CT: Wesleyan University Press, 2005.

Gregory, James. *American Exodus: The Dust Bowl Migration and Okie Culture in California.* Oxford: Oxford University Press, 1989.

———. *The Southern Diaspora: How the Great Migrations of Black and White Southerners Transformed America.* Chapel Hill: University of North Carolina Press, 2005.

Grossman, Barbara. *Funny Woman: The Life and Times of Fanny Brice.* Bloomington: Indiana University Press, 1991.

Guy, Roger. "A Common Ground: Urban Adaptation and Appalachian Unity." In Obermiller, Wagner, and Tucker, *Appalachian Odyssey,* 49–66.

Hamessley, Lydia. *Unlikely Angel: The Songs of Dolly Parton.* Urbana: University of Illinois Press, forthcoming.

Hamm, Charles. *Yesterdays: Popular Song in America.* New York: W. W. Norton, 1979.

Harkins, Anthony. *Hillbilly: A Cultural History of an American Icon.* New York: Oxford University Press, 2004.

Harrington, Beth. *The Women of Rockabilly: Welcome to the Club.* Seattle: M2kmusic, 2004.

Harrison-Kahan, Lori. *The White Negress: Literature, Minstrelsy, and the Black-Jewish Imaginary.* New Brunswick, NJ: Rutgers University Press, 2011.

Hartigan, John, Jr. "'Disgrace to the Race': Hillbillies and the Color Line in Detroit." In Obermiller, Wagner, and Tucker, *Appalachian Odyssey,* 143–158.

Haslam, Gerald W. *Workin' Man Blues: Country Music in California.* Berkeley: University of California Press, 1999.

Haytock, Jennifer Anne. *The Middle Class in the Great Depression: Popular Women's Novels of the 1930s.* New York: Palgrave Macmillan, 2013.

Hegarty, Marilyn. *Victory Girls, Khaki-Wackies, and Patriotutes: The Regulation of Female Sexuality during World War II.* New York: New York University Press, 2008.

Heidemann, Katie. "Remarkable Women and Ordinary Gals: Performance of Identity in Songs by Loretta Lynn and Dolly Parton." In Pecknold and McCusker, *Country Boys and Redneck Women,* 166–188.

Henderson, C. Phil. "San Francisco Area Takes Big Step toward Western Swing." *Tophand,* November 1946, n.p.

Hoberman, J., and Jeffrey Shandler. *Entertaining America: Jews, Movies, and Broadcasting.* New York: Jewish Museum, under the auspices of the Jewish Theological Seminary of America, 2003.

Hofstra, Warren R., ed. *Sweet Dreams: The World of Patsy Cline.* Urbana: University of Illinois Press, 2013.

Hubbs, Nadine. *Rednecks, Queers, and Country Music.* Berkeley: University of California Press, 2014.

Hurst, Jack. "Barn Dance Days: Chicago's National Barn Dance." *Bluegrass Unlimited* (March 1986): 56–69.

Jackson, Mark, ed. *Progressive Thought in Country Music: The Honky-Tonk on the Left.* Boston: University of Massachusetts, 2018.

Jellison, Katherine. *Entitled to Power: Farm Women and Technology, 1913–1963.* Chapel Hill: University of North Carolina Press, 1993.

Jenkins, Henry. *What Made Pistachio Nuts? Early Sound Comedy and the Vaudeville Aesthetic.* New York: Columbia University Press, 1992.

Jensen, Joli. *Nashville Sound: Authenticity, Commercialization, and Country Music.* Nashville, TN: Country Music Foundation Press; Vanderbilt University Press, 1998.

Johnson, Michael L. *Hunger for the Wild: America's Obsession with the Untamed West.* Lawrence: University Press of Kansas, 2007.

Jones, Karen J., and John Wills. *The American West: Competing Visions.* Edinburgh: Edinburgh University Press, 2009.

Kayes, Gillyann. *Singing and the Actor.* New York: Routledge, 2005.

Kennedy, David. *Freedom from Fear: The American People in Depression and War, 1929–1945.* New York: Oxford University Press, 1999.

Kessler-Harris, Alice. *Women Have Always Worked: A Historical Overview.* Old Westbury, NY: Feminist Press, 1981.

Kibler, M. Alison. *Rank Ladies: Gender and Cultural Hierarchy in American Vaudeville.* Chapel Hill: University of North Carolina Press, 1999.

Kimmel, Michael. *Manhood in America: A Cultural History.* New York: Free Press, 1996.

Knapp, Raymond. *The American Musical and the Performance of Personal Identity.* Princeton, NJ: Princeton University Press, 2006.

Knapp, Raymond, Steven Bauer, and Jacqueline Warwick, eds. *Musicological Identities: Essays in Honor of Susan McClary.* Burlington, VT: Ashgate, 2008.

Koegel, John. *Music in German Immigrant Theater: New York City, 1840–1940.* Rochester, NY: University of Rochester Press, 2009.

La Chapelle, Peter. *Proud to Be an Okie: Cultural Politics, Country Music, and Migration to Southern California.* Berkeley: University of California Press, 2007.

———. "'Spade Doesn't Look Exactly Starved': Country Music and the Negotiation of Women's Domesticity in Cold War Los Angeles." In McCusker and Pecknold, *Boy Named Sue,* 24–43.

Laird, Tracey. *Louisiana Hayride: Radio and the Roots along the Red River.* Oxford: Oxford University Press, 2005.

Lane, Geoff. "The Queen of Country Music." *Country Music,* December 1974, 43.

Lange, Jeffrey J. *Smile When You Call Me a Hillbilly: Country Music's Struggle for Respectability.* Athens: University of Georgia Press, 2004.

Lavitt, Pamela Brown. "First of the Red Hot Mamas: 'Coon Shouting' and Jewish Ziegfeld Girl." *American Jewish History* 87, no. 4 (December: 1999): 253–290.

Lawler, Stephanie. "Rules of Engagement: Habitus, Power and Resistance." In Adkins and Skeggs, *Feminism after Bourdieu,* 110–128.

Le Guin, Elisabeth. *Boccherini's Body: An Essay in Carnal Musicology.* Berkeley: University of California Press, 2006.

Leppert, Richard. "Gender Sonics: The Voice of Patsy Cline." In Knapp, Bauer, and Warwick, *Musicological Identities,* 191–203.

Leppert, Richard, and George Lipsitz. "'Everybody's Lonesome for Somebody': Age, the Body, and Experience in the Music of Hank Williams." *Popular Music* 9, no. 3 (1990): 259–274.

Levine, Lawrence. *Highbrow/Lowbrow: The Emergence of Cultural Hierarchy in America.* Cambridge, MA: Harvard University Press, 1988.

Lewis, George H., ed. *All That Glitters: Country Music in America.* Bowling Green, OH: Bowling Green State University Popular Press, 1993.

Lindberg, Ulf. "Popular Modernism? The 'Urban' Style of Interwar Tin Pan Alley." *Popular Music* 22 (October 2003): 283–298.

Linn, Karen. *That Half-Barbaric Twang: The Banjo in American Popular Culture.* Urbana: University of Illinois Press, 1991.

Lipsitz, George. *Class and Culture in Cold War America: A Rainbow at Midnight.* New York: Praeger, 1981.

———. *Time Passages: Collective Memory and American Popular Culture.* Minneapolis: University of Minnesota Press, 1990.

Logsdon, Guy William. *"The Whorehouse Bells Were Ringing" and Other Songs Cowboys Sing.* Urbana: University of Illinois Press, 1989.

Lott, Eric. *Love and Theft: Blackface Minstrelsy and the American Working Class.* 2nd ed. New York: Oxford University Press, 2013. First published 1993.

Mahon, Maureen. "Listening for Willie Mae 'Big Mama' Thornton's Voice: The Sounds of Race and Gender Transgression in Rock and Roll." *Women and Music: A Journal of Gender and Culture* 15 (2011): 1–17.

Malone, Bill C. *Country Music USA.* 2nd ed. Austin: University of Texas, 2002. Originally published by the University of Texas for the American Folk Society, 1968.

———. *Don't Get above Your Raisin': Country Music and the Southern Working Class.* Urbana: University of Illinois Press, 2002.

———. *Singing Cowboys and Musical Mountaineers.* Athens: University of Georgia Press, 1993.

———. *Southern Music, American Music.* Lexington: University Press of Kentucky, 1979.

May, Elaine Tyler. *Homeward Bound: American Families in the Cold War Era.* 1988. Reprint, New York: Basic Books, 2008.

Mazor, Barry. *Meeting Jimmie Rodgers: How America's Original Roots Music Hero Changed the Pop Sounds of a Century.* Oxford: Oxford University Press, 2009.

McBee, Randy D. *Dance Hall Days: Intimacy and Leisure among Working-Class Immigrants in the United States.* New York: New York University Press, 2000.

McKinney, James C. *The Diagnosis and Correction of Vocal Faults: A Manual for Teachers of Singing and for Choir Directors.* Long Grove, IL: Waveland Press, 2005.

McClary, Susan. *Conventional Wisdom: The Content of Musical Form.* Berkeley: University of California Press, 2000.

———. *Feminine Endings: Music, Gender, and Sexuality.* 1990. Reprint, Minneapolis: University of Minnesota Press, 2002.

McCracken, Allison. *Real Men Don't Sing: Crooning in American Culture.* Durham, NC: Duke University Press, 2015.

McCusker, Kristine M. "Gendered Stages: Country Music, Authenticity, and the Performance of Gender." In Stimeling, *Oxford Handbook of Country Music*, 355–374.

———. *Lonesome Cowgirls and Honky-Tonk Angels: The Women of Barn Dance Radio.* Urbana: University of Illinois Press, 2008.

———. "Patriarchy and the Great Depression." In Berry, *Hayloft Gang*, 153–167.

McCusker, Kristine M., and Diane Pecknold, eds. *A Boy Named Sue: Gender and Country Music*. Jackson: University Press of Mississippi, 2004.

McGinley, Paige. *Staging the Blues: From Tent Shows to Tourism*. Durham, NC: Duke University Press, 2014.

McLaird, James D. *Calamity Jane: The Woman and the Legend*. Norman: University of Oklahoma Press, 2005.

McNamara, Brooks. *The New York Concert Saloon: The Devil's Own Nights*. Cambridge: Cambridge University Press, 2002.

McNay, Lois. "Agency and Experience: Gender as a Lived Relation." In Adkins and Skeggs, *Feminism after Bourdieu*, 175–190.

McRobbie, Angela. "Notes on 'What Not to Wear' and Post-Feminist Symbolic Violence." In Adkins and Skeggs, *Feminism after Bourdieu*, 99–109.

Meyerowitz, Joanne, ed. *Not June Cleaver: Women and Gender in Postwar America, 1945–1960*. Philadelphia: Temple University Press, 1994.

Milkman, Ruth. *Gender at Work: The Dynamics of Job Segregation by Sex during World War II*. Urbana: University of Illinois Press, 1987.

———. *On Gender, Labor, and Inequality*. Urbana: University of Illinois Press, 2016.

Miller, Karl Hagstrom. *Segregating Sound: Inventing Folk and Pop Music in the Age of Jim Crow*. Durham, NC: Duke University Press, 2010.

Miller, Kiri. *Traveling Home: Sacred Harp Singing and American Pluralism*. Urbana: University of Illinois Press, 2008.

Miller, Richard. *The Structure of Singing: System and Art in Vocal Technique*. New York: Schirmer Books, 1986.

———. *Training Soprano Voices*. Oxford: Oxford University Press, 2000.

Morris, Mitchell. *Persistence of Sentiment: Display and Feeling in Popular Music of the 1970s*. Berkeley: University of California Press, 2013.

Neal, Jocelyn. *Country Music: A Cultural and Stylistic History*. Oxford: Oxford University Press, 2013.

———. "'Nothing but a Little Ole Pop Song': Patsy Cline's Musical Style and Evolution of Genre in the 1950s." In Hofstra, *Sweet Dreams*, 128–153.

———. *The Songs of Jimmie Rodgers: A Legacy in Country Music*. Bloomington: Indiana University Press, 2009.

———. "The Twang Factor in Country Music." In *Timbre in Popular Music: The Relentless Pursuit of Tone*, edited by Robert Fink, Melinda LaTour, and Zachary Wallmark, 43–64. Oxford: Oxford University Press, 2018.

Nelson, Daniel. *Farm and Factory: Workers in the Midwest, 1880–1990*. Bloomington: Indiana University Press, 1995.

Nies, Betty L. "Defending Jeeter: Conservative Arguments against Eugenics in the Depression-Era South." In *Popular Eugenics: National Efficiency and American Mass Culture in the 1930s*, edited by Susan Currell and Christina Cogdell, 120–139. Athens: Ohio University Press, 2006.

Obermiller, Phillip J., Thomas E. Wagner, and E. Bruce Tucker, eds. *Appalachian Odyssey: Historical Perspectives on the Great Migration*. Westport, CT: Praeger, 2000.

Ortner, Sherry B. *Anthropology and Social Theory: Culture, Power, and the Acting Subject*. Durham, NC: Duke University Press, 2006.

Palmer, Vivien Marie. *Social Backgrounds of Chicago's Local Communities*. Chicago: University of Chicago, 1929.

Parler, Samuel Jennings. "Musical Radicalism and Racial Nationalism in Commercial Country Music, 1915–1953." PhD diss., Harvard University, 2017.

Parrish, Michael E. *Anxious Decades: America in Prosperity and Depression, 1920–1941*. New York: W. W. Norton, 1992.

Pecknold, Diane. *The Selling Sound: The Rise of the Country Music Industry*. Durham, NC: Duke University Press, 2007.

Pecknold, Diane, and Kristine M. McCusker, eds. *Country Boys and Redneck Women: New Essays in Gender and Country Music*. Jackson: University Press of Mississippi, 2016.

Peterson, Richard. *Creating Country Music: Fabricating Authenticity*. Chicago: University of Chicago Press, 1997.

Plantenga, Bart. *Yodel-Ay-Ee-Ooo: The Secret History of Yodeling around the World*. New York: Routledge, 2004.

———. *Yodel in Hi-Fi: From Kitsch Folk to Contemporary Electronics*. Madison: University of Wisconsin Press, 2012.

Potter, John. *Vocal Authority: Singing Style and Ideology*. Cambridge: Cambridge University Press, 1998.

Pugh, Ronnie. *Ernest Tubb: The Texas Troubadour*. Durham, NC: Duke University Press, 1996.

Radway, Janice. "The Book-of-the-Month Club and the General Reader: On the Uses of 'Serious' Fiction." *Critical Inquiry* 14, no. 3 (1988): 516–538.

Rayburn, Jim. "No Sign of Controversy at Chicks Concert." *Deseret Morning News*, July 10, 2003, B-03.

Rodger, Gillian M. *Champagne Charlie and Pretty Jemima: Variety Theater in the Nineteenth Century*. Urbana: University of Illinois Press, 2010.

———. "Drag, Camp, and Gender Subversion in the Music and Videos of Annie Lennox." *Popular Music* 23, no. 1 (2004): 17–29.

Rubin, Joan Shelley. *The Making of Middlebrow Culture*. Chapel Hill: the University of North Carolina Press, 1992.

Rubin, Rachel. "Sing Me Back Home: Nostalgia, Bakersfield, and Modern Country Music." In Rubin and Melnick, *American Popular Music*, 93–109.

Rubin, Rachel, and Jeffrey Melnick, eds. *American Popular Music: New Approaches to the Twentieth Century*. Amherst, MA: University of Massachusetts Press, 2001.

Rumble, John W. "'I'll Reap My Harvest in Heaven': Fred Rose's Acquaintance with Country Music." In Tichi, *Reading Country Music*, 350–377.

Russell, Tony, and Bob Pinson. *[Country Music Records: A Discography, 1921–1942.]* New York: Oxford University Press, 2004.

Salamon, Sonya. *Prairie Patrimony: Family, Farming and Community in the Midwest*. Chapel Hill: University of North Carolina Press, 1992.

Sanjek, David. "Can a Fujiyama Mama Be the Female Elvis? The Wild, Wild Women of Rockabilly." In *Sexing the Groove: Popular Music and Gender*, edited by Sheila Whiteley, 137–167. London: Routledge, 1997.

Scharf, Lois. *To Work and to Wed: Female Employment, Feminism, and the Great Depression*. Westport, CT: Greenwood Press, 1980.

Sennett, Richard, and Jonathan Cobb. *The Hidden Injuries of Class*. New York: Knopf, 1972.

Shank, Berry. *Dissonant Identities: The Rock 'n' Roll Scene in Austin Texas.* Hanover, NH: University of Press of New England for Wesleyan University Press, 1994.

Sharp, Cecil. *English Folk Songs from the Southern Appalachians.* London: Oxford University Press, 1932.

Skeggs, Beverley. "Exchange, Value, and Affect: Bourdieu and 'The Self.'" In Adkins and Skeggs, *Feminism after Bourdieu,* 75–97.

———. *Formations of Class and Gender.* Thousand Oaks, CA: Sage, 1997.

Smart, Mary Ann, ed. *Siren Songs: Representations of Gender and Sexuality in Opera.* Princeton, NJ: Princeton University Press, 2000.

Smith, Graeme. "Australian Country Music." *Popular Music* 13 (October 1994): 297–311.

Smith, Henry Nash. *Virgin Land: The American West as Symbol and Myth.* Cambridge, MA: Harvard University Press, 1950.

Smith, Patricia Juliana. "Brit Girls: Sandie Shaw and the Women of the British Invasion." In Stras, *She's So Fine,* 137–162.

Stanfield, Peter. *Horse Opera: The Strange History of the 1930s Singing Cowboy.* Chicago: University of Illinois Press, 2002.

Stark, James. *Bel Canto: A History of Vocal Pedagogy.* Toronto: University of Toronto Press, 1999.

Steel, David Warren, and Richard H. Hulan. *The Makers of the Sacred Harp.* Urbana: University of Illinois Press, 2010.

Stilwell, Robynn J. "Vocal Decorum: Voice, Body, and Knowledge in the Prodigious Singer, Brenda Lee." In Stras, *She's So Fine,* 57–87.

Stimeling, Travis D. *Cosmic Cowboys and New Hicks: The Countercultural Sounds of Austin's Progressive Country Music Scene.* Oxford: Oxford University Press, 2011.

———. "Narrative, Vocal Staging, and Masculinity in the 'Outlaw' Country Music of Waylon Jennings." *Popular Music* 32, no. 3 (October 2013): 343–358.

———, ed. *The Oxford Handbook of Country Music.* Oxford: Oxford University Press, 2017.

———. "Taylor Swift's 'Pitch Problems' and the Place of Adolescent Girls in Country Music." In Pecknold and McCusker, *Country Boys and Redneck Women,* 84–101.

Stras, Laurie, ed. *She's So Fine: Reflections on Whiteness, Femininity, Adolescence and Class in 1960s Music.* Burlington, VT: Ashgate, 2010.

———. "Voice of the Beehive: Vocal Technique at the Turn of the 1960s." In Stras, *She's So Fine,* 33–55.

Sundberg, Johan, and Margareta Thalén. "What Is 'Twang'?" *Journal of Voice* 24, no. 60 (2010): 654–660.

Swan, Ellen. "People and Things." *Tophand,* November 1946, n.p.

Taylor, Paul S. "Again the Covered Wagon." *Survey Graphic* 24, no. 7 (1935): 345–351.

Taylor, Timothy D. "Music and the Rise of Radio in Twenties America: Technological Imperialism, Socialization, and the Transformation of Intimacy." In Greene and Porcello, *Wired for Sound,* 245–268.

Tichi, Cecelia ed. *Reading Country Music: Steel Guitars, Opry Stars, and Honky-Tonk Bars.* Durham, NC: Duke University Press, 1998.

Time. "Music: Bull Market in Corn." October 4, 1943, 49–50.

Trott, Walt. *The Honky Tonk Angels: The Kitty Wells–Johnny & Jack Story.* 1987. Reprint, Nashville, TN: Nova Books, 1993.

Tucker, Sherrie. *Swing Shift: "All-Girl" Bands of the 1940s.* Durham, NC: Duke University Press, 2000.

Tyler, Paul L. "The Rise of Rural Rhythm." In Berry, *Hayloft Gang*, 19–71.

Vander Wel, Stephanie. "The Lavender Cowboy and 'The She Buckaroo': Gene Autry, Patsy Montana, and Depression-Era Gender Roles." *Musical Quarterly* 95, no. 2/3 (Summer–Fall 2012): 207–251.

———. "The Singing Voice in Country Music." In Stimeling, *Oxford Handbook of Country Music*, 157–176.

———. "Weeping and Flamboyant Men: Webb Pierce and the Campy Theatrics of Country Music." In Jackson, *Progressive Thought in Country Music*, 74–101.

Votaw, Albert N. "The Hillbillies Invade Chicago." *Harper's*, February 1958, 64–65.

Walser, Robert. *Running with the Devil: Power, Gender, and Madness in Heavy Metal Music.* Hanover, NH: University Press of England, 1993.

Warren, Louis S. *Buffalo Bill's America: William Cody and the Wild West Show.* New York: Alfred A. Knopf, 2005.

Warwick, Jacqueline. *Girl Groups, Girl Culture: Popular Music and Identity in the 1960s.* New York: Routledge, 2007.

Webb, Chloe. *Legacy of the Sacred Harp.* Fort Worth: Texas Christian University Press, 2010.

White, B. F., and E. J. King. *The Sacred Harp: Facsim. of the 3d Ed., 1859, Including as a Historical Introduction: The Story of the Sacred Harp, by George Pullen Jackson.* Nashville, TN: Broadman Press, 1968.

White, John I. *Git Along, Little Dogies: Songs and Songmakers of the American West.* Urbana: University of Illinois Press, 1989.

Whiteside, Johnny. *Ramblin' Rose: The Life and Career of Rose Maddox.* Introduction by Woody Guthrie. Nashville, TN: Country Music Foundation Press; Vanderbilt University Press, 1997.

Wicks, Sammie Anne. "A Belated Salute to the 'Old Way' of 'Snaking' the Voice on Its (ca.) 345th Birthday." *Popular Music* 8, no. 1 (January 1989): 59–96.

Williams, Michael Ann. "Home to Renfro Valley John Lair and the Women of the Barn Dances." In Wolfe and Akenson, *Women of Country Music*, 88–108.

Williams, Roger M. *Sing a Sad Song: The Life of Hank Williams.* 2nd ed. Urbana: University of Illinois Press, 1981.

Wise, Timothy. "Jimmie Rodgers and the Semiosis of the Hillbilly Yodel." *Musical Quarterly* 93 (2010): 6–44.

———. *Yodeling and Meaning in American Music.* Jackson: University Press of Mississippi, 2016.

———. "Yodel Species: A Typology of Falsetto Effects in Popular Music Vocal Styles." *Radical Musicology* 2 (2007): 57 pars. 17 January 2008. http://www.radical-musicology.org.uk.

Wolf, Stacy. *A Problem like Maria: Gender and Sexuality in the American Musical.* Ann Arbor: University of Michigan Press, 2002.

Wolfe, Charles. *Classic Country: Legends of Country Music.* London: Routledge, 2001.

———. *A Good-Natured Riot: The Birth of the Grand Ole Opry.* Nashville: Country Music Foundation Press and Vanderbilt University Press, 1999.

Wolfe, Charles, and James Akenson, eds. *The Women of Country Music: A Reader.* Lexington: University of Kentucky Press, 2003.

Young, William H., and Nancy K. Young. *Music of the World War II Era.* Westport, CT: Greenwood Press, 2008.

Index

Note: Page numbers in *italics* refer to photos and music examples.

STEPHANIE VANDER WEL is an associate professor of music at the University at Buffalo.

Music in American Life

"Susanna," "Jeanie," and "The Old Folks at Home": The Songs of Stephen C. Foster
    from His Time to Ours (2d ed.)   *William W. Austin*
Songprints: The Musical Experience of Five Shoshone Women   *Judith Vander*
"Happy in the Service of the Lord": Afro-American Gospel Quartets
    in Memphis   *Kip Lornell*
Paul Hindemith in the United States   *Luther Noss*
"My Song Is My Weapon": People's Songs, American Communism,
    and the Politics of Culture, 1930–50   *Robbie Lieberman*
Chosen Voices: The Story of the American Cantorate   *Mark Slobin*
Theodore Thomas: America's Conductor and Builder
    of Orchestras, 1835–1905   *Ezra Schabas*
"The Whorehouse Bells Were Ringing" and Other Songs
    Cowboys Sing   *Collected and Edited by Guy Logsdon*
Crazeology: The Autobiography of a Chicago Jazzman
    Bud Freeman, as Told to Robert Wolf
Discoursing Sweet Music: Brass Bands and Community Life
    in Turn-of-the-Century Pennsylvania   *Kenneth Kreitner*
Mormonism and Music: A History   *Michael Hicks*
Voices of the Jazz Age: Profiles of Eight Vintage Jazzmen   *Chip Deffaa*
Pickin' on Peachtree: A History of Country Music in
    Atlanta, Georgia   *Wayne W. Daniel*
Bitter Music: Collected Journals, Essays, Introductions, and Librettos
    Harry Partch; edited by Thomas McGeary
Ethnic Music on Records: A Discography of Ethnic Recordings Produced
    in the United States, 1893 to 1942   *Richard K. Spottswood*
Downhome Blues Lyrics: An Anthology from the
    Post–World War II Era   *Jeff Todd Titon*
Ellington: The Early Years   *Mark Tucker*
Chicago Soul   *Robert Pruter*
That Half-Barbaric Twang: The Banjo in American Popular Culture   *Karen Linn*
Hot Man: The Life of Art Hodes   *Art Hodes and Chadwick Hansen*
The Erotic Muse: American Bawdy Songs (2d ed.)   *Ed Cray*
Barrio Rhythm: Mexican American Music in Los Angeles   *Steven Loza*
The Creation of Jazz: Music, Race, and Culture in Urban America   *Burton W. Peretti*
Charles Martin Loeffler: A Life Apart in Music   *Ellen Knight*
Club Date Musicians: Playing the New York Party Circuit   *Bruce A. MacLeod*
Opera on the Road: Traveling Opera Troupes in the United States,
    1825–60   *Katherine K. Preston*
The Stonemans: An Appalachian Family and the Music
    That Shaped Their Lives   *Ivan M. Tribe*
Transforming Tradition: Folk Music Revivals Examined   *Edited by Neil V. Rosenberg*
The Crooked Stovepipe: Athapaskan Fiddle Music and Square Dancing
    in Northeast Alaska and Northwest Canada   *Craig Mishler*

The University of Illinois Press
is a founding member of the
Association of University Presses.

———————————————————

University of Illinois Press
1325 South Oak Street
Champaign, IL 61820-6903
www.press.uillinois.edu

Printed by Printforce, United Kingdom